MADNESS AND LOSS OF MOTHERHOOD

SEXUALITY, REPRODUCTION, AND LONG-TERM MENTAL ILLNESS

Ronit Rothman

MADNESS AND LOSS OF MOTHERHOOD

SEXUALITY, REPRODUCTION, AND LONG-TERM MENTAL ILLNESS

Roberta J. Apfel, M.D., M.P.H.

Maryellen H. Handel, Ph.D.

American Psychiatric Press, Inc.

Washington, DC
London, England

Note: The authors have worked to ensure that all information in this book concerning drug dosages, schedules, and routes of administration is accurate as of the time of publication and consistent with standards set by the U.S. Food and Drug Administration and the general medical community. As medical research and practice advance, however, therapeutic standards may change. For this reason and because human and mechanical errors sometimes occur, we recommend that readers follow the advice of a physician who is directly involved in their care or the care of a member of their family.

Books published by the American Psychiatric Press, Inc., represent the views and opinions of the individual authors and do not necessarily represent the policies and opinions of the Press or the American Psychiatric Association.

Copyright © 1993   American Psychiatric Press, Inc.
ALL RIGHTS RESERVED
Manufactured in the United States of America on acid-free paper
First Edition
96 95 94 93   4 3 2 1

American Psychiatric Press, Inc.
1400 K Street, N.W., Washington, DC 20005

Library of Congress Cataloging-in-Publication Data
Madness and Loss of Motherhood: Sexuality, Reproduction, and Long-
    Term Mental Illness / by Roberta J. Apfel, Maryellen H.
    Handel.—1st ed.
    p.   cm. — (Clinical practice : no. 26)
    Includes bibliographical references and index.
    ISBN 0-88048-183-8 (alk. paper)
    1. Mentally ill—Care. 2. Mentally ill—Sexual behavior. 3. Chroni-
cally ill—Care. 4. Chronically ill—Sexual behavior. 5. Pregnancy in
mentally ill women. I. Apfel, Roberta J., 1938–   . II. Handel, Maryellen H., 1939–   . III. Series.
    [DNLM: 1. Long-Term Care. 2. Mental Disorders—in
pregnancy. W1 CL767J no. 26 / WQ 240 S518]
RC455.4.S45S49 1992
616.89—dc20
DNLM/DLC   92-10958
for Library of Congress   CIP

British Library Cataloguing in Publication Data
A CIP record is available from the British Library.

To our mothers,
Rena Sperling Hurwitz
and
Polly Gurian Apfel,
who were our first teachers about
motherhood

Clinical Practice

Number 26
Judith H. Gold, M.D., F.R.C.P.C.
Series Editor

Contents

About the Authors

Dr. Apfel is Associate Professor of Clinical Psychiatry at Harvard Medical School, the Cambridge Hospital, and the former Metropolitan State Hospital in Waltham, Massachusetts. She is on the faculty of the Boston Psychoanalytic Institute and is in private practice in Newton, Massachusetts.

Dr. Handel is Director of Psychiatric Ambulatory Services, Newton-Wellesley Hospital, Newton, Massachusetts, and Clinical Assistant Professor of Psychiatry at Tufts University School of Medicine. She is in private practice in Newton, Massachusetts.

Introduction
to the Clinical Practice Series

*O*ver the years of its existence the series of monographs entitled *Clinical Insights* gradually became focused on providing current, factual, and theoretical material of interest to the clinician working outside of a hospital setting. To reflect this orientation, the name of the Series has been changed to *Clinical Practice.*

The Clinical Practice Series will provide books that give the mental health clinician a practical, clinical approach to a variety of psychiatric problems. These books will provide up-to-date literature reviews and emphasize the most recent treatment methods. Thus, the publications in the Series will interest clinicians working both in psychiatry and in the other mental health professions.

Each year a number of books will be published dealing with all aspects of clinical practice. In addition, from time to time when appropriate, the publications may be revised and updated. Thus, the Series will provide quick access to relevant and important areas of psychiatric practice. Some books in the Series will be authored by a person considered to be an expert in that particular area; others will be edited by such an expert, who will also draw together other knowledgeable authors to produce a comprehensive overview of that topic.

Some of the books in the Clinical Practice Series will have their foundation in presentations at an annual meeting of the American Psychiatric Association. All will contain the most recently available information on the subjects discussed. Theoretical and scientific data will be applied to clinical situations, and case illustrations will be utilized in order to make the material even more relevant for the practitioner. Thus, the Clinical Practice Series should provide educational reading in a compact format especially designed for the mental health clinician–psychiatrist.

Judith H. Gold, M.D., F.R.C.P.C.
Series Editor
Clinical Practice Series

Clinical Practice Series Titles

Treating Chronically Mentally Ill Women (#1)
Edited by Leona L. Bachrach, Ph.D., and Carol C. Nadelson, M.D.

Divorce as a Developmental Process (#2)
Edited by Judith H. Gold, M.D., F.R.C.P.C.

Family Violence: Emerging Issues of a National Crisis (#3)
Edited by Leah J. Dickstein, M.D., and Carol C. Nadelson, M.D.

Anxiety and Depressive Disorders in the Medical Patient (#4)
By Leonard R. Derogatis, Ph.D., and Thomas N. Wise, M.D.

Anxiety: New Findings for the Clinician (#5)
Edited by Peter Roy-Byrne, M.D.

The Neuroleptic Malignant Syndrome and Related Conditions (#6)
By Arthur Lazarus, M.D., Stephan C. Mann, M.D., and Stanley N. Caroff, M.D.

Juvenile Homicide (#7)
Edited by Elissa P. Benedek, M.D., and Dewey G. Cornell, Ph.D.

**Measuring Mental Illness: Psychometric Assessment
for Clinicians (#8)**
Edited by Scott Wetzler, Ph.D.

Family Involvement in Treatment of the Frail Elderly (#9)
Edited by Marion Zucker Goldstein, M.D.

Psychiatric Care of Migrants: A Clinical Guide (#10)
By Joseph Westermeyer, M.D., M.P.H., Ph.D.

Office Treatment of Schizophrenia (#11)
Edited by Mary V. Seeman, M.D., F.R.C.P.C., and
Stanley E. Greben, M.D., F.R.C.P.C.

The Psychosocial Impact of Job Loss (#12)
By Nick Kates, M.B.B.S., F.R.C.P.C., Barrie S. Greiff, M.D., and
Duane Q. Hagen, M.D.

New Perspectives on Narcissism (#13)
Edited by Eric M. Plakun, M.D.

**Clinical Management of Gender Identity Disorders in
Children and Adults (#14)**
Edited by Ray Blanchard, Ph.D., and Betty W. Steiner, M.B., F.R.C.P.C.

Family Approaches in Treatment of Eating Disorders (#15)
Edited by D. Blake Woodside, M.D., M.Sc., F.R.C.P.C., and
Lorie Shekter-Wolfson, M.S.W., C.S.W.

Adolescent Psychotherapy (#16)
Edited by Marcia Slomowitz, M.D.

Benzodiazepines in Clinical Practice: Risks and Benefits (#17)
Edited by Peter P. Roy-Byrne, M.D., and Deborah S. Cowley, M.D.

Current Treatments of Obsessive-Compulsive Disorder (#18)
Edited by Michele Tortora Pato, M.D., and Joseph Zohar, M.D.

Children and AIDS (#19)
Edited by Margaret L. Stuber, M.D.

Special Problems in Managing Eating Disorders (#20)
Edited by Joel Yager, M.D., Harry E. Gwirtsman, M.D., and
Carole K. Edelstein, M.D.

Suicide and Clinical Practice (#21)
Edited by Douglas Jacobs, M.D.

Anxiety Disorders in Children and Adolescents (#22)
By Syed Arshad Husain, M.D., F.R.C.P.C., F.R.C.Psych., and
Javad Kashani, M.D.

Psychopharmacological Treatment Complications in the Elderly (#23)
Edited by Charles A. Shamoian, M.D., Ph.D.

Responding to Disaster: A Guide for Mental Health Professionals (#24)
Edited by Linda S. Austin, M.D.

Psychiatric Aspects of Symptom Management in Cancer Patients (#25)
Edited by William Breitbart, M.D., and Jimmie C. Holland, M.D.

**Madness and Loss of Motherhood: Sexuality, Reproduction, and
Long-Term Mental Illness (#26)**
By Roberta J. Apfel, M.D., M.P.H., and Maryellen H. Handel, Ph.D.

Treatment of Adult Survivors of Incest (#27)
Edited by Patricia L. Paddison, M.D.

Foreword

*T*he authors of this interesting, readable, and timely book share with us their experience and an extensive review of the literature on sex and reproductive issues in patients with long-term mental illness. From the burgeoning number of articles on sex in the past decade, and from a longer look over 50 years, Drs. Apfel and Handel demonstrate how the subject of sex and reproduction has moved from no mention and little understanding to being the focus of detailed studies on important and relevant issues. Particularly valuable to readers of this book are the guides to management of patients with long-term mental illness who are sexually active and of those who are pregnant. The many illustrative cases cited will be most helpful to clinicians.

When I began my residency in psychiatry, in 1931, at the Worcester State Hospital (WSH) in Massachusetts, my first assignment was to the Medical and Surgical Service. The WSH was the obstetrical center for women in all mental and correctional institutions in the state. With the help of an attending obstetrician, several nurses, and three psychiatrists, I gave prenatal care, delivered babies, and cared for them and their mothers afterward. Memory for details after 60 years is not reliable. I don't recall any major problems in either mothers or babies. It was a time before antipsychotic medication was available and before widespread substance abuse.

It was assumed that mothers who were confined in the criminal justice system and those institutionalized for psychosis or mental retardation were unable to care for their babies. All the infants were placed in some kind of foster care.

What amazes me is that it did not occur to us to seek the answers to such questions as

- What was the attitude of the mother toward her pregnancy?
- What was her attitude toward giving birth?
- Did becoming a mother exacerbate or ameliorate the mental illness?
- What was the mother's response to the child?
- Was bonding permitted?

- What was the mother's feeling toward loss through adoption? loss of contact with the infant?
- Why did we miss the opportunity to investigate how the criminal mothers differed from the psychotic ones?

Worcester State Hospital was a nationally known research center studying schizophrenia. Most clinicians, including myself, were engaged in research of some kind. We missed an unusual opportunity to increase understanding of reproduction in persons with mental illness.

Perhaps part of the reason for our failure was society's attitudes toward sex in those individuals segregated from the world outside. Because of society's disapproval, pregnancy and severe sexual behavior within this population were surrounded in secrecy. No thought was given to providing a time and place for conjugal relations. If it was proven that a member of the staff was responsible for the pregnancy, he or she was promptly dismissed.

Some 30 years later when I was the superintendent of the Boston State Hospital, I wrote that there was no evidence that sexual intercourse among patients was a greater problem in the mental hospital than in the community: an unwanted child caused distress to many people—spouse, parents, the administrators, and society in general. I noted the frequency of sexual manifestations and of homosexuality. My own attitude also showed 30 years ago when my commentary on patients' sexual fantasies and activities in my book appeared under the heading of "Sexual Misconduct."[1]

Much has changed, particularly in the past decade or two, with regard to social attitudes toward sexuality. The authors of this book have traced these changes. They give us the state of current knowledge and its application in specific situations.

This is a good book on an important topic often ignored. The book should be read by clinicians both in the field of obstetrics and in the mental health professions if they are responsible for prenatal care, delivery, and postnatal care for patients with long-term mental illness.

All who care for mentally ill persons will profit from a greater understanding of sexual and reproductive issues and patients' feelings and attitudes. The authors have produced an excellent practical guide that

---

[1]Barton WE: *Administration in Psychiatry.* Springfield, IL, Charles C. Thomas, 1962.

will aid in both the understanding and the management of sexual expression and pregnancy in people with mental illness.

Walter E. Barton, M.D.
Hartland, Vermont

Acknowledgments

*T*his book began in Dublin at an interdisciplinary international women's conference in 1987. We were amazed by the intense response to our presentation of a clinical paper about women with long-term mental illness and their many losses of opportunities to mother. Our audience had no knowledge of psychiatry and yet was deeply moved and interested in the case studies we presented. We realized that we had touched on something important for our own field of psychiatry and decided to write about this subject for our colleagues. Over 4 years and numerous continents, we have talked with and learned from many people who have contributed significantly to this book. American Psychiatric Press Editor-in-Chief Carol Nadelson, colleague and friend, saw the need for this monograph and encouraged us then, as now. Judith Gold, our helpful series editor, Claire Reinburg, and Greg Kuny have seen the book to fruition.

Since Leona Bachrach indicated the need for public policy about motherhood in mentally ill persons in 1984, she has continued to inspire us personally and professionally. Some pioneering efforts have been launched by Anna Spielvogel and Joanne Wile, Laura Miller and Valerie Raskin, Lee Cohen and Deborah Sichel, Penelope Krener, Ann Massion, Mary Seeman, Sally Severino, Donna Stewart, Nada Stotland, and Katherine Wisner. Henry Grunebaum, Carole Hartmann, Richard Lannon, William Miller, Tamar Kron, Saralee Glasser, Joyce Maguire Pavao, Jeffrey Geller, and Alicia Lieberman had already been at work in related areas. Thus, we have had a growing group of colleagues with whom to share ideas and enthusiasm. All of them have participated in our project. As we explored, we discovered that significant work is being done by people in other fields: Anitra Pivnick and Brenda Schwab in medical anthropology; Gerald Grob, Judith Leavitt, and Ellen Dwyer in history; Loretta Finnegan in pediatrics; Vicki Heller and Molly Clark in obstetrics; and Robert Like in medicine.

Consumer interest and enthusiasm has been crucial: Nancy Bertchold in patient advocacy (Depression After Delivery) and Agnes Hatfield, Harriet Lefley, and Peggy Straw in family advocacy (Alliance for the Mentally Ill) encouraged us along the way. Colleagues working with mothers with schizophrenia—Haven Miles and Fredericka Bettinger in Rhode Island and Peg Grandison in New Jersey—inspired us to realize that there are realistic options

There were colleagues who helped us to trace the unrecorded history of the treatment of psychotic pregnant women in the past. Alvin Becker directed us to the history of treatment of pregnancy in state hospitals in Massachusetts. Mona Bennett, then Deputy Commissioner of Mental Health, introduced us to Mary Remar, who gave us access to her informal repository of history for the Massachusetts mental health system. Walter Barton, who has been a central person on the frontlines of clinical care and administrative psychiatry, read an early draft of the manuscript and stimulated us with his recollections of the treatment of pregnant patients and insights about their care.

Throughout this journey, our interest has been spurred on by residents and staff colleagues at Metropolitan State Hospital and Cambridge Hospital and by the Aftercare staff at Newton-Wellesley Hospital.

We have had enormous support in our workplace: from office manager Louise Neiterman; from the Cambridge Hospital Department of Psychiatry, and especially its chairperson, Malkah Notman, who also read the manuscript; from Hadassah Hospital; from the Boston Psychoanalytic Institute; and from the Countway Library and its archivist, Richard Wolff. This project, most of all, was sustained and nurtured by the Department of Psychiatry at Newton-Wellesley Hospital, which has provided a base for our work. Above all, we thank our chairman and colleague Alvin Becker for making available departmental resources to facilitate our research. We are deeply grateful to Dace Skulte, who typed the manuscipt with skill and care and continued to support us with her ongoing interest in the subject matter; and to Chris Bell in the library and her wonderful staff who did literature searches and provided ongoing technical support to help amass our extensive bibliographies.

Our extended families have believed in this project and cheered us along when our spirits flagged. David Apfel, Kalman Apfel, and Ira Hurwitz provided advice and counsel. Our husbands, Bennett Simon and Sidney Handel, read the manuscript thoroughly and provided in-depth editing and thought-provoking questions that helped shape the finished product. Our children—Amy, Ari, Celia, Jonathan, Michael, Molly, Shoshana, and Zev—make us realize the value of reproductive and productive activity in everyone's lives. Each has contributed in a unique way.

Finally, we want to thank our patients, who have taught us about their lives and touched us with their own human experiences. They reminded us that they are women and men, and not just mental patients. We have presented their stories in a way that protects confidentiality, but we have felt moved and personally encouraged in this endeavor by our patients and feel grateful to be able to give them a voice.

Introduction

*T*hose of us who work with psychotic patients are increasingly aware of how crucial issues of sexuality, reproduction, and parenting are in their lives. It is precisely because of the progress we have made in the treatment of long-term mental illness, including progress in realizing the humanity and the individuality of each patient, that we are increasingly encountering the fact that seriously mentally ill persons wish to and frequently do become mothers and fathers. Coupling and reproducing— expectable milestones of normal development—are complicated enough under the best of circumstances. For these long-term mental patients and their families, they become areas of confusion, ambivalence, and painful moral dilemmas. Nor are mental health professionals caring for these patients exempted from such distress, and there is little available in professional lore and literature to reliably guide us.

This book brings together literature and accumulated clinical experience on topics that are subsumed under the heading of reproductive health. We use numerous case examples that are based on published reports and on our combined experience in various hospitals and communities where we have worked and taught. Of course, the cases are disguised to protect the identity of the patients.

We take a distinctive stance about reproduction among those individuals with long-term mental illness. We have found, in discussing the preparation of this book with colleagues and friends, that many people assume it is a bad thing for women with schizophrenia to have babies— bad for them, but more so bad for the general genetic pool of the world. Some people thought we might acknowledge the universal female fantasy of pregnancy but focus on its prevention in this population. Others, who also work closely with patients with long-term mental illness and know their wishes, assume we will say it is a good thing for the patients to get pregnant. We want to say we do not think it can be judged universally as either good or bad. It inevitably happens. Pregnancy in a woman with long-term mental illness is always complicated for everyone concerned and needs to be understood and negotiated case by case; that is our moral and clinical principle.

Long-term mental illnesses are persistent and painful for the caregivers as well as for the patients. In the current climate, the job can seem impossible at times when the problems of limited resources and imperfect treatments are compounded by a rage to blame and sue the doctor. The challenge of meeting the reproductive health needs of the patients adds enormously to the complexity of treatment of the mental illness itself.

We ourselves are practicing clinicians—a psychologist (M.H.H.) and a psychiatrist/psychoanalyst (R.J.A.). We know from our own experience how hard it is to be clear, balanced, and compassionate about these cases. We are also both women and mothers and know about how compelling childbearing is. From our own perspective we try to understand the role of reproductive issues in human life and how they are refracted through the lens of mental illness. We bring a psychodynamic approach that is sometimes different from the management planning approach used in the settings where we work. Both of us have worked in reproductive health areas in the past: in childbirth education and birth control services, and in obstetric and gynecology liaison psychiatry. We are aware of the realities of cost-benefit ratios and the multitude of health professionals with varied training and perspectives. We continue to believe primarily in the value of listening and responding to the individual needs of each patient while working within the complex milieu of the staff and patients and the communities where we practice. We know there are no easy answers and no panaceas; yet we have felt the need for more mastery in clinical situations that have been intriguing, complicated, and, at times, overwhelming. Our own attempts to learn have resulted in this effort to inform and guide our colleagues striving to provide optimal care for patients with long-term and severe mental illness. Our intention is to stimulate dialogue, as well as to transmit information and opinion.

This book is written at a particular point in time when mental illness is becoming less stigmatized and it is easier to discuss sex more openly. In the decade of the 1980s, literature on schizophrenia started to reflect increasing awareness of gender and sexuality (Goldstein 1988). Hopefully, this climate of greater acceptance will permit clinicians to listen to the themes of reproduction and sexuality that have been there all along.

Deinstitutionalization (1950s to the 1970s) has made sex and pregnancy more possible and more visible. Young adult patients now spend most of their lives in the community, where they share the expectations and hopes of their nonmentally ill peers; they are no longer convinced that they will inevitably be social outcasts and failures (Chamberlin 1988; Pepper and Ryglewicz 1987). Patients of both sexes live in the community, where they form couples, have sex, experience pregnancies, and care for children and families (Schwab et al. 1991; Stewart 1984; Test et al. 1990). Persons with long-term mental illness want as much of a normal life as they can have. In the past, the person with mental illness was housed in an isolated state hospital where little attention was paid to gender or sexuality (Geller 1985). When sexual activity was acknowledged in the state mental hospital, it was in reference to women patients as sexual prey of strangers who wandered onto the grounds of the hospital (Barton 1962). Never was the woman with mental illness seen as a sexual person herself (G. Grob 1985; personal communication, 1989).

An illustration of this mindset was found by Dwyer (1987; personal communication, 1989), whose research on 19th-century New York State mental hospital records yielded only one mention of pregnancy: a debate about how long a pregnancy could last. A woman gave birth 15 months after entering the hospital, and the medical staff assumed she must have conceived prior to admission!

This attitude of denial regarding patient sexual activity and identity began to change as the psychosocial rehabilitation movement, which followed deinstitutionalization, emphasized the unique qualities of each patient and demanded that treatment plans reflect the individual's own strengths and strivings. Once the individuality of persons with long-term mental illness is acknowledged, gender identity can no longer be ignored.

The women's movement (1960s to the 1980s) was another major event that increased awareness of the developmental psychology of women (Notman and Nadelson 1978). As more professional women with families began to work with mentally ill persons, they have been more acutely sensitive to the voices of women patients and to stories that resonate with universal aspects of the female experience (Martin 1987). The fact that patients with mental illness are now exposed to female staff members who are pregnant also focuses attention on issues of female reproductive life.

Historically, there has been an association between women and mental illness (Sandler 1978). Reproductive organs have been seen as the site of madness: the wandering uterus of ancient Greece, the ovary in the 19th century, the raging hormones in this, the 20th, century (Simon

1978). When Pinel freed the mental patients from their shackles, the men were freed first, the women several days later. The women were depicted in illustrations of the event as young, sexual, crazed, immodest creatures compared with the competent and rational men (Showalter 1985). These views of mad women reflect fantasies and fears more than realities. Stereotypes of the relationship between women and madness are changing. In the past two decades there has been more scientific attention paid to the actual biological and psychosocial experiences of women in the genesis of mental illness (Kaplan and Sadock 1989). Insofar as reproduction affects women more than men, this topic could only be fully discussed once the larger subject of women's lives had come to center stage (Notman and Nadelson 1991).

During the past decade, the National Alliance for the Mentally Ill (NAMI) and other advocacy organizations have provided a forum for families of patients with long-term mental illness in which they can express their pain without shame or blame. The families have gained a greater sense of their power and of a community from which to demand greater societal attention to their concerns. These parents and grandparents, especially the grandmothers, have been requesting help with their adult children with severe and long-term mental illness who want to get pregnant, who bring home babies, or who want custody of children whom they are at risk of losing. The families of these patients want recognition of the fact that their adult children want to be pregnant and that pregnancies do occur (Jennings et al. 1987).

Motherhood wishes and fantasies are universal and central to female identity. The possibilities and actualities of motherhood for women with mental illness may not be the same as for women who are not so disabled. The discrepancy that exists between their desires for this normal experience and the realities of their ability to carry out the role of motherhood creates additional emotional pain for the patients. Therefore, this book is written so as to be accessible to women patients we have known, who have told us about their fantasies and their experiences, as well as to the many with whom we have not worked.

The therapy team needs to work closely with other specialties, particularly obstetrics and gynecology, which may not be receptive or cooperative. Today, one pregnancy in one psychotic inpatient can require more than a psychiatric-medical team. For example, at least two lawyers—one for mother, one for unborn child—may be called when the patient is under commitment. Sometimes additional attorneys for the father, the family, the treatment team, and the hospital will become necessary. What may seem to be fulfillment of a life's dream for the patient can be a nightmare for clinicians, diminishing their sense of mastery and competence. Indeed, even for outpatient pregnant patients with long-term mental illness, caregivers and community services can scarcely keep up with realistic needs.

In this book we focus on childbearing from the perspective of the mental health professionals who work with patients who become parents rather than from the viewpoint of the children. Children who have parents with mental illness are also in need of attention and work, but their concerns are outside the scope of this book.

For the purposes of this book we will define long-term mental illness according to Bachrach's (1988) tripartite conception of diagnosis, disability, and duration. Thus, we refer to those who have 1) a diagnosis of a major mental illness; 2) a disability involving "the erosion or the lack of development of their functional capacities in three or more major areas of daily life," including interpersonal relationships, employment, self direction, learning, and recreation; and 3) a duration of the disability for more than 2 years.

We begin, in Chapter 1, to explore the search for normality that we believe underlies the wishes of those persons with long-term mental illness to have families. Then, in Chapter 2, we examine staff issues and the complex responses of mental health professionals to these difficult cases. In Chapter 3, we talk about sex, safe sex, and birth control, and discuss the impact of medication in men and women. In Chapter 4, we review female patients' menstruation and reproductive life cycle, sexuality, gynecological care, and contraceptive choices. Pregnancy is the subject of the following four chapters (Chapters 5–8). The puerperium is a time of high risk for first and recurrent psychoses for all women and for some vulnerable men, and this is the subject matter of Chapter 9. The extreme tragedy of infanticide is considered in Chapter 10 because it is a common fear about this population. In Chapter 11 we focus on the specific parenting experience of men with long-term mental illness and describe both the fantasies and the realities of fatherhood. Long-term treatment strategies and options for parenting by people with major mental illness, beyond the pregnancy, are the focus of Chapter 12. We conclude, in Chapter 13, with recommendations for further research and clinical and programmatic work.

Chapter 1

Sex and Reproduction: Ways of Being Normal for Patients With Long-Term Mental Illness

For too long, mental patients have been faceless, voiceless people. We have been thought of, at worst as subhuman monsters, or at best, as pathetic cripples, who might be able to hold down menial jobs and eke out meagre existences, given constant professional support. Not only have others thought of us in this stereotyped way, we have believed it ourselves . . .

. . . [but, now, we have begun to] see ourselves for what we are—a diverse group of people, with strengths and weaknesses, abilities and needs, and ideas of our own.

Judi Chamberlin *On Our Own* (1988)

Schizophrenia is a lonely and difficult disease.

Patricia Ruocchio "How Psychotherapy Can
Help the Schizophrenic Patient" (1989)

*T*he literature on what is abnormal in major mental illness is vast, and much clinical and experimental research work has gone into documenting, classifying, and attempting to understand the confusing welter of symptoms and disturbances that attend and characterize long-term psychotic illnesses. Much less has been written from the perspective of what is "normal" in people with long-term psychosis. Clinical and research-based observation has established that no one is psychotic 24 hours a day, 365 days a year, in every sector of his or her personality. Since Freud's essay on Schreber (1911), there has been a growing realization that many schizophrenic symptoms are attempts at restitution—that is, attempts to rebuild a shattered internal world—and emergency efforts to maintain contact with the outer world.

Clearly, in our current state of understanding, we do not have a comprehensive picture of the relationship between the normal and the abnormal in the person with long-term psychosis. But even more painful and more poignant is that our patients often struggle with this same question. "Twas not Hamlet, but Hamlet's madness that spoke and acted so outrageously"—thus pleads Hamlet, begging forgiveness, in Shakespeare's play. Many patients do not have such a clear picture of their inner life and the source of their behavior. Nor do their families— we know how the families of people with long-term mental illness struggle to reconcile the person they knew and the person who now is.

Our thesis in this chapter is twofold:

1. That facing up to our patients' uncertainties, including their wishes, yearnings, and fears to be normal, is a crucial part of building a working alliance with patients and their families.
2. That exploring and understanding patients' feelings and behaviors in the area of sexuality and reproduction is a vital and necessary way to work with both their yearnings and their fears about being normal.

In general, as clinicians and policy-makers, we have erred in the direction of viewing issues of sexuality and reproduction as trouble-some intrusions of the normal into the decidedly abnormal world of the patient. We wish to redress this imbalance by recognizing the normal without denying the abnormal.

In this chapter we will discuss 1) patients' experiences of them-selves as normal despite their realizations of how abnormal and im-paired they are; 2) ways in which these experiences and patient wishes for normalcy clash with the views of their therapists; 3) the nature of abnormalities stemming from the mental illness itself; and 4) the qual-ity of abnormalities associated with any high-risk chronic illness.

Patients' Experience of Themselves as Normal

Normal has the meaning of being usual or regular, and free from mental or emotional disorder. Paradoxically, the very people we consider abnormal because of their mental illness have a subjective sense of self revolving around normality. Their desire to be ordinary and usual is often quite clear, even in the midst of a thought disorder; and normality is clearly a central life goal for many individuals who have chronic mental illness (Feinberg 1988).

Psychiatrists and other mental health professionals are taught to focus on the pathological and therefore have more training and experience with the deviant and the abnormal than with the normal. Yet individuals whom we consider deviant or abnormal define themselves as no different from others whom they wish to emulate (Goffman 1963). What does it mean to be normal or like everyone else? What do human beings need universally? In an elegant study, Godschalx (1987) has demonstrated how young adults with chronic mental illness seek the same normal human experiences as everyone else. She defined these needs in the following way:

1. We seek security—psychological, physical, economic, and interpersonal.
2. We want to find meaning in life through work—a sense of accomplishment and usefulness.
3. We want to ameliorate the emotional pain of whatever losses we experience.

Godschalx studied 30 young adults with schizophrenia who were living outside the hospital. These 15 men and 15 women were randomly selected and were queried about their lives, perceptions, and coping mechanisms. When the data were analyzed, Godshalx concluded that for her sample group the wish to be like others transcended and pervaded all other concerns and dimensions of life. Normality for people with schizophrenia was both a goal and reality. She showed how patients sought interpersonal relations in order to have company and care and to avoid loneliness. Sex was sometimes no more than a way of belonging. The desire to have a child was sometimes the wish to have someone to care for, and someone to care about them, after aging relatives passed on. (In fact, 10 of the 15 women Godschalx interviewed had married, and 5 were primary caregivers for their children.)

Clash of Patients' Wish to Be Normal and Therapists' Perspective of Pathology

To interpret a normal wish as pathological may set a distance between therapist and patient. This distance allows us as therapists to treat an illness—that is, function in familiar ways. We may, however, be avoiding a clash of values with the patient and may, indeed, be forcing the patient to hold onto her insistence of normality as one side of her ambivalence because we take the opposite pole. Many women in our society are not optimally fit to be mothers (e.g., women with psychotic illnesses; those with life-threatening medical illnesses, including those with HIV antibodies; and those with drug or alcohol addiction). Ethical issues are always raised in such situations, and inevitably, we, as health caregivers, feel concern about abetting danger if we assist such women to have babies. If we see the patient's wish for a baby only as pathological, we may be able to treat the woman's illness and resolve our own conflict (Arras 1990), but we may lose the complexity of the patient's feelings and the alliance with her.

Some authors argue that our patriarchal social system has bias against women and that even women with few resources deserve opportunities to mother and assistance for that natural task (Chesler 1987; Levine and Dubler 1990). At the personal level, when the therapist feels the patient's conflict, the therapist feels the patient's enormous suffering and pain.

The benefit, however, of trying to understand the patient's wishes as one's own is that one might feel genuine empathy and even admiration for the woman who at first glance only seemed unfit to mother. Effective counseling for reproductive decisions requires an understanding of the point of view and values of the individuals who are involved (Arras 1990). The following case is an example of a clinical dilemma and clash of values:

Case 1: The Wish to Be Normal

A psychiatric consultation was requested by the medical/high-risk obstetrical team on the treatment of a young mother of two who refused to use contraception and take medication for her chronic hepatitis. The staff, concerned for her health, saw her refusal of needed medication as "crazy" and "self-destructive." In 4 years, she had had five pregnancies, three abortions, and two babies.

The patient presented herself for the psychiatric consultation, along with her baby and 3-year-old child. She seemed to take great pride and pleasure in these offspring, who were clearly well-cared-for, alert, and engaging children. They became the initial focus of the interview. The patient reported that she had felt most alive when giving birth and most in control of her life during labor and delivery. "I am infatuated with pregnancy," she said, adding, "it's something I can do right." Naturally, she wanted to repeat the experience as often as possible. Indeed, as difficult as the realities of being black and poor, young and single, medically and allegedly mentally ill, were, the presence of her children made her feel loved and normal.

The patient had gotten into a struggle with the medical team, whom she perceived as wanting to remove her right and desire to make life. No matter what names the doctors called her or what medicines they wanted her to take, she would do nothing to prevent the conception of further children. She had had so many losses, she could not give up her children too.

When the importance of her mothering was acknowledged and the necessity of improving her physical health was explained to her in terms of preserving her childbearing capacity, she was able to accept the temporary prescription of birth control and other needed medications. The contraception and medication became a vehicle for mastery of life goals rather than a deterrent. The doctors were able to enlist the healthy, life-affirming part of her in caring for herself as well as she wanted to care for her children.

Indeed, the power of the female wish to bear children can be so great that it can surpass even the most extreme circumstances (Sorel 1984). This powerful wish is observed in women who continue to become pregnant after losing custody of their children due to neglect. It is seen in those HIV-positive women who are able to become pregnant in spite of their drug addiction, AIDS-related complex, and multiple losses; many refuse to have recommended abortions and are willing to take the risk that the baby will be normal (only 30% of the babies born to HIV-positive mothers will have been infected in utero) (Arras 1990). Of the women who became pregnant again after knowing their seropositivity, more than half already had a child infected with AIDS (Willoughby and Sutherland 1988). Our usual perception of HIV-positive women who become pregnant is that they do not fully comprehend the danger to the fetus or that they are, at least, unconsciously hostile to their existing and unborn children (Navarro 1991). Yet further discussion with these patients can reveal the same wish to affirm life (Klass 1990). The power of the wish to bear children is enormous, even, or especially, in the face of previous losses of children and one's personal health. Wherever there is the physical ability remaining to get pregnant, this powerful wish might be translated into a reality.

Certain human characteristics are universal across different circumstances, cultures, places, and populations. These characteristics are also present in people with long-term mental illness: yearnings of the heart and soul, developmental stages of human growth, and significant differences in the male and female experience. Those with long-term mental illness also suffer from all the necessary and usual losses of life, but mental illness itself represents a major loss that can be the substrate in which the desires for reproduction are generated.

The need to nurture is present and apparent even in those who are mentally ill. On a state hospital ward, it is quite usual and moving to see older and more experienced patients care for those who are younger, newer, and more psychotic. Most individuals have many outlets for their generativity; the possible avenues for expression of nurturing feelings are, however, limited in those persons with mental illness. Childbearing seems generative and possible even when childrearing is not a reality. The need to be nurturant is recognized alongside or as underlying the need to be nurtured; both are present in our patients.

Pregnancy and birth are times when women consolidate their identity as women, crucial times to create the social dimension of women's lives (Leavitt 1986). The experience of pregnancy can bind women to each other across the inherent barriers between a patient with mental illness and her professional caregiver, as illustrated in the following case (Forcier 1990):

Case 2: The Bond of Pregnancy

An agitated unidentified psychotic woman was brought to the emergency room by the police and placed in four-point restraints. When the psychiatry resident, who was pregnant, came to speak with her, the patient interrupted her screaming and wistfully said, "Oh, I was once pregnant too, 15 years ago. If you untie my hands, I will tell you about it." The young psychiatrist was so taken with this moment of normal contact that she did undo the hand restraints. The patient sat up and talked coherently and vividly about her own experience of pregnancy, woman to woman. After she had described her pregnancy, labor, and delivery in great detail, she said, sadly, that the baby had been given up for adoption, and she resumed more assaultive and psychotic talk. The island of sanity in the midst of this crisis was remarkable and gave the resident a glimpse of another person, a woman more like herself in some ways. Although the patient continued to present a management problem and needed to be restrained again, the doctor felt more empathy and was able to take more care with the case.

Several authors have noted the significant gender differences in schizophrenia (Bachrach and Nadelson 1988; Childers and Harding 1990; DeLisi and Crow 1989; Goldstein 1988; Goldstein and Kreisman 1988; Goldstein and Link 1988; Goldstein and Tsuang 1990; Goldstein et al. 1989; Lewine 1979, 1988; Lewine et al. 1989; Mogul 1985; Seeman 1982, 1983a, 1983b, 1989a, 1989b; Seeman and Lang 1990; Seeman et al. 1982; Wyatt et al. 1989). In the earlier literature, women with schizophrenia were found to be more overtly hostile, physically active and dominating, seductive, and sexually delusional, and, in general, to be louder, more emotional, and more visible. Recent well-designed studies tend to support these observations (Bennett et al. 1988; Test et al. 1990). The incidence of schizophrenia is relatively equal in women and men, but the expression of the illness is different, with women tending to be more schizoaffective (Seeman 1989b). Different treatment strategies are necessary for men and women patients (Lewine 1988; Seeman 1983b; Shelter 1991). In one study, in which deinstitutionalized patients were assessed for coping style, women were able to integrate more successfully based on their greater social sensitivity and responsivity to support in the environment (Segal and Everett-Dille 1980). The current observation is that the course for the male with schizophrenia is apt to be more isolated and downhill; women, on the whole, tend to have a relatively benign course and to behave in a way that elicits more support from other people (Bardenstein and McGlashan 1986; Goldman and Ravid 1980; Mowbray and Chamberlain 1986).

Females, compared with males, are known to be more affective and affiliative, and this is also true of females with schizophrenia. Schizophrenic illnesses in females have a later onset on the average, and the illness picture is different than that of men, with more sociability and affect evident. Females with schizophrenia are more apt to marry, to want to have babies, and to parent than are males with this disorder (Test et al. 1990).

Babies provide a social and community context for their parents. Raising a child connects a mother with other mothers and pediatricians, and with playgrounds and schools. The role of motherhood provides meaningful work and a social situation with easy access to those persons with a mutual interest. Babies are joyful and life-affirming, and their vitality is contagious, even to depressed and self-absorbed people.

Losses of children, real and imagined, are devastating to the parents or would-be parents. Astrachan (1983) has movingly described the devastation in a couple who suffered a stillbirth, showing how the fetus was already a fantasied child for the parents-to-be. Lazare (1979) describes how he wept when he learned of the crash of a plane that was bringing a child from Vietnam whom he had never met but was planning to adopt. Similarly, people who have mental illness can experience an enormous sense of loss when they talk of children who might have only existed for them in hopes or fantasy (Hilgard and Newman 1959). Biological mothers who have given up babies for adoption continue to think of those children over their entire lives (Rynearson 1982).

Abnormal by Virtue of Mental Illness: Loss of Identity

The mind's dysfunction inhibits the person with mental illness in his or her quest for normalcy. This dysfunction involves both cognition and affect. The psychotic inability to distinguish fantasy from reality may be reflected in the patient's fantasy of being normal, while, in fact, he or she is very far from acting and appearing normal. The continual therapeutic challenge is how to acknowledge both fantasies and realities and to help the patient to realize whatever dreams of normalcy can be implemented and to mourn those that cannot be (Chapman and McGhie 1963).

Internal struggles, ambivalence, indecision, distortion, and pain are apparent in those persons with long-term mental illness ("Recovering Patient" 1986; Strauss 1989). Part of the disease schizophrenia is a disturbance in the person's inner sense of whom or what he or she is (Hatfield 1989). This commonly encountered difficulty with identity is evident in one example of a mother with schizophrenia who writes about her anxiety concerning her son (DuVal 1989). She poignantly describes the small boy's social isolation and backwardness, and her fear and pain that he would be just like her instead of being normal. Doubts that are normally associated with parenting are amplified in a mother with schizophrenia.

These identity problems are part of the illness (Estroff 1989), part of experiencing the sense of being abnormal while wanting to be normal. A mental illness, especially schizophrenia, can overwhelm a person so much that a redefinition of the sense of self becomes necessary (Strauss and Estroff 1989). The schizophrenic person's inner disturbance of self is *the* most profound loss. The sense of self also grows out of social roles that are severely damaged by a schizophrenic illness (Estroff 1989). Kinship ties that permit a sense of belonging can be weakened in families who can get worn out by years of living and working with a family member who has a long-term mental illness (Strauss and Estroff 1989). Additionally, once the person with mental illness is identified as a patient, that identity can become primary for the person as well as the caregiver and may supplant all other identities. The mental health system, especially hospitalization, tends to promote and reinforce dependency and weakness. However, the disabling characteristics of the disease process itself are fundamental; at best, mental health care in the community can halt or ameliorate the disability rather than potentiate it. Living in the community even with optimal treatment is still difficult. Those persons with mental illness are reminded of their deviance and dysfunctions daily.

Families, who may be the only people with whom the person feels truly safe, can become estranged (Seeman 1982). Siblings present the contrast of an enviable, more normal life. There are families in which the siblings can become strong advocates for their family member who is mentally ill. But, for others, the conflicting emotions experienced by both sibling and patient may provide less than optimal safety and support. While for all adults the loss of parents is a developmental milestone, it can be an especially devastating loss to a person whose illness has so limited other personal and social ties (Lefley 1987). People with mental illness need the chance to live with dignity in the community, but the lives they lead can be very difficult for them and for their caregivers (Minkoff 1987).

For people with severe mental illness, social disablements, the tertiary level of disability, get established and then persist, creating their own disadvantage even for people who are able to spend most of their years of illness outside of hospitals. The diminished social networks, the stigma of mental illness (Flynn 1987), the downward mobility, the inevitable poverty and unemployment—all contribute to a general deviance from the mainstream of society (Bachrach 1986–1987).

Estroff (1981), in an anthropological study of people with chronic mental illness, was able to learn intimately about the personal agonies and incapacities of these individuals. She writes poignantly about the conflict and loneliness, disconnectedness, resignation, and passivity that characterize so many of the people she studied, and about their sorrow, courage, fear, and hope. The additional stress of street life and drug abuse is noted in that over half the group of young adult men and women with schizophrenia used alcohol, marijuana, and other street drugs on a daily basis. The clients classified themselves as "crazies" (or "freaks" or "nuts") as distinct from "normies" or "regular people."

Schwab, a medical anthropologist working with a research team, also studies young adult schizophrenic people in the community and has been particularly impressed by their social relationships and involvement with children (Schwab et al. 1991). For some persons with mental illness, parenthood can potentially overcome the major problems of isolation, identity confusion, and stigma that are associated with long-term mental illness. By becoming a parent, one can travel from outcast to a valued and honored status.

Case 3: The Patient's Pregnancy as Vicarious Pregnancy for the Therapeutic Community

The patient was a 32-year-old woman with bipolar disorder who had a chaotic course, with many suicide attempts and hospitalizations. The patient had been married for 2 years, to another patient, but they lived separately in all-male and all-female cooperative apartments. When the patient became pregnant, she and her husband decided that she would carry the baby to term and then relinquish the baby for adoption.

At the day program she attended, the patient became the special member of the community for both staff and her peers, although she had previously been considered somewhat troublesome. The other female patients looked up to her in awe and asked about her experiences. "How does it feel to be pregnant?" "How did you decide to give up the baby?" "How will you be able to give the baby up?" "Can you feel the baby move?" The patient became the pregnant woman for all the other patients.

The patient's experience had a profound effect on staff also. Some staff members felt a sense of pride that she was so stable during this period of pregnancy and that this previously difficult patient was cooperative and making progress. They praised her as being mature and sensible in her decision to relinquish the baby. One female staff member began to talk of her own yearnings for a baby during supervisory sessions and felt that she envied the patient's fertility.

The patient's ambivalence about her decision to relinquish the baby emerged only with her individual therapist and not in the context of the day-program milieu. She even asked that her therapist accompany her during labor and delivery. The individual therapist worried that once the baby was given away, the patient would lose not only the child but her status as the special patient. A good deal of time was spent in therapy about these issues, and care was taken that the patient and her husband spend some days with the baby before the infant was given to his adoptive parents. Two months after the baby was adopted, the patient and her husband moved together, as a childless couple, to an apartment in a nearby state. After providing for the appropriate clinical linkages for the transfer of both patients, the treaters never heard about the couple again. The pregnancy and baby, it seemed, had been a farewell gift; the whole community felt the loss.

Abnormal by Virtue of Chronic Illness: A High-Risk Situation

Any and all chronic illnesses present the individual with a burden. Life is permanently altered and must be lived with and around the illness. Whenever a new event or illness occurs, the chronic illness must be taken into account. Medications required to maintain and enhance life with the chronic illness inevitably have side effects that also affect other body systems, including the mind. Any chronic illness in pregnancy can create a high-risk situation. Naturally, this is especially true of those illnesses in which hormones, reproductive organs, and mental functioning are concerned.

Chronic illnesses, in general, require different means for coping and adaptation than acute medical illnesses. The former are harder to define and limit and more difficult to treat, and the goal of treatment is amelioration and coping strategies rather than cure. The very nature of chronic illness is the rhythm, often unpredictable, of relapses and remissions, of new symptoms in new places. The demands on the individual and on the treatment team are quite different. The individual must manage himself or herself in the world, hoping to regulate stress and maximize quiescence. Developing a relationship with not just one, but often several professionals for different aspects of care is essential and requires skills for organization and relatedness from the patient (Hubner 1989).

The patient must become aware of his or her body and must be able to learn early warning signs to minimize damage and pain in relapses. For the person with chronic mental illness, this can be a major problem. The thought disorder in schizophrenia itself interferes with the recognition of relapses in the mental illness and in incidental physical illnesses. Severe mental illness often has as one of its characteristics a distorted body awareness. Patients who have been mentally ill for years may fail to recognize themselves in the mirror, or they may relate delusionally to parts of the body rather than to the body as a whole. Furthermore, schizophrenia is associated with failure to register important bodily sensations, especially pain (Talbott 1978). This inability of the patient with chronic illness to be an ally in his or her own care puts more burden on the treatment team and may dangerously delay needed treatment.

The chronic illness of schizophrenia has impact on other systems besides the mind. Even before the advent of psychotropic drugs, amenorrhea and movement disorders were described as part of the picture of the disease of schizophrenia. This disease is based in the brain and is associated with neurotransmitters that have impact throughout the human organism. In addition to the illness itself, the medications used to treat schizophrenia typically affect sexual functioning, creating changes in libido and performance.

Because women have been shown to cooperate with drug treatment, as well as with social role and psychological treatments that are offered, they have significantly more favorable outcomes than do men (Hogarty et al. 1974a, 1974b). Women premenopausally tend to respond faster and better to lower doses of neuroleptic drugs, suggesting that estrogen has a potentiating effect on the medication; following menopause, the female patient requires more medication (Seeman 1989a, 1989b; Seeman and Lang 1990).

Psychotropic drugs can affect many systems in a woman when she is in a nonpregnant state. With the addition of pregnancy, itself a condition affecting many bodily systems, the effects of these drugs are even more complex. Even without considering the severe psychosocial aspects of mental illness, the fact of its chronicity and of the physical aspects of the disorder make for highly complicated and risky situations. There is a high risk of losing the pregnancy. There is also high physical risk to the mother and high risk to the professionals who treat these most complex pregnant patients.

With all their physical and mental abnormalities, women with mental illness still sometimes opt to have pregnancies. The outcome of these pregnancies is not sufficiently and consistently negative to routinely advise against them, even if this were possible and ethical (Arras 1990; Robinson 1933). Therefore, we have to learn how to understand and better manage women with mental illness who are making such complex and complicating reproductive choices.

The reality of the high risk (for mother and child) associated with pregnancy in this group of patients, coupled with their strong desires for normalcy and parenthood, creates a most difficult situation for treaters. Next, we will explore the responses of clinicians who must confront these two often-opposing forces when treating pregnant patients with severe mental illness.

Chapter 2

Sex and Reproduction in the Care of Patients With Long-Term Mental Illness

*C*aring for a psychotic woman who is pregnant can be a harrowing experience. The intensity of the staff members' feelings and fantasies make this work especially difficult. Disentangling and understanding our own complex and powerful emotional response patterns can be a key to the treatment of such complicated and disturbing cases. In this chapter we will look more closely at how staff, including 1) general ward staff, 2) individual therapists, 3) women clinicians, and 4) pregnant staff, react to pregnant women who suffer from long-term mental illness.

General Ward Staff Reactions to a Pregnant Psychotic Woman: Parallel Process

Treating pregnant women who have long-term severe mental illness may activate negative or positive attitudes among caregivers. Beyond individual attitudes some reactions can involve the entire staff on a ward. Negative feelings may be voiced, when conscious, in informal settings, during coffee breaks, or in private conversations. Sometimes unacceptable staff reactions may remain unconscious, only to emerge through projections onto others or, indirectly, to be expressed by the patients on the ward. Unit leadership has a major role in making the ward milieu one in which it is safe for staff and patients to express and explore these views. It is important to find ways to bring staff feelings such as confusion, anger, and ambivalence into conscious awareness so that they are not acted upon (Wile et al. 1988).

Case 4: Hatred of a Pregnant Patient

A 28-year-old woman with a chronic schizoaffective disorder was readmitted to an inpatient unit after she was found arguing loudly with people on a busy city street corner and picked up by the police. Upon evaluation, it was noted that she was 7 months pregnant and a polydrug abuser, and that she earned money through prostitution. Although the woman did not want any treatment, she was evaluated by the courts and admitted to a locked unit against her will.

During the first month of her hospital stay, she refused prenatal care, cursed at professional staff, and did not participate in unit activities. The baby's father, who was also addicted to multiple substances, visited her often. The couple made plans to keep the infant but showed no intention of changing their present life-style.

When the patient's case was first brought up in staff meetings, there was little comment. In fact, there was no discussion about conflicted feelings among the staff about the patient's pregnancy, her prostitution, or her court-ordered commitment. Privately, staff members muttered and fumed and wished the patient had been admitted in time to solve the problem via abortion. Only after comments from vocal patients on the ward emerged did the staff members have to confront their own strong negative feelings.

"She shouldn't be a mother!"

Staff on the unit felt angry that they were obliged to care for this pregnant patient when she acted in ways that were not healthy for her or the unborn child. Staff members were unable or found it difficult to identify with this woman's desire for a baby; they identified, instead, with the maltreated unborn child. They also felt frustrated and helpless and did not feel connected to this patient who rebuffed their efforts to care for her. The more they felt powerless, the more they turned away from the patient.

The staff discussion reflected the difficulty of maintaining an empathic stance with a patient whose illness and behavior character-ized her as the antithesis of the stereotypical good mother. One clini-cian asked that the patient be transferred to another hospital so that the clinician's discomfort in treating a drug-addicted pregnant prostitute with a long-term mental illness could simply disappear.

In time, guidance from the team leader and from an invited outside consultant allowed another side of the staff members' feelings to emerge: I wonder how this patient found herself in such an impossible and painful situation. I wonder what her sense of her ability to mother is. I wonder if she had a "bad mother" herself. I wonder why she is trying to keep us distant from her.

"Isn't there still a way for her to have an abortion?"

This astonishing denial of the reality of a near-term pregnancy signaled the team's impasse. Some clinicians expressed the feeling that taking care of this pregnant patient was too difficult and that they wanted to make the pregnancy go away. Societal, moral, and religious values were discussed, with excessive intellectualizing, by the staff, but most of the discussion focused on the angry feelings that were engendered by this patient on the ward. The pregnancy was seen by some as a problem and by others as a reproductive process. What rights did the mother have? What rights did the unborn baby have? And, ultimately, what rights did the anguished staff have to be free of their ambivalent feelings?

Staff response over time changed to: I wonder what the patient thinks about abortion. I wonder what her religious and ethical values are. I wonder if she considered abortion earlier in her pregnancy. Did she discuss this issue with the baby's father or with other family members? I wonder if she feels ambivalent about the pregnancy. Gradually, the patient became a real, individual person to the staff.

"You can't lock up a pregnant woman!"

Some staff members remarked that it was difficult for them to simultaneously contain the image of a pregnant woman and the image of a psychotic "madwoman." Societal values that honor and elevate the pregnant woman are in direct conflict with a court-ordered incarceration. Mental health workers and nurses felt terrible when they had to physically restrain a pregnant psychotic woman. They blamed the psychiatrist, the court, and/or the patient for the painful situation they were in.

Staff response over time changed to: I wonder if this patient feels frightened to be pregnant and in a mental hospital. I wonder how she feels about her involuntary commitment. I wonder what it is like for her and the baby's father during this time.

"Why should she have special treatment?"

The anger and jealousy expressed by other patients because of the pregnant patient's special status on the ward began a staff discussion about their own rage at the extra workload that she required. All patients should be treated equally, but it was also true that the pregnant woman required more attention. The patient's special status was also enhanced by resistance to treatment and refusal to cooperate. As staff anger mounted, it became more difficult to empathize with or approach the patient with the nurturing stance that was their professional pride. They did not want to collude with her "evil deed"—bringing a baby into the world under these circumstances. They felt angry, guilty, unsympathetic, and deprived of gratification in their work.

Staff response over time changed to: I wonder if this patient feels special because she is pregnant. Does her special status on the unit make her feel good? How does she regard her pregnancy? Is this the most honored role that she has ever experienced? Does the anger of the other patients because of her status repeat any family issues she had as a child? After this discussion, the staff could start to treat this patient with more empathy.

"At least let's save the baby!"

Anger at the mother coexisted with a positive identification with the baby. Some clinicians felt hopeless in connection with the care of the pregnant patient but hoped that the hospitalization would at least serve to protect the fetus from harm. They could feel successful if the baby were healthy. Positive feelings were expressed about the baby, and elaborate fantasies about the baby's future were detailed by some staff members. They wanted to address their patient's negative behaviors in order to encourage her to accept prenatal care.

Staff response over time changed to: I wonder if she has positive fantasies about the baby. What hopes and dreams does she imagine for the baby's future? How do those fantasies connect to her refusal to have prenatal care? Does the baby's father care about the baby's prenatal care and future health?

In response to changes in staff attitudes, the patient began to accept prenatal care during her second month of hospitalization. She also allowed a nurse to coach her and the baby's father about the process of labor and delivery. The patient became a more active member of the ward community and was able to discuss her pregnancy, her drug addiction, and her prostitution. She shared her hopes and fears about her pregnancy in community meetings and was given support by other women who had had babies in the past.

"Do you take babies away?"

The issues of loss and abandonment came into focus at staff meetings as the time for the patient's confinement drew near. The fact that the baby would be leaving the hospital soon after delivery elicited a good deal of sadness among the staff. Some staff members were surprised to realize how emotionally involved with the fantasy baby they had become. They wanted so much for the baby to be healthy that they had even stopped thinking of the likelihood that the baby would have health problems secondary to drug exposure.

It was another patient's question about babies being taken away that initiated a discussion about a requirement for professional staff to file reports with the child welfare agency about possible neglectful or abusive parenting. Much anguish was expressed by both patients and staff about this mandated reporting role. The attachment to this pregnant patient made some staff members hopeful she would alter her way of life, be able to keep the baby, and not have to be reported as a neglectful or abusive parent. Others hoped that the baby would be removed and set up in a good adoptive home. Some staff members said that they felt that babies should never be removed from their mothers.

Staff response over time changed to: I wonder how the patient can manage to keep her baby. I wonder how she can ever bear to relinquish her baby if she is required to do so. I wonder if she is so wounded by her past experiences that she may not have the hope or strength to adhere to a plan that will enable her to be a mother to the baby. Staff were finally able to see the situation with compassion and not blame the patient for her limitations.

After the baby was born, this woman was able to hold and provide some care for her baby. She agreed to accept foster care while she attempted to stay off drugs and enroll in both a mental health outpatient clinic with a program for mothers with major mental illness, and a 12-step program for recovering addicts. The ward staff never saw her again, and they still wonder how successful she was in her attempts to parent. The clinicians learned about themselves as they listened to the patients on the ward, discussed their feelings and fears, and provided optimal care for this pregnant woman. The ongoing discussions of staff reactions to this complicated and difficult clinical situation provided a forum in which mutual support enabled staff to tolerate their differing points of view and bear the difficulties and demands of the work together. Often, the frustrations, fears, helplessness, and sadness surrounding these cases not only reflect staff issues but also mirror the inner experience of the pregnant psychotic woman herself.

The Therapist's Idiosyncratic Reactions

When a therapist is individually treating a woman with a long-term mental illness who becomes pregnant, the therapist may have an idiosyncratic response, in addition to the common patterns that were highlighted in the previous section. Whereas the ward staff meeting is a better vehicle for airing the common patterns, individual supervision (even on a ward) is a better context for discussion of a therapist's idiosyncratic reactions. Supervision will be especially necessary to help the therapist understand strong personal reactions that are out of conscious awareness.

Case 5: The Therapist's Hidden Wishes

A 32-year-old unmarried woman with a bipolar disorder was a practicing Catholic. She had given birth to two children who were living with adoptive parents. She had been seen at an outpatient clinic for 10 years and recently started to work with a new female psychiatrist. The patient did not have a steady partner but often hitchhiked to other cities and had sexual relations with men she met in bars. She had been hospitalized many times, but her condition was now stable—living in a co-op apartment and working for a dry cleaning store near the clinic.

Within months of meeting her new therapist, the patient announced that she was pregnant again and intended not to have an abortion, due in part to her religious beliefs, but would give up this baby, too, for adoption. The therapist was extremely upset and after the session talked to other clinic staff about this dilemma. The next time she was to meet with the patient, the therapist was uncharacteristically late and found that she had difficulty sitting through the session. When the therapist discussed the case in supervision, she began to realize how much she herself wanted a baby and was jealous of the patient's fertility. She understood that she felt it was unfair for this patient to have so many pregnancies, to endanger the unborn babies with environmental toxins, and to then give up the babies, while she herself had none. She objected to a woman with long-term mental illness having a baby and was having trouble helping the patient explore her fantasies of motherhood.

After this personal insight, gained in part through working with her supervisor, the therapist began to wonder about the patient's positive reactions to her pregnancy. As she heard the patient describe her condition, the doctor could hardly contain her own yearnings for a pregnancy. The therapist fantasied that the patient might have noticed her barren therapist's wishes for a baby. The patient talked about wanting to be pregnant but did not have any positive thought about motherhood; she had quickly arranged to relinquish the unborn child without exploring any ambivalent feelings connected with this decision. The therapist's new awareness of her own fantasies about having a child helped her to work with the patient. The therapeutic sessions began to flow as explorations of the patient's positive and negative feelings about her pregnancy, and the patient's plan to give up her baby was examined. Continuing supervision was crucial for the therapist because it opened the way for both patient and doctor to explore the intense and complex issues of pregnancy and motherhood. The patient had the baby and acknowledged the birth and the loss in therapy; she relinquished the baby for adoption and, some months later, had a tubal ligation.

Women Clinicians Treating Women Patients

Female professionals who have a self-image as good, caring, therapeutic, self-sufficient, and rational may find it especially difficult to be confronted by women patients who are the opposite (male professionals, on the other hand, may not have the same problems with such patients) (Zambrana et al. 1987). The Women's Issues Consultation Team at San Francisco General Hospital (SFGH), as reported by Eastwood et al. (1989), has addressed the unconscious responses of female clinicians. Female staff on the SFGH inpatient unit, which specialized in treating psychotic pregnant women, found that there were certain pregnant patients who were particularly hard to treat and who stimulated strong negative responses. They described four types of women who stimulated intense, disturbing responses in their all-female staff: 1) the aggressive woman; 2) the sex trade worker; 3) the dependent woman; and 4) the bad mother. These types of women evoked reactions that diminished optimal treatment of their psychological distress. The authors concluded that these patients represent for the clinicians negative aspects of the feminine psyche, and, therefore, the clinicians have greater difficulty working with such women who are mentally ill.

We recommend examination of these issues in staff meetings and in supervision so that staff members can be more comfortable with female patients who set off strong countertransference responses. Female professionals doing this work may also require their own personal psychotherapy to allow them to accept disavowed parts of themselves. Disentangling these specific woman-to-woman negative countertransference issues may also require outside consultation when there is collective staff response to particular patients on a ward (Eastwood et al. 1989). It is important that women professionals be as open and honest with each other as possible in order to provide the insight and support needed to fully explore these intense feelings.

The Pregnant Therapist

When therapists are pregnant, they are able to gain insight into emotions that surround the sexual/reproductive experiences of women with major mental illness and feel the tension between their patients' desire for normalcy and the reality of their disabilities. Through the experience of pregnancy, the therapist is better able to connect to her patients' profound experiences of loss. The hidden aspects of the reproductive life both of the therapist and of patients with major mental illness are thrust into the open; it can be both a shattering experience (for which many are unprepared) and an opportunity to work on issues that have been deeply buried (Bridges and Smith 1988; Statlender 1990).

Several authors have shown that there are typical countertransferential themes that occur for pregnant therapists. Benedek (1973) and others (Paluszny and Poznanski 1971) noted that as the therapist approaches term, there is a decrease in her interest in the intellectual side of the work and a tendency to withdraw. Nadelson and her colleagues (1974) noted an added sense of vulnerability in the pregnant therapist caused by her bodily changes, her attention to the baby, and her fears that something may go wrong. There are special considerations for those pregnant therapists working with people with long-term mental illness. Some specific issues are discussed below.

Guilt

Staff who are pregnant often feel guilty when they leave their patients, even when thoughtful coverage has been arranged. Baum and Herring

(1975) found that pregnant residents may be especially anxious and guilty; in the third trimester, they withdrew libido from patients and work, causing feelings of guilt. McCarty and her colleagues (1986) commented that pregnant therapists may feel guilty because of fantasied wishes about leaving their patients entirely to devote themselves to their own unborn children.

If other staff acknowledge their own ambivalent feelings about the pregnant therapist's leave, it will be easier for the therapist to value her personal as well as professional needs (Auchincloss 1982). A pregnant therapist may feel that she is leaving very sick patients to other staff members who must carry on her work during her absence (Baum and Herring 1975). Some therapists may take on extra duties while they are pregnant and working in order to compensate for the burden they feel they later will be placing on others (Frank 1990; Leibenluft 1984). They may also feel guilty because of their own reproductive opportunity in the face of the profound losses experienced by their patients.

Disruption of Boundaries

The therapist's pregnancy breaks down the normal barriers between patients and staff by removing the anonymity of the therapist's personal life (Bassen 1988; Browning 1974). For the patient with long-term mental illness, these barriers and clear role demarcations foster safety, clarity, and the distinct reality of each person. Pregnancy is a manifest acknowledgment of the therapist's active sexual life. A female patient may even identify with her therapist and become pregnant; then her pregnant therapist, after realizing that identification is one motive for the pregnancy, must either find a way to continue working with the patient or find someone else to reclarify the boundaries between patient and therapist.

Ambivalence

Pregnant therapists may worry about how they will be able to care for a new baby and continue on with their professional lives. "Will I be a good mother?" "Will I continue to be a good therapist?" Because of the ambivalence about the coexistence of these two roles, therapists may find it difficult to make clear plans to terminate with patients, begin maternity leave, or set a date for return to work. Therapists who are pregnant may doubt both their own abilities to be a mother and their ability to continue to be effective with patients. Pregnant therapists, like all pregnant women, can be confused about how their role as mothers and their professional role can be reconciled and uncertain about which role they would rather emphasize.

Safety Issues

Pregnant women often feel physically as well as emotionally vulnerable. Movements of the baby and other bodily preoccupations may distract the pregnant therapist. Psychotic patients may be acutely aware of these differences in the therapist and may feel intense and primitive feelings of rage toward the therapist and/or the unborn baby. Therapists must trust their instincts; if and when they become fearful of patients, consultation and supervision can help to ascertain if it is safe to continue working with a patient who arouses a new sense of fearfulness. In some cases, the therapist or patient may have to be transferred to ensure everyone's basic safety. Pregnant therapists often feel increased sensitivity to protecting their unborn babies from harm in the work setting. They may be less able to tolerate the emotional impact of psychotic patients and psychotic transference responses that are accelerated by the pregnancy. Often they feel shaky about their professional competence when they are faced with amplified problems at a time when they feel less able to cope.

We are learning more about how pregnant mental health clinicians respond to working with patients who have major mental illness. Just as patient reactions can help us to understand staff responses, the pregnant staff member's feelings give us insight into the pregnant patient's condition. A pregnant therapist is usually middle class, educated, and planning a pregnancy under the best circumstances. The pregnant therapist may, however, have many feelings in common with the pregnant patient: feeling vulnerable, feeling proud, being looked upon by both staff and other patients as sexually active; being envied by her peers; feeling guilty about exceeding her peers; feeling special; and worrying about her ability to mother and what negative traits she will transmit to her child (DuVal 1989).

The challenge for staff is to continue to try to balance the normal wishes of the patients with the very real treatment issues that the mental illness and the pregnancy present. By looking at the complex issues surrounding any pregnancy, we can learn a great deal about ourselves and our patients. How that listening and learning translate into practical considerations is the subject of the next several chapters.

Chapter 3

Talking With Patients About Sexuality

> Sexual performance is not disturbed in schizophrenia. What may
> frequently be disturbed is the ability to conduct a courtship.
>
> M. V. Seeman "Gender Differences in Schizophrenia" (1982)

*W*omen and men with severe and long-term mental illness have
basic gender-related preoccupations about sex: sexual fantasies, urges
and feelings, and a need to express themselves sexually as others do.
They have the right to this sexual expression, free of the fear of
contracting venereal illness or conceiving an unwanted baby. Because
people who have severe mental illness have been considered genderless
and not able to take responsibility for the consequences of their sexuality, historically, their right to be sexual has been denied or diminished.

Views about sex are determined by the historical times and by the
cultural context (Bancroft 1983). Sex in special populations reflects
and exaggerates these views. In this chapter, we will review 1) the data,
and the problems encountered in collecting data, related to the sexuality
of people with major mental illness; 2) the effects of psychotropic
medication on sexual functioning; 3) staff attitudes regarding sexuality
in their patients' lives; 4) inpatient management of sexuality; 5) the
problem of sexual exploitation of people with major mental illness; and
6) examples of sex education training for staff and patients.

Sexuality in Persons With Major Mental Illness

In recent years, we have extended our awareness of the sex-related
needs of men and women with long-term mental illness (Bachrach and
Nadelson 1988; Friedman and Harrison 1984; Morgan and Rogers
1971; Raboch 1984). Aside from Barton's 1962 matter-of-fact recognition of the presence and expectation of sexuality in the mental hospital,
there has been, heretofore, scant mention of sexuality in the histories
detailing the daily lives of patients in asylums in this country (G. Grob,
personal communication, 1989). In earlier decades, when mentioning

sexuality in psychosis at all, researchers lumped all those patients with long-term mental illness together as "schizophrenics" and referred to them as "endocrinologically inferior" and "sexually deficient" (see, e.g., Mott 1919). The distinction was not made between those who lived much of their lives in the community and those who were institutionalized. Groups of people with mental illness were studied only retrospectively, after they had already been selected as a pathological diagnostic group. It is difficult to know which of these observations were the effects of the illness per se, what were the effects of the institutionalization and diminished opportunities for more normal and mature expression of sexuality, and what might have been the problems of the observers who gathered the data (Lukianowicz 1963). For example, women who had puerperal psychosis who were studied were judged retrospectively to be "frigid" or "chronic masturbators" (Anderson 1933).

Akhtar and Thomson (1980a, 1980b) have reviewed the literature on schizophrenia and sexuality and their own patients who had been hospitalized long term. They concluded that sexual themes are prevalent in the thoughts of people with schizophrenia, as they are in the thoughts of adolescents and of adults of all ages. These authors noted four areas of sexual dysfunction among men and women with schizophrenia: 1) disorders of thought, 2) disorders of perception, 3) disorders of behavior, and 4) those disorders associated with psychotropic medication. The illness of schizophrenia itself produced a quantitative rather than a qualitative change in sexuality, ranging from autoeroticism and mutual masturbation, to oral and anal sex, to expression of immature sexual desires such as incestuous wishes and exhibitionism, and often to sexual apathy and celibacy. Patients' sexuality covers the same range as found in the general population. Some clinicians have observed that changes in sexual symptomatology forecast changes in mental status (Donlon 1976; Loeb and Loeb 1987).

Several studies showed the ordinariness of sexual functioning among those individuals with major mental illness (Brown and Heidelberg 1985). Grunebaum et al. (1971) found that schizophrenic patients grappled with the usual sexual questions and dysfunctions. Verhulst and Scheidman (1981) discovered that their patients could be interviewed reliably about their sexuality and that they had a low incidence of sexual dysfunction; there were no sexual symptoms peculiar to the person with schizophrenia. Long-term mental illness, with its concomitant social inhibition and withdrawal, usually decreases opportunities for sexual expression and intimacy. A major variable seems to be the protective and restrained environments in which most chronic patients live. Another factor may be cultural—for example, coupling of inpatients may coincide with marriages of staff members (Hartocollis 1964; Lyketsos et al. 1983).

Sometimes, recognition of patient sexuality requires the fresh view of a newcomer to the inpatient unit. The following story was written by a resident in psychiatry on her rotation at a state hospital (Ely 1990):

> Many years ago, on a sidewalk near my house, someone scratched five words into a slab of wet cement. Though moss is growing into the words now, I read them when I walk to the mailbox, or to the dry-cleaners, or the hospital. With each tilted reading, they seem to me more inspired and more struck with truth: I LOVE YOU BIG DUMMY.
>
> They remind me of the most eloquent—and also the most inarticulate—lovers I know. For 10 years, this couple has lived across the hall from one another: devoted, compelled, monogamous, and unwavering. . . . They are committed by heart to one another and by court to the state hospital.
>
> Maybe they seem an unlikely pair: He is large and moist, with a face of perpetual sorrow. He is like the sequoia through whose heart tourists drive, measuring its diameter and remarking on the centuries of petrification. Occasionally, he weeps; he never speaks.
>
> She is fragile and electric, with hair fanning out over her eyes, blocking out vision of her—and, more to the point, hers to us. Razor slashes decorate one cheek. She is especially fond of a pair of tap shoes she found in the clothing room; syncopation precedes her everywhere.
>
> Her technical diagnosis is multiple personality, and truly she is lived by several persons. Sometimes she speaks in a large and dangerous voice; sometimes she is too soft to understand; sometimes she telegraphs; sometimes babbles. Often, one or another person misplaces a season. "Mewwy Cwismas," she said all last summer in the middle of the heat wave; "Mewwy, mewwy Cwismas."
>
> No one knows exactly how they came together. Sex between patients is obviously discouraged in a hospital (raising many worthy questions for those who spend their lives behind locks). But when she kisses him in the hallway, moving one strand of hair aside to become accessible, it is clear that they have escaped what another patient once called "the wounds of boredom, the wounds of loneliness." With all her selves, she loves him; in all of his immobility, he receives her.

It is not clear whether they are aware that a compression of force is coming down hydraulically around them. The state plans to edit this hospital's population . . . Surplus patients who cannot safely be discharged will be distributed to distant hospitals. The ones most likely to be moved first and sent farthest will be those with the fewest family ties. No one knows, though, what will constitute a sufficient definition of family.

. . . when he leaves the unit these days—for the dentist, or a rare shopping trip, or perhaps to scratch her name in a slab of wet cement— she waits by the door. Sometimes she lets out a high lament over a vast desert. At those times, the personality she speaks from is not quite human.

When he comes back, she takes both his hands. She is an assemblage of joyful personalities, all of them in tap shoes. It doesn't matter what has happened to him out there. It doesn't matter which one of her persons has been waiting.

When he comes back (and for now, he still does), she dances around him. I have seen her, and she does not dance as if he were a sequoia—she dances as if he is a maypole.

Rozensky and Berman (1984) studied day center patients and showed that they were more restricted by their own ignorance and anxiety about sexuality than they were by their living environments. On self-administered questionnaires, patients revealed lack of knowledge, as in the 20% who believed they could not get pregnant at first intercourse, and the 30% who believed they could catch venereal disease from dirty towels and toilet seats, and the 39% who believed that homosexuals and heterosexuals are physiologically different. Basic anatomical questions were answered incorrectly. Alarmingly, at the same time patients reported that they knew about sex, they responded that it was all right to engage in sex but not to have sexual thoughts or feelings.

Not surprisingly, however, most patients stated that sex per se was not a rewarding part of their lives. They tended to be sexually inactive (33% not at all and 80% having intercourse less than once a month). Only 34% of those who had coitus used birth control regularly. This study demonstrated a clear need for sex education for patients with long-term mental illness that must include vocabulary, anatomy, functioning, attitudes, values clarification, birth control, and the sexual side effects of psychotropic medications.

Medications and Their Effects on Sexual Function

Almost all neuroleptic medications have some sexual side effects, many of which are mediated by increased prolactin (Sullivan and Lukoff 1990). These side effects have been largely underreported because psychiatrists do not ask for this information and patients do not readily volunteer it. In the *Physician's Desk Reference* (PDR), there is no reproductive or sexual section for side effects on any drugs. A partial list compiled from endocrine, genitourinary, and autonomic side effects includes adverse effects on all the phases of the sexual response cycle (i.e., desire, arousal, and orgasm). Both female and male patients may experience side effects from the psychotropic medications that affect the reproductive system.

Female patients may experience the following:

1. Amenorrhea and other menstrual abnormalities, such as oligomenorrhea, menorrhagia, and menopause
2. Increased or decreased desire for sex
3. Urinary impairment
4. Qualitative change in orgasm
5. Pelvic pain
6. Dyspareunia (painful intercourse)
7. False pregnancy tests (especially those based on urine)
8. Breast engorgement, cysts, pain, and lactation
9. Vaginitis and discharge

Male patients may experience the following:

1. Decreased or increased desire for sex
2. Difficulty achieving and maintaining an erection
3. Inflamed, painful testes and epididymis
4. Occasional priapism
5. Inhibition of ejaculation
6. Retrograde ejaculation (back into the bladder)
7. Delayed ejaculation
8. Inability to achieve or experience orgasm
9. Painful orgasm
10. Enlarged breasts and lactation

There is a large literature on the effects of psychotropic medications on sexuality (Dorman and Schmidt 1976; Gartrell 1986; Gottlieb and Lustberg 1977; Mitchell and Pipkin 1982); however, there has not yet been optimal collaborative research between sexuality and psychopharmacology researchers. Segraves (1989) hypothesized, based on available human and animal data, that increased dopaminergic activity is associated with erectile response. The complex mechanism of erection seems to involve inhibition of alpha-adrenergic influences and beta-adrenergic stimulation as well as the release of a noncholinergic vasodilator substance, all of which are neurochemicals affected by neuroleptic medications. Ejaculation is probably mediated via alpha-adrenergic fibers and inhibited by serotonergic transmission. Ideally, in the future, research will allow for more specific design and clinical selection of medications, taking into account the sexual side effects.

Patients who are having trouble with their own sexual functioning are not aware of the complex chemical mechanisms of the medications that they are taking. They may feel too embarrassed, ashamed, and inferior to bring up the topic of sex with their doctor and may not even think that it is the medication that is affecting their sexual functions. Or, they may make the association with the medication, feel angry about it, and not comply with the recommended drug, with or without telling the prescribing physician. The significant correlation of sexual problems with psychotropic medications holds true especially for older males and younger females, probably because of the marginal loss of sexual function in the older man and the keen awareness of reproductive cycles in the younger woman. Another correlation is that the longer patients have been taking psychotropic medications, the more enduring is the change in their sexual functioning.

Case 6: Balancing a Couple's Relationship and Medication Side Effects

Two patients developed an intimate sexual relationship in the state hospital where they were acknowledged as a couple, and took adequate birth control precautions. After discharge to the community, they were not able to live together. The woman made a better adjustment than did the man, who became increasingly isolated and paranoid. His psychiatrist prescribed more neuroleptic medication, which enabled him to engage his woman friend more but diminished his sexual potency; he could not maintain an erection. The couple saw the psychiatrist together and decided that their priority was personal closeness; they chose to maintain their relationship without sexual intercourse. They mourned this loss, but gained pleasure in shared activities, conversations, and sexual playfulness. As a couple, they were strengthened and required few hospitalizations over the years. The brief couples therapy intervention permitted a place for the patients to affirm their sexuality, express the pain and anger at their mental illness and need for medication, and affirm their security with each other's company.

Ghadirian et al. (1982) have developed a simple self-rating questionnaire about sexual dysfunction side effects of medications prescribed for men and women with long-term mental illness. Men and women are asked to describe any current sexual problems. Men are also asked to compare their experience of achieving and maintaining an erection, and of orgasm and ejaculation, with a previous time when they were not on medication. Women are also directed to respond about whether their menstruations have become more irregular or changed in quantity of blood loss. They are asked to compare the present quality and frequency of orgasm with their response at a time before medication.

Sexual side effects have been observed since an early series of medicated patients was studied by I. M. Cohen in 1956. In general, the most offending medications regarding sexuality are the phenothiazines, and especially thioridazine, which is most apt to produce ejaculatory and erectile dysfunction for men and amenorrhea for women (Kotkin et al. 1976). A long time passes before these case reports appear in the medical literature, and an even longer time elapses before they are discussed in the psychiatric literature, and then only lastly do they appear in the official drug company package insert and the PDR.

Thioridazine is a case in point. First marketed (as TP21, then later as Mellaril, by Sandoz) in the late 1950s for the treatment of schizophrenia, it became very popular because patients showed fewer overall side effects than with other medications in use at the time. By 1976, thioridazine was the most frequently prescribed major tranquilizer on the market, possibly used by as many as 12 to 15 million people. Only 31 cases of sexual dysfunction had been filed with the manufacturer. When Kotkin and his colleagues (1976) interviewed 115 men with schizophrenia, they asked the 87 who said they had masturbated or had intercourse since starting the medicine specifically about any sexual side effects. Of the thioridazine group, 60% said they had trouble: 49%

had ejaculation problems (one-third of them experiencing retrograde ejaculation), 44% had trouble getting an erection, and 35% had trouble maintaining an erection. (One-fourth of a comparison group on other tranquilizers reported overall sexual dysfunction.) Furthermore, 34 men who were taking thioridazine had previously taken other medications, and 20 said they only had the dysfunction with this drug. Dysfunction occurred in doses as low as 30 mg/day (Shader 1964). One of the authors of the 1976 Kotkin study was so impressed with the patient reports that he voluntarily took a 50-mg dose of thioridazine and masturbated 4 hours later. He experienced what is called retrograde ejaculation, a tearing suprapubic pain at orgasm and no ejaculation.

In an earlier study of thioridazine, up to 50% of women patients in the childbearing years had amenorrhea. One of the few (four) women patients who were queried reported less pleasurable arousal and less satisfying orgasm since being on thioridazine (Sandison et al. 1960). Lactation in both men and women is another disturbing side effect.

Strange or atypical sexual functioning can produce anxiety and/or shame. By inquiring matter-of-factly about sex, the clinician gives the patient permission to speak about something that may seem too private or shameful to volunteer. These effects are best discussed with the patient in advance so that the side effects can be anticipated and, thereby, prove to be less frightening if they do occur. If a particular side effect is intolerable to the patient, then perhaps another drug can be substituted.

Case 7: Powerful and Frightening Impact
of a Medication Side Effect (Lactation)

A mental health counselor met with a 24-year-old schizophrenic woman just after breakfast on the ward of a state hospital. The patient was a single parent with a 4-year-old son. She lived with her parents, who were helping her raise the child. The patient had become acutely psychotic after a miscarriage at 12 weeks gestation. She had intense paranoid thoughts for which her psychiatrist prescribed haloperidol, 10 mg tid, an increase from her usual dosage of 10 mg hs.

When approached by the therapist, the patient appeared terrified and, after some time, whispered the following story to the counselor. She was afraid that her condition had worsened and that she would never be able to go home and see her family. Then she described the events of the night before. "I woke up in the middle of the night and my sheets were quite wet. Soon I realized that I didn't wet the bed at all, but that milk was running from my breasts and soaked all the bedding. I am sure that this has happened because of my mental illness. I am afraid to tell the nurse or the doctor because they will never let me leave here. Please help me."

The mental health counselor explained calmly to the patient that the lactation she had experienced was due to her medication and that it was a known drug side effect and was not connected with pregnancy or childrearing. When the therapist reviewed the side effects of halo-peridol in the PDR with her, the patient was relieved. She spoke to the psychiatrist to request a change in her medication regime as well as a pass to see her parents and child.

Influence of Knowledge, Attitudes, and Training of Clinicians on Studies About Sexuality

Pinderhughes and his colleagues (1972) published an interview survey of doctors and psychiatric inpatients that revealed a striking disparity in attitudes and knowledge between the two groups about the relationship between sexuality and psychiatric disorders. The doctors were clearly more ignorant, or worse, filled with pseudoknowledge. The authors concluded that there is a need for hard data and education in this area. Most psychiatrists and 20% to 50% of patients believed that 1) sexual functioning does contribute to psychiatric disorder, 2) psychiatric disorders would interfere with sexual functioning, and 3) sexual activity would retard recovery from psychiatric illness. Psychiatrists said that they would tell 25% of their patients to limit sex upon discharge from the hospital, whereas 60% of the patients said that they planned to resume regular sexual relations on discharge. Psychiatrists said that they initiate discussion of sex with 80% to 89% of those patients with major mental illness; of the patients, however, only 40% had had such discussions. When patients were asked if doctors should talk with them about sexual functioning, 66% of the entire group, and 74% of those with psychotic illnesses, said yes.

Unfortunately, many psychiatrists in this survey, when referring to patients, seemed to classify sexual functioning as a psychiatric-medical disorder rather than as a part of all human life. We believe that similar attitudes and practices prevail in many psychiatric settings in the early l990s. Sexual topics are frequently omitted in the training and ongoing work of mental health professionals. Thus, it is not surprising that when staff are confronted with issues of sexuality in patient care, there are a variety of dysfunctional staff responses. For example, Akhtar et al. (1977) found that staff members reacted strongly to sexual topics, sometimes with overt anger, disbelief, and punitiveness, or sometimes with covert denial or an appearance of indifference. The absence of neutrality about sex can take the form of silence and passive non-acknowledgment of sexuality in the care of those patients with major mental illness.

However, in our experience, when the topic of sexuality is discussed openly, even people whose illness is severe enough to require long-term hospitalization do not appear to be so apathetic about sex. Even patients who have chosen celibacy or who feel relatively asexual have very strong feelings about their choices.

Management of Sexuality on an Inpatient Unit

Keitner and Grof (1981) surveyed 70 psychiatric units in Canada to learn how emotional and sexual intimacy among patients was managed. They discovered that none of the general and provincial hospitals had a written policy but that they all had a philosophy or an approach to sexuality among the patient population. Longer-term units tended to be more tolerant of patient intimacy and coupling, and to respond to them more therapeutically than did short-term units.

Most important is to evaluate each patient and his or her mental status. Patient variables include age, marital status, intellectual ability, medication, and a psychodynamic understanding of the situation. For instance, impulsive hypersexuality can be a sign of mania or early schizophrenia. Sexual relationships between patients can reflect more general problems on an inpatient unit, such as problems within the staff, that must be analyzed and directly confronted.

Any policy about sexuality is difficult to achieve and enforce. An all-inclusive policy puts staff in the position of ignoring some obvious and even appropriate intimacies that develop. Paradoxically, when AIDS is a concern, staff may be required to distribute condoms even though there is a written policy prohibiting sex among patients (Cournos et al. 1990). Staff members can feel vulnerable and uncertain about how to proceed.

Sexual Exploitation of Patients
With Mental Illness

The existence of sexual activity among patients in psychiatric hospitals is inevitable. Every person who has worked in a mental hospital knows that sexuality is a topic of great importance to the patients and to the staff and affects the relationships between these two groups. In the hospital settings where there are long-term patients, the potential for abuse of the staff-patient relationship is well known. The fact that both women and men patients have been sexually abused is also known, though not officially and openly talked about. However, it is usually the female patients who are involved sexually with male staff. Relationships can develop in which the woman patient gives some sort of consent, trading physical favors for some special holding or attention, sometimes for something as small as a cigarette or soda.

Although no one overtly condones this sexual abuse, silence on the part of hospital administration has provided covert acceptance of patient exploitation. Male mental health attendants, especially those who cover the long night hours, are the primary offenders. These attendants are typically low paid, poorly trained, and relatively powerless within the system; the sexual abuse of patients can be a way to exert power over those who are even lower in the hierarchy. The offenses are difficult to prove. The patients are, after all, mentally ill and easily dismissed as incompetent. Unfortunately, the realities of staff needs and loyalties can take priority over the truth. Abuses are most common in isolated public mental health facilities and less so in more open systems of care.

Barton, in his 1962 book on administration in psychiatry, includes a section on "sexual misconduct" in which he realistically describes the range of sexual practices in hospitals for mentally ill persons. The author indicates that he, as an experienced administrator, has seen them all. The problems in the mental hospital reflect

> fornication and adultery in the general community: sexual intercourse between male and female patients, sexual intercourse of female patients with male staff or citizens who drive onto the grounds and take the patient for a ride. Both the male and female patients expose their genitals. Employees who make sexual advances usually fondle a passive female patient on the breasts and genitalia; frank rape is rarely charged. The patient or female employee who is a nymphomaniac may make herself available. Males always seem willing to oblige. (p. 219)

Women who have been sexually abused in the past are more apt to become psychiatric patients and also to repeat the traumatic experience when they are patients (Carmen et al. 1984). In a study of 105 women in a state hospital in Illinois, 51% revealed having been sexually abused as children or adolescents; many of the patients had never before told of the abuse because they had never been asked (Craine et al. 1988). Another study indicates that patients with a history of abuse are more likely to be those who approach staff members and interact in ways that may be interpreted as sexual overtures (Beck and Van der Kolk 1987). Because so many needs for affection and dependency can be expressed in sexual behavior, a sex act that patients participate in may be followed by some misgivings and regret. These are situations that we expect to deal with clinically, and the goal is the optimal care of the patients involved. However, in the present litigious climate, secret acts can become public knowledge and public scandals.

One case report from Rochester, New York (Holbrook 1989) particularly dramatized how the pendulum could swing from avoiding any acknowledgment of sex among patients to exposing every detail to public scrutiny. In this case, the state became the prosecutor as well as the protector of patients. An allegation by a patient that he was sodomized by another patient was not reported to the family or police at the victim's request. He then reported it to his parents several days later. They reported it to the police and filed a suit against the hospital and the state. The grand jury produced no civil or criminal indictments but did instigate a demand that the hospital report every incident of sexual activity involving a mentally incompetent person. After this incident, the police demanded to be informed of every homosexual or heterosexual act.

This mandatory reporting was an overreaction that was neither fair nor clinically prudent. Whereas a few months before, no one talked to patients about sex at all, interrogation was initiated that must have been at least confusing, and probably, at times, quite traumatizing, to the patient. Such overly strict reporting requirements make the problem appear even larger and add to the public's fear about mental hospitals and mentally ill persons (Steadman 1981). Administrators of psychiatric hospitals and mental health professionals need to find some middle ground between the use of policing policies to govern sexual activity among patients and clinical discretion. The current climate always requires assessment of legal responsibility. Governing sexual abuse is necessary; clinical judgment and team decision making are essential.

Fear of legal reprisal should not be used as an excuse for not dealing with sexuality in a ward milieu. In spite of the Rochester example, we believe that the open discussion of sex with patients is most apt to lead to clinically responsible behavior. Patients do not get new ideas for sexual acting out from talking with a concerned therapist. On the contrary, when there is confusion and secrecy, it is more likely that situations will arise that can become legal problems. We believe that training and education for all staff and patients are essential and will decrease the abuses that now occur.

Talking About Sex: Some Examples

Staff Training

An important innovative sex education program for staff in long-term public psychiatric hospitals has been developed by Cohen and Tanenbaum (1985). This interdisciplinary and balanced course is aimed at increasing comfortable discussions about sexuality and patient care, and guiding personnel in assessment and intervention strategies. Material covered includes privacy, masturbation, sexual self-esteem, fantasy, and inquiries about sexual function or dysfunction. The nonjudgmental attitude of the instructors encourages curiosity and facilitates discussion.

Sex Education for Patients

Sex education for patients has been initiated in treatment settings in the past (Lukoff et al. 1986), but at present, in response to the AIDS epidemic, the need is more urgent (Sacks et al. 1990a, 1990b). Carmen and Brady (1990) instituted a course in a state hospital that got the attention of staff as well as patients. They described how time-consuming the process was and how concrete the information had to be. (For example, patients needed to practice unrolling a condom onto an anatomically correct model of an erect penis.) Questions that seemed basic were discussed: Why is the condom sticky? When do we put it on? When do we take it off? Why do my hands shake when I try to unroll it? (Akathisia and lack of confidence are the answers.)

Because resistance is inevitable and may come from any quarter, those who implement this education must be prepared to overcome criticism. In the experience of the authors, patients were much less re-sistant than staff to participating in this type of educational experience.

The sex education program for patients must be quite explicit and specific and thus may make staff members uncomfortable. The details of sexual activity need to be considered in a way that was not necessary before. For instance, what of anal sex and oral sex? Should women patients having oral sex wear the type of rubber bridge that dentists are using for AIDS prevention?

This training has made a difference. Some patients who have participated in the educational programs have learned about the need for safer sex, carried their own condoms, and used them correctly.

Now that we have discussed the fact of sex in the lives of people with long-term mental illness, as well as some of the research that has documented attitudes and approaches on the part of mental health professionals, we will turn to more specific issues. If we are to ade-quately treat and counsel patients, we must understand in greater detail how the female reproductive cycle is manifested for the patient with severe mental illness.

Chapter 4

The Female Reproductive Cycle and Long-Term Mental Illness

*I*n this chapter we will focus on a neglected topic in mental illness: the female reproductive cycle, and especially on menstruation as a crucial feature of that life-cycle experience. Menstruation is a central part of female identity. While menarche may be surrounded with special customs and practices in different cultures, it universally marks a girl's entrance into the world of normal adult womanhood (Gold 1985). When a woman is asked about her menses, it is a sign that her gender is recognized and that something about her feminine identity is appreciated. Menstruation can also be an area of distress for some women, and the menstrual period can be a regularly occurring natural event around which other anxieties are timed and focused. Women in the menstruating years have higher rates of morbidity for physical and mental illness, and utilize more health services than do men in that same age bracket (Clare 1983).

A woman who has long-term mental illness may be surprised to be asked about such a personal matter as menstruation. However, it is important to ask, to know how to ask, and to be alert to the important meanings of menstruation to the woman patient. Sometimes answers will be nonchalant, but more often one learns about 1) times of amenorrhea (perhaps including the present) that are of concern to the patient, and 2) periodic fluctuations in mental illness that follow the menstrual cycle but may not be in a pattern that is evident to the patient. In this chapter we will address 1) amenorrhea and major mental illness, 2) cyclic exacerbations of psychosis, and 3) menopause.

Amenorrhea in Major Mental Illness

Amenorrhea, a loss of the menses sometime after menarche lasting at least 60 days (some studies use 90 days), is a known, though inadequately understood and appreciated, consequence of psychosis (Drew

1961). Psychogenic amenorrhea has been described at the time of a sudden shock, the death of a loved one, or a change of environment, or accompanying an intense desire for pregnancy. Amenorrhea is a prominent symptom in two specific psychiatric disturbances: anorexia nervosa and pseudocyesis. In anorexia, the amenorrhea may occur early in the illness prior to the weight loss, even if the patient is not evidently psychotic; but amenorrhea always occurs by the time the weight has decreased to less than it was at the time of menarche (Frisch 1987, 1988).

A range of explanations is proffered for amenorrhea: neurotic psychosexual conflict, inability to take on the feminine role, or problematic relationships with mothers. None of these is a sufficient reason for amenorrhea, and there are many regularly menstruating women who share these emotional problems. Some physiological links are understood, such as the role of the hypothalamus, wherein the suppression of luteinizing hormone produces ovarian deficiency. All in all, the pathogenesis is not known.

The association of amenorrhea and psychosis has been observed for a long time (Cutting 1980) and was formerly even thought to be causal—that is, the psychosis was understood to be a result of unexpressed menstrual blood being forced into the head. Gregory (1957), in his literature review, cites an 1874 paper by Schroeter, who noted amenorrhea at the onset of psychosis and resumption of normal menses at the time of clinical improvement; if amenorrhea persisted while the clinical picture improved, this boded poorly for the patient's future.

Ripley and Papanicolaou (1943) did a thorough study of the menstrual cycle in psychiatric inpatients. Because self-reports of menstruation are notoriously unreliable, these investigators elected to examine a group of psychiatric inpatients prospectively and to do vaginal (Papanicolaou) smears on a sample of them. They studied the menstrual interval, amount, and duration of bleeding in 221 patients, ages 13 to 40: 114 with schizophrenia, 81 with depression, and 26 with elation. Menstrual irregularity correlated with the beginning of the psychiatric illness, and improved mental state was accompanied by a more regular menstrual cycle. Because this study was done in the era before neuroleptic medications were available, the results cannot be accounted for by drug effects.

More recent studies (Flint and Stewart 1983) indicated a high incidence of amenorrhea (27.3%) in psychiatric inpatients (with schizophrenia and affective disorders) compared with the average of 5% reported in gynecological textbooks. Interesting, and deserving of further investigation, is the finding that the majority of psychiatric patients with amenorrhea had simultaneous major medical illness such as diabetes, hypothyroidism, or renal disease. The physical illness itself accounted for more of the secondary amenorrhea than did the psychiatric illness or the psychotropic medications.

The clinical significance of these findings is that many women with mental illness will also have serious menstrual abnormalities. In our experience, patients experience these abnormalities with confusion and a personal sense of further defectiveness. Additionally, psychotropic medications affect the menstrual cycle (Halbreich et al. 1991). (Electroconvulsive therapy [ECT] is also known to disrupt menstruation.) Unfortunately, it is difficult to predict with certainty which drug will have which effect on a particular patient's cycle. Although it is impossible to give specific anticipatory guidance, a general matter-of-fact warning may be helpful.

A general normative statement is useful to patients who are beginning to receive neuroleptic medications or who are being treated with ECT—for example, "Many women find that this treatment changes their menstrual periods in some way; let's make note of what your periods are like now, and please make notice if anything changes with your cycle so you can let me know the next time I see you." When changing the treatment regimen, also mention these expectable interruptions in the normal menstruation. Such an exchange does not induce menstrual abnormalities in the patient; rather, it is instructive, and women are more apt to worry if something unforeseen happens to this residual normal function. In our experience, open discussion of menstruation with women with major mental disorders has positive effects beyond the very useful one of fact gathering. Discussion of this topic fosters collaboration between doctor and patient around concern for normal functioning.

Regular menstruation can be an indicator of potential improvement, and it is important for both clinician and patient to know about that. To discuss menstruation too is to talk of sex and reproduction. (The French call menstruation the *cycle sexuale*.) Patients can confuse amenorrhea with pregnancy and the possibility of a child, or with menopause and the end of the possibility of reproduction. Urine pregnancy tests can produce seemingly false negative results for patients who are taking psychotropic medications. The serum pregnancy test is more accurate (Hodgson 1959). If the patient is not pregnant and had great hopes to be pregnant, discuss her disappointment.

Patients who do not want to be pregnant must receive birth control and instruction even if they have amenorrhea, because ovulation and pregnancy can occur (erratically) during the amenorrheic time. If there is no pregnancy and the woman is puzzled and longing for her period, consider arranging for her to receive less medication, or even to have a drug holiday. This can bring on the menses, and she may feel more normal and better for it. If a drug holiday is contraindicated because of her mental state, the patient with secondary amenorrhea can be helped to menstruate pharmacologically in two ways:

1. Medroxyprogesterone acetate (Provera), 10 mg for 5 to 10 days, inducing progestin withdrawal bleeding within 3 to 7 days. It is not safe to use in cases of amenorrhea when pregnancy is suspected because of progesterone teratogenicity in the first trimester.
2. Bromocriptine mesylate (Parlodel) in daily doses of 1.25 to 80 mg is also used to suppress galactorrhea and reinstate normal ovulatory menstrual cycles. It has been used for hyperprolactinemia (usually when secondary to prolactin-producing tumors), but can be used in women with mental illness and appears safe even during pregnancy (Weil 1986).

Case 8: A Patient Who Missed Having Her Periods

A young woman confided to her doctor that, with her new medication regimen, the "voices are gone but I miss having my periods." She felt like a "freak" not to get her periods, and she felt excluded from casual women's complaints about "the friend" and "the curse," and sad when she saw tampons in the drugstore. With this new medication and dosage, her thinking seemed clearer and less psychotic, but her mood appeared more subdued. The psychiatrist talked with her at length about the value and importance of her period to her. Together, they agreed to slowly reduce the medication dosage until menstruation resumed, but that if she became more psychotic, the reduction would have to stop. Several months later, the alliance with the therapist had strengthened, which also reduced the patient's need for as much medication. She appeared with a big smile and a bouquet of flowers for the therapist: "I got my friend back!" she said. "Thanks!"

Menstrual Cycle Exacerbations of Psychosis

The relationship between menstruation and mood has increasingly been studied (Fava et al. 1982; Gitlin and Pasnau 1989; Halbreich et al. 1983; O'Boyle et al. 1988; Rubinow et al. 1984; Severino and Moline 1989a, 1989b, 1990; Severino and Rado 1988; Severino and Yonkers 1991). There is continuing investigation of the late luteal-phase dysphoric disorder (LLPDD) (Eckerd et al. 1989; Hurt et al. 1992; Severino et al. 1989). Whether it is a psychiatric diagnosis, and whether it merits classification in the upcoming DSM-IV, it has been described and included in the *DSM-IV Options Book: Work in Progress* (American Psychiatric Association 1991) as a severe dysfunctional state with mood lability and dysphoria. Transient psychotic symptoms have also been described for years (Kramer 1977; Teja 1976; Williams and Weeks 1952), and Severino and Yonkers (1991) have recently reviewed the literature. Zola and colleagues (1979) carried out a careful study of psychiatric admissions that failed to show any general relationship between admission to a mental hospital and premenstrual syndrome. There have been numerous clinical reports in the literature of patients who received a primary diagnosis of menstrual psychosis. This is an admitting diagnosis that was used especially in the last century for young psychotic women who had recurrent psychotic illnesses coinciding with a phase (usually premenstrual) of the menstrual cycle and remitting with the onset of the menses.

There is no doubt that there are psychotic illnesses that are primarily endocrinologically based, notably the psychoses accompanying the thyroid disorders of myxedema and thyrotoxicosis. There are also some women who experience major psychiatric symptoms in one phase of the menstrual cycle. Such symptoms must always be taken seriously and evaluated, including in women with a history of major mental illness. Evaluation and treatment involve self-monitoring and diary keeping that give the patient an active role in her diagnosis and care (Hamilton et al. 1984). Some of these women will be found to have depressive disorders that are mild enough to be asymptomatic except when defenses are lowered because of the hormonal changes premenstrually (Endicott et al. 1981).

Endo and his colleagues (1978) documented seven cases of women who had treatment-resistant major psychosis with an onset and exacerbations occurring in relation to the menstrual cycle. In these young unmarried women, ages 13 to 23, hospitalization, medication, and ECT did not provide the anticipated relief of symptoms. Five showed abnormalities on their electroencephalogram. All remitted within a decade, as the young women became more physically and mentally mature. Glick and Stewart (1980) found three schizophrenic women who had severe premenstrual exacerbation of their psychosis who did not respond to hospitalization or antipsychotic or hormonal medications, but did respond well to the addition of lithium; again, these were young women with onset of illness in their teens. Some investigators speculate that these treatment-refractory conditions result from monoamine oxidase (MAO) metabolism; MAO activity in the hypothalamus is known to fluctuate fourfold within a menstrual cycle (Endo et al. 1978). This refinement and specification of behavioral-hormonal linkages can potentially provide treatment breakthroughs, and the linkages must not be confused with the age-old stereotyping belief that women's hormones cause mental illness.

Admission records from the last century include menstruation among the more common admitting diagnoses, always referring to young psychotic women. These menstrual psychoses continue to represent 1% of the mental hospital admissions in modern China; they are resistant to the usual medications as well as to naturopathic remedies such as herbs and acupuncture (Shanghai Psychiatric Hospital, personal communication, 1980). In the West now, these women would probably present with behavioral gynecological disorders; if they were seen by psychiatrists they would be diagnosed as having "atypical" or "periodic" or "cycloid" or "hysterical" psychois.

Hamilton and Parry (1983) have demonstrated the importance of looking at medication levels in women patients considering their menstrual state. For instance, the lithium level decreases premenstrually, so a therapeutic level can become subtherapeutic and the patient can become symptomatic for several days a month. These authors provide a practical guide to evaluation and treatment of premenstrual complaints that can be adapted for use with the psychotic patient.

Premenstrual psychosis seems to correlate with postpartum psychosis in some published case histories, but there are no definitive studies. Hormonal treatments, and even oral contraceptives, seem to be effective for some women with severe premenstrual symptoms (Felthous et al. 1980).

Menopause and the Patient
With Long-Term Mental Illness

In our society, which overvalues youth and undervalues old age, the cessation of the reproductive cycle for a woman can be a sign that she has reached old age (Gold 1985). For many women, reaching menopause brings with it a sense that a certain potential for personal fulfillment is gone (Notman 1984, 1985) The psychological implications of this additional loss for women with long-term mental illness, who have already had so many losses in their lives, must be explored by the clinicians who are working with them. For example, menopause may mean not being a normal female; the end of childbearing might mean loss of sexual attractiveness to men.

Case 9: The Meaning of Menstruation

A 40-year-old patient with a diagnosis of schizoaffective disorder and a history of 20 hospitalizations in a 10-year period had been stable for several years. She had made a good adjustment to the community, with support from weekly psychotherapy and a drug regimen that included lithium carbonate and a phenothiazine. Her psychiatrist was sensitive to the patient's wish to have normal periods and was, therefore, careful to keep the patient's phenothiazine dosage below the threshold that would cause her menses to stop. However, when life stresses threatened to upset her current equilibrium, her psychiatrist increased the dose of the antipsychotic medication.

During the course of a therapy session, just weeks after an acute exacerbation of her illness, the 40-year-old patient began to talk about aging. "I am old. I am no longer attractive to men. I can't have babies any more, and men want women who can give them babies, and I know I am too old for that." When the therapist inquired further, the patient indicated that because she no longer had her period, she must have had menopause, thus making her old, past the childbearing age, and unattractive. She was depressed and felt that time had passed her by. The therapist took the opportunity to explore some of these issues with the patient, but also informed the patient that menopause probably was not yet the cause of her amenorrhea and reviewed the fact that her medication dosage had recently been increased. The patient, still unconvinced, arranged an appointment with her psychiatrist. To the patient's delight, the medication was changed and her periods returned. In therapy, she continued to explore the meaning of aging and menopause in relation to her sense of herself as a woman.

Postmenopausal women may require more antipsychotic medication than they did premenopausally, and even more than their male counterparts in the same age range do. Estrogen seems to potentiate antipsychotic treatment (Seeman 1983a, 1989a, 1989b; Seeman and Lang 1990). It also seems to have some protective value against tardive dyskinesia, which becomes more of a problem after menopause when doses of medication are higher and natural estrogen is depleted. In addition to the usual considerations for estrogen replacement therapy for prevention of osteoporosis and heart disease, the use of exogenous hormones to supplement neuroleptics may have special use in the postmenopausal woman with severe mental illness.

Having discussed the reproductive cycle in women with long-term mental illness, we will now turn to gynecological care and birth control for this special population.

Chapter 5

Gynecological Care, Birth Control, and Safe Sex

Women with long-term mental illness have the same (or more) needs for gynecological care as other women have (McBurney 1966). The psychiatric care they receive is often their primary medical care and may be limited to psychiatric and social problems (Roca et al. 1987). Gynecologists who see these women may have problems understanding them and their ways of communicating, and may thus, unwittingly, shortchange the patients. Women patients can get lost in between the gynecological system and the mental health system. It is important to develop team approaches and referral arrangements that permit optimal care of these women who have both mental illness and continuous gynecological medical needs. In this chapter, we will discuss areas of normal gynecological care as they pertain to working with women who have long-term mental illness. These areas include 1) a model program for gynecological care; 2) management of routine pelvic examinations; 3) approaches to birth control choices, including sterilization; and 4) sexually transmitted diseases.

Model Program for Gynecological Care

Gynecological care for people with long-term mental illness has developed under the framework of birth control services. The group of clinician-researchers in the late 1960s who developed these programs did so because of the push of deinstitutionalization. They wanted to provide protection against pregnancy for women patients who were leaving the state hospitals, especially because of the observed increase in conception rates. They also wanted to give women with long-term mental illness the same opportunity for sexual and social freedom that other women of the times enjoyed. Grunebaum, Abernethy, and their colleagues in Boston developed a state hospital program for family planning and gynecological services that endures to this day; they have written about their experience extensively (Abernethy and Grunebaum 1972, 1973; Grunebaum and Abernethy 1975; Grunebaum et al. 1971, 1975). In this group of patients, all of whom needed gynecological care, it was documented that two-thirds were sexually active, but only half had ever used birth control, and only 18% were protected at the time of the most recent coitus (Abernethy 1974). Two decades later, the same need was documented (Coverdale and Aruffo 1989). It is important for psychiatrists to recognize this need for both inpatients and outpatients, and help provide programs that have the following features:

1. Invitation to utilize birth control and gynecology services to all new and returning female inpatients. All women patients who are hospitalized long-term are seen regularly for yearly Papanicolaou smears and pelvic examinations, and also whenever they are symptomatic (Handel 1985; Handel and Bennett 1988).
2. Availability of birth control and safe sex counseling, information, and devices.
3. Follow-up procedures for recommendations made by the gynecological physician in the clinic.
4. Monitoring of annual and semiannual exams.
5. Continuity of gynecological care as patients go between inpatient and outpatient services, especially when there is a question of sexually transmitted disease or when a woman is at high risk of cervical or breast cancer.
6. Information and inservice educational programs for both staff and patients on topics related to sexual health.
7. Access to mammograms for the early detection of breast cancer. Mammograms are now routine at 50 years of age and beyond every year, at 2-year intervals from 40 to 50, and one time prior to age 40.
8. Documentation of gynecological and reproductive history of women patients in the psychiatric record (D'Ercole et al. 1991).

In addition to the specific goals related to women's physical health, the very existence of these clinics conveys to both patients and staff that a woman's concerns about her body are important. Especially for women in the state hospital, where so much of the treatment is genderless and so many of the concerns are focused on thought processes and behavior, the visits to the gynecologist can become a place for patients to discuss anxieties and delusions about their bodies.

In the Grunebaum-Abernethy model, a typical state hospital is set up with a patient advocate/assistant and a female gynecologist. The advocate does outreach by scouting for patients in need of services, by talking with staff, by going to team meetings, and, most importantly, by developing informal relationships with the women patients. The advocate then serves as an explainer, anxiety reducer, and personal assistant to the patient for dressing and undressing during the gynecological examination. The advocate is a young and attractive woman who is seen by the patients as a peer and a nonthreatening friend. She is casual, joking, and matter-of-fact in manner, and she herself feels somewhat identified with the patients. She gives frank permission to be sexual in a setting where sex is secretive or illicit.

This type of confidante provides an example of a young woman who can be sexual without being pregnant to patients who may desire birth more than they want birth control. As part of the team, the gynecologist can be more strictly factual and less involved personally with the patients. She is the authority who does the physical examination, and her more-technical words are translated into patient's vernacular by the advocate.

Management of the Routine Pelvic Examination

It is worthwhile to use the occasion of the routine pelvic examination as an opportunity to gather history about previous pregnancies and losses. This history, as we have noted, is not routinely taken and highlighted elsewhere in the psychiatric patient record. The woman patient expects to discuss her body and her physical self at the physical examination. It is an excellent time to review all the pertinent history—menstruation, birth control, and venereal diseases, as well as each pregnancy. Then a line can be recorded about the event of each pregnancy: Did it end in miscarriage or abortion? When? Patient's reaction? Did the pregnancy come to term? What happened to the baby? Any stillbirths or other losses? Mother's reproductive history? These significant events of life remain most vivid for all women.

Women with mental illness are often glad to know of someone else's interest in their reproductive histories and are ready to discuss their experiences in as much detail as the interviewer wants. This is a time that unresolved grief and longing for the lost babies may be revealed. Several cases will illustrate how the routine pelvic examination can be an opportunity for patient care and education.

Case 10: Middle-Aged Woman Worried About Sexual Activity

In the course of examining a 53-year-old woman, the routine question "How many pregnancies have you had?" revealed significant and previously unknown history and led to current anxieties being expressed and clarified:

> *Patient:* I dunno [looking distracted and uncomfortable].
> *Interviewer:* Tell me about each one . . .
> *Patient:* Oh yes, once I had one—with Bill—what was his last name? at 19, I was, uh, just out of the hospital. [Wistfully] . . . I had an abortion . . . and I was 4 months along. I was living at home and I didn't want my parents to have another mouth to feed . . . never talked to anyone about it . . . still wonder about that kid . . . (was a kid . . . that was when I was working and had all my parts).
> *Interviewer:* That was a tough experience, and lonely.
> *Patient:* Yeah, but then I had two; they're now 30 and 17 years old. They're doing well, I hear, and I have a grandson—I've never seen him, but I write and I once talked on the telephone to him . . . and I think of him all the time. Oh yes, now I remember, my daughter is getting married soon. I have to be all done in the hospital by then . . . Another time in the hospital I thought I was pregnant, but it was just my parts weren't working . . . My periods stopped. Now I don't even have my parts . . . Look! (pointing to a relatively unhairy cheek) I still have hair on my face after that hysterectomy 6 years ago. That operation made my blood stop flowing and so no blood comes to my cheeks where ordinarily young women are pink . . . My skin is dying and old and I am losing my eyesight too . . .
> *Interviewer:* It is normal to get dryer skin and need glasses at your age; not so nice, but normal. Let's examine you and see how we can help.

The patient brightened at being called "normal" and having her physical anxieties addressed. During the exam, she could be assured that her hysterectomy scar was well healed. She also was offered cream for her dry skin and an appointment to have her eyesight checked. Her secret abortion of long ago was now revealed. Her current anxiety about her attractiveness and fears about bodily deterioration were identified for her treatment team. She conveyed her attachment to her children and grandchild, and her wish to be out of the hospital by the time of the wedding. Misinformation and ignorance about the normal reproductive cycle are rampant in a general population but are even more severe among individuals with the delusional distortions of schizophrenia.

Case 11: Dialogue About Sexual Fears and Fantasies

Patient: I was messing around while I had my period; maybe I have an infection or got knocked up.

Interviewer: Of course you want to mess around sometimes. Usually, you're not likely to get "knocked up" at the time you have your period; it's actually a pretty safe time to have sex that way. I'll give you something to make messing around safer.

Patient: Where is the bleeding from anyway?—my hemorrhoids or vagina?

Interviewer: When you get your period, the blood comes from the vagina; when we examine you we'll show you in the mirror where the vagina is and the anus is. We can check and see if you have hemorrhoids.

Patient: Yeh, I need to know what went in—foam or suppositories— and where to put it all—Maybe the whites I got are from the foam, maybe the infection . . .

Interviewer: We'll also check to see if you have "the whites" [slang term for vaginal infection or discharge]. White discharge from the vagina can be confusing. You might want to try some of these new brightly colored condoms we have, instead of the foam; they're better than foam and help prevent AIDS and stop infections. Has the guy you had sex with gotten an infection?

Patient: I don't know. He's not in the hospital, and I don't know if and when I'll get out to see him again.

Even with a psychotic patient, it is possible to have a frank and productive interchange. When the patient is hostile and paranoid, her feelings can easily transfer to the gynecological examination and the personnel performing it. It is wise to postpone the visit until a patient is less agitated, but sometimes that is not feasible, as when there is some emergent need for an examination. This is not an unusual predicament in a setting where there are patients with severe and long-term mental illness who may not clearly and easily identify physical pain and complain (Rosenthal et al. 1990; Talbott 1978).

Case 12: Examining a Paranoid Woman

When a postmenopausal woman with long-term paranoid schizophrenia started to bleed vaginally, she was referred by the ward nurse to the
gynecologist with a question of uterine cancer. The patient mutely
refused to talk with the gynecologist and eyed the clinic setup with
suspicion. The ward aide who accompanied her and the clinic assistant
helped her up onto the table, explaining the need for the exam as they
went. The gynecologist talked her way through the examination and
gently used the smallest possible speculum and her smallest finger for
the bimanual examination. Another function of the two assistants present was to steady the patient and restrain her physically to enable the
doctor to make the diagnosis. In this situation, as the assistants whispered instructions to each other, the patient blurted out, "Don't blab
about me . . . and don't tell that other patient [referring to a male
patient with whom she might have had sexual relations] about my skin
graft." She was apparently focusing her anxiety on exposure of a
different sort, concentrating on her shame about a self-mutilation earlier in life that had required a skin graft. The prospect of a tumor and
the possible need for surgery were recalling for her that prior time.
Because the staff understood the background, they were able to manage the situation swiftly and competently, and to not take the patient's
remarks personally.

At times, a patient will at first seem cooperative about the pelvic
examination, only to become quite panicky, frozen, or even violent on
the table. This happens usually in patients who have had a previous
experience with sexual abuse, rape, or incest. The helpless posture and
manipulation of the genitals produce a flashback to a traumatic experience that was perhaps repressed or suppressed, and the patient feels
attacked. She then reacts as a small, terrified child or strikes out in an
unpredictable manner. One patient also screamed, "Protect me, that
damn bastard!!!" thus giving a clue that she had had such a trauma and
was now mistaking the gynecologist for a villain. A gynecologist who
is caught in this situation can be frightened and injured herself. Sitting
vulnerably at the perineum, the doctor is in danger of being injured by
the violently kicking patient. It is best in these situations to proceed
cautiously and to show the patient in a mirror what is being done. It is
essential to talk with the patient about how this exam may remind her
of a terrible time in the past but to clarify that this is a different situation
and that the people are different. This is a time-limited exam for a

particular purpose. It may be necessary to stop and then talk and return to another time if the patient is too upset. Occasionally, it is necessary to sedate or even to anesthetize the patient. This is best done with the patient's consent, lest it further the sense of being out of control and repeating the earlier trauma.

A quite explicit fear of cancer can have a real basis or be a metaphor for revealing feelings of being dirty or falling apart, or of being eaten inside (Sontag 1978). One example was a woman who barged into her appointment, saying, "I'm afraid I have breast cancer." She was gaudily made up for a field day outing. It seemed that the more she acted social and sexual, and made herself attractive on the outside, the more she became convinced internally that she was dark and bad. Such somatic anxiety is not unlike what is found in other women without severe mental illness; it can be discussed and physical reassurance can be easily provided. The more difficult task is to deal with the underlying anxiety, shame, guilt, and inner conviction of badness; this is the work of ongoing therapy. Coordinating the therapy with periodic physical checkups is reassuring to both patient and therapist.

At times, a patient becomes convinced of a physical problem, and the conviction begins to take on the quality of a fixed physical delusion. This can be a sign of worsening mental illness, a focus of underlying despair, or a harbinger of a suicide attempt. It can also be a sign of an actual, as yet undetected physical illness, such as a tumor. It is always better to err on the side of repeating the physical workup. Particularly in women patients, and especially in those women with long-term mental illness, it is too easy to dismiss a complaint as part of the "hysterical style." Those who suffer with mental illness are also able to feel anxiety and guilt about having caused a problem themselves because of their behavior or their wishes. Sexual thoughts, fantasies, and actions can all produce guilty feelings that can then lead to concerns about retaliation or punishment. In this population, we see an exaggerated form of the normal fantasies seen in any illness—for example, "What wrong did I do to deserve this? Why me?" Common fears are more freely expressed in the primary process of the person with schizophrenia. For instance, "My boyfriend left me . . . I must be too big for him . . . give me surgery," from an aging woman trying to explain her boyfriend's infidelity by taking responsibility for the size of her vagina. Or, "I need penicillin; I know I'll get the clap this time from having a good time."

The basic guidelines for gynecological services for women with mental illness are the same as for other women. Overall, it is the role of the clinician to be an active listener and to hear in the patient's language the emotional need that underlies the physical complaint. One question is whether it makes a difference to the woman patient to have a woman or a man gynecologist. Whereas a male doctor can (concretely) elicit terror more quickly in a woman who has had an abuse history, there can be homosexual transference reactions with a woman physician (Apfel and Fisher 1984). What is essential is an empathic manner and gentle touch, and the presence of a patient advocate and guide to accompany the doctor (of either gender) and the patient through the examination.

Approaches to Birth Control Choices, Including Sterilization

Decisions about the method of birth control to be used should be made collaboratively with the patient, and always with respect for her personal values. It is the responsibility of the mental health professional to know whether their patients are sexually active and whether they are using birth control and safe sex, and to refer them to services that provide nonjudgmental prescription of birth control. It is also important for mental health personnel to be aware of contraceptive choices to help counsel their patients about options and to help advise their gynecological colleagues on behalf of the patients (Stotland 1985).

Choices today are realistically influenced by the AIDS epidemic, which necessitates the use of condoms whenever possible. Mechanical devices such as the condom and the diaphragm present special problems for the long-term mental patient whose fine motor coordination is impaired by illness and medication. The diaphragm is usually not a realistic choice for a woman with mental illness because it requires planning and considerable comfort in touching one's own body that many of our patients do not have. Condoms can and should be used, but only after explicit instruction and practice. Intrauterine devices can be the treatment of choice for monogamous couples not at risk for contracting AIDS; they require least input from the patient, but they are currently limited in availability.

Birth control pills and hormonal contraceptives are also useful for those patients who are at low risk for AIDS. These contraceptives are contraindicated for those over 35 who are smokers (because of the high risk of cardiovascular accidents), and this eliminates many of our patients. The physician must be aware of drug interactions of hormonal contraceptives and other medications and of the total medical-pharmacological picture. Hormonal contraceptives can also be a primary cause of depression, a drug side effect that can be confused with a mental illness (Kane et al. 1969; Royal College of General Practitioners 1974). The patient's preference and willingness to use any method are crucial. The patient's contraceptive preferences need to be repeatedly reassessed in view of her current life situation.

Sterilization or permanent birth control (i.e., tubal ligation) is a choice that many mentally ill women will want to make for themselves, just as many other women do. In the past, forced sterilization of mentally ill persons, and sometimes now too-forceful focus on this one option, can, paradoxically, prevent a woman with mental illness from making this valid choice easily for herself. Also, barriers exist within our current system of medical care, with fear of lawsuits and insurance regulations conspiring against a surgical and relatively expensive procedure. Forced sterilization still occurs in some places where clinicians are feeling pressed to eliminate the possibility of pregnancy and their responsibility for it.

The guidelines for voluntary sterilization are as follows:

1. The decision should be independent of other major life events (e.g., an abortion) to allow for the necessary emotional response to each event.
2. The patient should fully participate in making the decision. If the patient is not competent to make the decision, it must be postponed because it must be considered a permanent life change. (Very rarely, reversals of sterilizations can occur, but they are expensive and not to be expected.)
3. There should be a waiting time from the decision to the surgery in order to allow for a change of mind and exploration of the ambivalence. Wherever feasible, work with the woman to allow her to see how sterilization is a positive choice that can increase rather than decrease her options.

Ironically, it is not always easy to arrange a tubal ligation for a woman with mental illness, even when she desires it voluntarily:

Case 13: Bureaucratic Impediments to Tubal Ligation

By age 27, one patient had tried many types of birth control and had two children. She lived in a halfway house, and her children were living with their father. She continued to be sexually active and requested a tubal ligation so she would not have to bother with birth control any more. Her therapist was delighted at this responsible decision but dismayed to discover that Medicaid might not pay for the procedure. Three hospitals turned down her request. Repeatedly asking for the sterilization and telling her story made the patient feel unsure of her decision, ashamed and humiliated. It was not until many months later after talking about this permanent decision in therapy and having an advocate at one of the hospitals that the procedure was accomplished. By then, much of the ambivalence and grief had been expressed, and she felt mostly relief.

Sexually Transmitted Diseases

There are numerous sexually transmitted illnesses to which people with mental illness, as well as the general population, are exposed. It is the responsibility of the mental health clinicians to inquire about physical discomfort, including genital symptoms such as itching or discharge. Patients' worries should be validated, and referrals to the appropriate medical clinics or specialists should be made. Most people with mental illness have learned to recognize more common and longer-known venereal diseases. Too few women, however, know that sexually transmitted diseases can be asymptomatic and are aware of the need to be tested (e.g., for gonorrhea and syphilis); these illnesses still abound, and they are treatable.

A complete discussion of sexually transmitted diseases is beyond the scope of this book. However, the AIDS epidemic concerns everyone. Staff and patients both need to be more open in talking and teaching about sex. Psychiatric inpatients claim to know quite a bit about AIDS already (Aruffo et al. 1990; Sacks et al. 1990a, 1990b). In one study, 93% of patients said they had learned from nonstaff sources such as media and posters, whereas only 40% had received their information from hospital personnel (Baer et al. 1988). Ironically and sadly, it is in the course of AIDS education that the general psychiatric lack of attention to sex has become obvious. AIDS education programs are exposing some of our limitations and producing some of the best sex education in many decades. It is becoming clear that most mentally ill patients can and will have to learn about AIDS. Also, some 80% of AIDS patients will have some organic brain disease during their illness that may require psychiatric hospitalization (Minkoff et al. 1988).

There is an urgent need to maintain and expand safe sex and birth control programs in the 1990s. Patients and staff must be trained in the proper use of condoms, and condoms must be made easily available. This education should be done by staff who are comfortable with the discussion of sex and AIDS, and are familiar with people with long-term mental illness who are also at risk for AIDS.

AIDS, in addition to mental illness, may create an untenable sense of loss and unwillingness to continue active treatment for either disease. In their desperation, some patients may become highly promiscuous. Their judgment may be triply impaired by the depth of their fears, their unmedicated mental illness, and the AIDS-related dementia. In these cases, staff are limited by all of the legal protections of privacy and confidentiality for AIDS patients and psychiatric patients and often feel totally helpless; they cannot help their own patients or protect those who are potentially at risk. This is an area in which new and flexible public policy decisions are badly needed.

We have discussed sexuality, the reproductive cycle, and regular gynecological care for patients with mental illness. The next section focuses on pregnancy, another aspect of the reproduction life cycle for women with long-term mental illness.

Chapter 6

Early Pregnancy:
Diagnosis and Decisions

*P*regnancy incidence among those women with major mental illness has not been completely or accurately reported. From the retrospective fertility studies and interview studies, it is not possible to tell reliably what has been the pregnancy rate for this population as a whole. This is understandable for many reasons. The population of women with mental illness is not uniform in time, place, or diagnosis. Pregnancy outcome, especially for women with high-risk illnesses, depends on the availability of early diagnosis and good prenatal and obstetrical care. Very early (first month, prior to diagnosis) pregnancy losses are frequent in the general population but are probably more prevalent among women with major mental illness because of the mental illness itself and the medications used in treatment. Pregnancy is also a common delusion in mental illness; women with schizophrenia, and some men too, develop the delusion that they are pregnant. Pregnancy among those who are unmarried, hospitalized, and mentally ill is illicit; therefore, stigma is attached to it. Such pregnancies have often not been noticed and have not been officially documented. Thus, fertility rates that are recorded must be lower than the actual rates, and the actual rates are impossible to ascertain retrospectively.

In this chapter, the first of three chapters on pregnancy, we will critically review the literature on fertility and major mental illness; discuss the problems of pregnancy diagnosis, pseudocyesis, and psychotic denial; and present the legal issues surrounding the pregnant woman who has a history of psychotic illness. Finally, we will discuss the clinical dilemmas of abortion.

Fertility in Major Mental Illness: Multiple Losses

Fertility in major mental illness has been a topic of great interest for much of the 20th century (Burr et al. 1979; Eaton 1975; Haverkamp et al. 1982; Propping et al. 1982, 1983a, 1983b). *Fertility* is defined as live births (e.g., per 1,000 women) as opposed to *fecundity,* which is the comparable number of pregnancies. The larger question is how major mental illnesses affect fecundity and fertility. There are no simple answers. One impetus for discussing this topic in the early part of the century was eugenic: the fear that the mental illness would be inherited as a simple Mendelian dominant and result in deterioration of the human race (Lewis 1967). Those who expounded these eugenic beliefs also stated explicitly, or implied, that people with mental illness copulated in an unrestrained manner and would overpopulate the world. In many places, this belief was translated into action with compulsory sterilization laws.

Currently, a more complex polygenetic, biological, and psychosocial model is used for understanding the origin of severe mental illness. In addition, more careful studies have been done to ascertain fertility and fecundity in people with mental illness. The studies differ from one another in time period, methodology, and control group used, and even in results. However, almost all of the studies show fecundity in major mental illness to be significantly lower than in the general population. In addition to fecundity and fertility rates, several other measures have appeared in the literature—for example, the number of infant deaths, the number of offspring who were given away to adoption or foster care, and the number of offspring who eventually became psychotic. These data yield a larger picture of the losses endured by schizophrenic women. In the course of the following discussion, we shall take note of these various kinds of losses, all of them involving a complex interplay of biological, psychological, and social factors.

As recently as 1973, it was generally accepted that people with schizophrenia have lower fertility than their unaffected siblings, and that the fertility of men with schizophrenia is significantly lower than that of women with the illness (Reed et al. 1973). The order of magnitude of the differences in live births was quite large when a hospitalized population from early 20th-century Pennsylvania was considered: 64% of schizophrenic females reproduced compared with 83% of their unaffected sisters, and only 27% of schizophrenic males reproduced compared with 63% of their unaffected brothers. The net number of children without mental disorder per individual was 0.80 for schizophrenic women and 2.51 for sisters; 0.59 for schizophrenic men and 1.73 for brothers.

Haverkamp and his colleagues (1982) critically reviewed 13 other studies from 1935 to 1982 that compared fertility rates of men and women who had schizophrenia with those of a normal group. They concluded that there were many methodological problems in selection of comparison groups and in case definition. A major problem in many studies was the recording of fertility only among married patients, and, because relatively few people with schizophrenia marry (Wignall and Meredith 1968), their reproductive rates were falsely deflated. Another problem is in using a pooled series. There may be a wide range of fertility among the participants that has implications beyond the overall average: if some women with schizophrenia have no pregnancies, but others have many, then it is not the schizophrenic illness per se that is responsible for the lowered fertility.

Erlenmeyer-Kimling and his colleagues (1968) compared two large cohorts of all patients admitted to 11 New York State hospitals, one in the years 1934–1936 and one in 1954–1956. They found that fertility did increase in the second time period, although the rates were still lower than those in a matched control group reported in the United States Vital Statistics. They attributed the increase in reproduction to changing attitudes toward those persons with mental illness and to shorter hospitalizations. Shearer et al. (1967, 1968) noted a 355% increase in fertility among Michigan state hospital women patients over the time period 1935 to 1964. As a result of these trends, it might now be assumed that birth rates among mentally ill persons are becoming more comparable to those of the general population.

However, when Hilger, Propping, and Haverkamp (1983) in West Germany set out to answer the question about whether reproductive rates are increasing in persons with schizophrenia, they concluded from their carefully designed and matched study that there was no evidence of an increase in fertility between 1949–1950 and 1965–1967. A defect in this study is that none of their measurements included the total population of people with schizophrenia—that is, the unmarried as well as the married.

Psychotic women, especially those with schizophrenia, are known to have more illegitimate babies than women in the general population, precisely because of their relatively low probability of marriage (Kallmann 1938). At least one study (Stevens 1970, 1971) indicated that births were a result of serious relationships rather than casual promiscuity.

An excellent review of fertility in major mental illness was published recently by Saugstad (1989), whose central hypothesis is that the etiology of major mental illness is neurodevelopmental, and that this etiology is intertwined with the differences observed in fertility rates. Thus, people with schizophrenia tend to be late maturers, and they may mature so late that some of the men who become schizophrenic have not yet and may never reach sexual reproductive maturity after the onset of the illness. Manic-depressive illness, by contrast, is a disease of early maturers, who have normal childbearing potential and performance prior to the onset of the mental illness.

Our impression is that the recorded studies must all be viewed with some skepticism. Our experience in reading medical records of patients whose histories we know from other sources is that mention of pregnancy and birth is frequently omitted. This distortion is motivated by many factors: stigma of illicit pregnancy in the mental hospital, the wish to protect the patient or the wish to protect the hospital, the wish to protect the child who is later adopted, and a lack of interest in this subject on the part of the caregivers.

Patients reflect the climate of their times. When birth rates are dropping, there is greater interest in contraception; when rates are increasing, patients report intensified wishes to have babies. There may be a significant difference between schizophrenia and manic-depressive illness as far as attitudes toward pregnancy. Patients with manic-depressive illness are apt to have had a child prior to the first psychotic episode and are more likely to request sterilization or birth control because of their illness. Schizophrenic women, on the other hand, are not likely to voluntarily curtail their fertility (Odegard 1980).

Coverdale and Aruffo (1989) were among the first to report on a different type of study of the fertility of women with major mental illness. Instead of looking at the records retrospectively, they interviewed 80 outpatients, ages 18 through 40, at a public mental health clinic. These few interviews revealed data that raised further questions about the aforementioned statistical surveys. Of the women interviewed, 27% had never been pregnant. Of the 73% who had been pregnant at least once, 23% had had at least one spontaneous miscarriage (compared with about 10% in the general population), and 31% had had at least one induced abortion. Seventy-five children were born to these 36 patients (2.4 average): 1 died, 4 grew up and were on their own, 25 were being reared by their biological mothers, and 45 were being reared by the biological fathers or an adoptive family. Diagnosis did not make the crucial difference in having a pregnancy, in losing or keeping the child, or in adequate contraceptive planning.

Spielvogel and Wile's (1986) series of 13 pregnant patients with major mental illness included eight different diagnoses and six women who were abusing alcohol and/or drugs. All of these 13 women, ages 23 to 45, had been pregnant before, and they had given birth to between one and five children previously; only nine of the women had delivered normal infants, two had stillbirths, and two had premature births, with one baby having died of Ebstein's anomaly secondary to maternal lithium. Five of the nine women with normal infants had to relinquish their babies.

In the most recent tabulation, at San Francisco General Hospital's psychiatric unit, Scheidt et al. (1990) showed that 62 of 124 female patients admitted had been pregnant at some time. Almost no one was married. Of the 62, 52 had children, and only 27% of those 52 women were caring for their children at the time of admission.

As we have seen, reproductive losses are multiple for the woman with psychotic illness. When prenatal and obstetric care is controlled, however, there may be no significant difference between the obstetrical complications for psychiatric patients and those for nonpsychiatric patients (McNeil 1986). Sociocultural factors clearly contribute to the high rate of loss. However, it is also postulated that there may be a genetic or microscopic cellular effect (Reider et al. 1975). Although a physiological advantage theory has been postulated (Erlenmeyer-Kimling 1968), prospective matched data show that a significant number of fetal and neonatal deaths occur among births to mothers with schizophrenia compared with those among control subjects (7.5% vs. 3.8%). Spontaneous abortions occur two to three times as frequently in the pregnancies of women with schizophrenia, many probably related to genetic problems, age, previous miscarriage, and drug effects (Leridon 1987; Modvig et al. 1990; Parnas et al. 1982). Furthermore, perinatal losses, stillbirths, and neonatal deaths were more common in women with schizophrenia, as were fetal malformations and multiple congenital anomalies (microcephaly, hydrocephaly, anencephaly) (Sobel 1961).

There are many possible reasons for the additional losses: the possible genetic effect, an adverse intrauterine environment secondary to maternal schizophrenia, the toxic effect of psychotropic medications, frequent usage of alcohol and street drugs, poor self-care and diet, and smoking. Stress itself may induce reproductive loss via cate-cholamine production (Istvan 1986; Katz et al. 1991; Loeser 1943). Whatever the causes, the mother with schizophrenia faces more actual reproductive losses, with an accompanying loss of a sense of adequacy and normality; with schizophrenia there is even more reality to the universal fear of producing a "monster."

We do see a consistent theme of reproductive losses at many levels for the population of women with schizophrenia:

1. More choose celibacy (or have it imposed on them).
2. Those who do couple and get pregnant experience more spontaneous miscarriage and abortion.
3. Those who carry the pregnancy have more stillbirths.
4. Those who give birth have a high likelihood of losing the baby through adoption or illness.

Pregnancy Diagnosis

Diagnosis of pregnancy is particularly difficult in psychotic patients, who may be poor self-observers and unreliable informants, and who may have reason to deny a pregnancy or to unconsciously fabricate one. There may be conscious avoidance of mental health professionals, who they (correctly) anticipate would disapprove of a pregnancy. A psychotic patient who has had previous pregnancy losses may be motivated to forget to tell about the pregnancy until she deems herself past the possible time of abortion. Early, nonjudgmental diagnosis is needed to have a full range of treatment options and to best provide for all the patients at hand—the psychotic woman, her unborn baby, and the baby's father, who may be another patient.

Diagnosis of pregnancy can produce further problems for the mentally ill woman; she may ironically find herself discriminated against (e.g., in housing) because of her pregnancy, as in the following:

> The other women worried about Gwendolyn alone on the park bench. They knew what Gwendolyn refused to admit. She was pregnant. They begged local churches to take her in. They explained why they were so concerned. But no one offered Gwendolyn any other place to live. Gwendolyn gave birth on the bench outside the locked building where she had once lived. (Bachrach 1985)

In spite of such potential burdens of pregnancy diagnosis, early recognition and planning are advisable. The need for pregnancy diagnosis is another reason for routine pelvic exams for all women with long-term mental illness and justifies monitoring the menstrual cycles of the hospitalized patient (Handel 1985). When the pregnant psychotic patient is already hospitalized, supervision is in place, and the diagnosis may be easier. When the patient is living in the community, diagnosis of pregnancy is a problem for those who are treating her. The pregnancy puts an extra responsibility of self-care on the woman with mental illness, often exceeding her coping abilities. Housing, nutrition, and social relations that are marginal in the nonpregnant state become totally inadequate with a pregnancy (Spielvogel and Wile 1986). Pregnancy is a time when more intensive care is needed, and yet when patients may, wittingly or unwittingly, retreat from care.

Sometimes women with mental illness will psychotically deny a pregnancy (Milstein and Milstein 1983; Slayton and Soloff 1981). The pregnancy may be discovered only incidentally or at the time of labor and delivery. In our experience, such denial usually occurs because of fear of loss. Many of these women have felt traumatized by previous pregnancy losses, and the psychotic denial is in the interest of protection against further loss. They may be able to acknowledge the pregnancy and accept care only after previous losses have been acknowledged and mourned. Miller (1990) has reported on how pregnancy denial has potential dire consequences because of lack of prenatal care, precipitous and unassisted delivery, fetal abuse, and neonaticide. She noted psychotic denial of pregnancy in 12 of 26 women admitted in 1 year to her special inpatient program for pregnant mentally ill women; compared with those who did not deny, the women who denied pregnancy had experienced significantly more losses of children in the past as well as the high likelihood of losing the baby to foster care at birth.

Case 14: Psychotic Denial of Pregnancy After Pregnancy Losses

A homeless black woman was admitted in the 28th week of gestation with the delusion that she was not pregnant, in spite of all evidence to the contrary. She was acutely confused and was diagnosed as having an acute exacerbation of her chronic undifferentiated schizophrenia. She showed increasing anxiety when questioned about the pregnancy;

she refused to wear maternity clothes, called the fetal movements "gas," and refused pelvic examination and ultrasonography. She had three previous uncomplicated pregnancies and had lost custody of the children, because of maternal neglect, to family members.

With medication, supportive psychotherapy, and family intervention, the patient's denial gradually faded. When she finally consented to an ultrasound examination, a question of congenital anomaly was raised. The denial resumed, interspersed with panicky demands for tests because she was worried about her baby.

Such motivated denial is a protection against further loss and, perhaps, protects the fetus against the unconscious maternal aggression that had led to neglect and loss in the past. The denial is usually not complete; typically, it waxes and wanes over time and coexists with normal prenatal attachment to the baby, nurturant fantasies, and paranoid beliefs about an intruder (Cook and Howe 1984). The opposite side of denial is the overanxiety with which denial can fluctuate. Eleven of the 12 women with pregnancy denial in Miller's (1990) series had a diagnosis of chronic schizophrenia; other women on that ward had diagnoses more representative of a general hospital psychiatry unit.

Pseudocyesis, or false positive diagnosis of pregnancy, is a condition known from antiquity. It is not uncommon to see women in mental hospitals who are hallucinating being pregnant by someone famous or supernatural. There are also women who are not known to have long-term mental illness and appear at obstetrical clinics falsely claiming to be pregnant. In current terminology, pseudocyesis is most likely to be a variant of monosymptomatic hypochondriasis, or a hysterical situational psychosis, in someone who has not been previously psychotic (Starkman et al. 1985). An enlarged abdomen and amenorrhea in the absence of an actual pregnancy must be worked up for a physiological neuroendocrine disorder, especially galactorrhea-amenorrhea hyper-prolactinemia syndrome (Cohen 1982).

Couvade is childbearing behavior at the time of a birth in a person other than the mother, usually in the baby's father (Treethowan and Conlon 1965). Psychotic inpatients may demonstrate couvade in sympathy or in mourning for a lost baby among them. This is especially likely to occur in the presence of a pregnant patient whose pregnancy is terminated and not discussed with the ward community, or when there is a pregnant therapist who takes leave without adequate discussion.

Legal Issues and Decisions of Pregnancy Once the Fetus Is Viable

It is absolutely critical that clinicians undertaking the care and treatment of severely mentally ill pregnant women understand the legal imperatives that circumscribe that care (Cohen and Taub 1989). In the *Roe v. Wade* decision (1973), the United States Supreme Court held that at the time of fetal viability (about 6 months gestation), the state may have a strong interest in the lives of both mother and unborn fetus (DalPozzo and Marsh 1987). The essential concept is that the clinicians' legal duty is to provide for the health and well-being of both the mother and her fetus once the fetus is considered viable (Chervenak and McCullough 1989). This dual commitment potentially creates a conflict of interest between the rights of the mother and the right of her unborn fetus "to be well born" (Gallagher 1989; Paltrow 1990; Robertson 1989; Rosenthal 1990; Soloff et al. 1979).

The dual obligation of the psychiatric staff to both the unborn fetus and to the mother creates special problems in evaluation and treatment planning. The staff must not only ascertain whether or not the patient presents a danger to herself and others, but also whether her mental condition may endanger the normal development of the unborn child that she is carrying (Harrison 1990). For example, the mentally ill pregnant patient's right to refuse treatment may directly conflict with the fetus' right "to be well born." After an assessment of the clinical situation that gives rise to these conflicting rights, the psychiatric caregivers must petition the courts, which then will decide whose interest will prevail.

Soloff and his colleagues (1979) at the Western Psychiatric Institute and Clinic in Pittsburgh, Pennsylvania, reported on a case of a schizophrenic pregnant woman who was brought to the emergency room in an acute psychotic state, 7 months pregnant. After a thorough evaluation on the psychiatric unit, the patient's continued denial of the pregnancy and her consistent refusal to participate in any type of prenatal care obliged the treating physicians and staff to petition the court to restrict the mother's right to leave the hospital. Although the pregnant patient objected, the treaters sought a civil commitment lasting until the time of the delivery of the child. The psychiatric staff presented their argument on the grounds that 1) involuntary hospitalization was needed in order to ensure that the fetus would survive to term, and 2) the civil commitment and confinement of the mother in a hospital was the least-restrictive setting that would allow for appropriate monitoring of the pregnancy and provide for a medically safe delivery. The Allegheny County Court of Common Pleas granted this commitment.

The legal obligations of psychiatric professionals to the rights of the fetus have increased in the last decade and are expanding due to the ability of modern medical technology to provide an environment in which babies can survive after fewer days of gestation (DalPozzo and Marsh 1987). In addition, there is a rapidly changing legal environment in the arena of fetal rights as the courts have begun to find pregnant women who behave in ways that are believed to be harmful to an unborn fetus criminally liable. As of March 1990, 35 women nationwide have faced criminal charges for using drugs or alcohol while pregnant (Landers 1990; Paltrow et al. 1990; Popovits 1991; Roberts 1990).

To date, women who are not mentally ill cannot be denied personal freedom in anticipation of acts that are deemed harmful to fetal health, but they can be subject to criminal prosecution once such harmful behaviors are proven. However, the matter is different for pregnant mentally ill women whose personal freedom can now be limited prior to any harmful acts. Psychiatric clinicians are legally obligated to act to protect fetal life by petitioning courts to impose restrictions on the personal freedom of pregnant women with serious mental illness in anticipation of their actions. Both the mentally ill pregnant patient and the psychiatric staff who are responsible for her care are obliged to act in accordance with these court rulings. Thus, access to legal counsel for guidance for patient and staff is essential in providing appropriate psychiatric care for this population of patients (Kaplan 1989).

In many states, once involuntary commitment is granted to the hospital, the court will assign legal counselors: one for the mother and one for the unborn fetus. These advocates will monitor the care that the psychiatric team gives to the mother, noting what impact these treatments will have on the health of the unborn child. To this end, the advocates may also oversee medications, frequency of room checks, and obstetrical and prenatal care. They act as advocates for their clients and as representatives of the court. The legal sanctions and surveillance add enormously to the stress of caring for these patients. Teamwork and mutual support of clinicians and legal counsel can help keep the focus on the best care for the patient.

Abortion

With early diagnosis, there is the possibility of abortion, an option that carries some risk but may well be the most humane and least traumatic for the psychotic patient, her family, and the caregivers. Abortion is not an innocuous procedure for any woman, and especially not for a woman with schizophrenia. Postabortion psychological reactions have been reported in a general population: 1) feelings of mild sadness, guilt, and regret that are transient and common; 2) mild to moderate depression requiring outpatient treatment; and 3) severe depression and psychosis occasionally necessitating hospitalization (Brewer 1977, 1978). The more severe reactions are most likely to appear in women who have the fewest social supports (David 1985), which includes those women with long-term mental illness. One study showed a 40% risk of postpartum psychosis and a 30% risk of postabortion psychosis for schizophrenic women (Hidas et al. 1989). Recurrences of psychosis in the months postabortion are not unusual. Also, depression and psychosis can recur months later at the date that would have been the expected date of delivery.

Any decision to abort the pregnancy is ideally made in collaboration with the woman patient who is mentally ill and pregnant. If possible, it is also wise to involve the father of the baby and the mother's guardian or family (if the patient has been judged incompetent) in discussions with the caregiving team. The team itself will need to air its views on this pregnancy, on its meaning for the woman, and on her current situation. It is often tempting for the staff to bypass these discussions and to rationalize that the abortion will be in the best interest of both the baby and the mother. However, clinically it is important for the patient to address her ambivalent feelings with a nonjudgmental staff, especially at these critical junctures.

The choice of abortion for pregnant mentally ill women may not be unlike the decision-making process for pregnant HIV-positive women, in that a past history of loss of children may be a key factor. The hypothesis is that the more past losses there are, the more likely the woman will choose to keep the pregnancy to term. Anitra Pivnick, an anthropologist at Montefiore Hospital in the Bronx, New York, found that HIV-positive women who did choose to terminate pregnancies were more likely to have had custody or had lived with a child for at least 85% of his or her life (Pivnick et al. 1991). Pivnick's work has led her to conclude that women's reproductive decisions are influenced by their histories of separation from, and profound yearnings for, their lost children (Levine and Dubler 1990). We also find that an examination of past losses for pregnant women with mental illness can help to shed light on their decision making in early pregnancy.

There is no reason to routinely advise abortion in a psychotic woman who gets pregnant (Robinson 1933). When time is taken to discuss the options and to validate the side of the woman that wishes to be pregnant, abortion may be chosen with more information and less likelihood of a repeat pregnancy. Much therapeutic work can be done around this agonizing decision about whether to abort; such work may decrease the psychosis and grief following the abortion (Spaulding and Cavenar 1978) and can also increase the woman's cooperation with a subsequent birth control measure. If the decision is made to keep the pregnancy, then many of the fears and fantasies have already been put on the table for therapeutic work during the pregnancy.

The following case illustrates how facing the ambivalence surrounding abortion helped one patient to end a pattern of repeated pregnancies and abortions.

Case 15: Multiple Abortions

The patient was a 30-year-old lesbian woman who had a manic-depressive disorder. She had become pregnant three times and followed the same pattern: she would become acutely psychotic at 8 weeks gestation, hospitalization would follow, and then abortion would be performed, with her consent. No one on the inpatient staff talked about the patient's desires to be pregnant, the fact that she had heterosexual relations to become pregnant even though she was a committed lesbian, or her sadness after each abortion; all staff were relieved when she decided to abort. The patient's acute psychosis cleared after the abortion, and she was discharged to outpatient therapy. There she began to talk about her yearnings for a baby, and how she would get drunk and find a man to sleep with when she was midcycle and had the fantasy of conceiving a baby. During her fourth hospitalization, her outpatient therapist helped inpatient staff to work with the patient to help her, while still pregnant, to fantasize about the possibility of having a baby and to mourn her loss after the abortion. She began to work with her therapist on identifying times when she became hypersexual, and she was willing to take additional medication (lithium) to prevent the drinking and sexual promiscuity (Donlon 1976; Loeb and

Loeb 1987). The wish for a baby became less pressing after she and her partner adopted a puppy, and she has not become pregnant again.

Finally, and unfortunately in our view, the reality of the choice of abortion may well be limited in the current legal, political, and cultural context. Recent court decisions may limit the ability of counselors and caregivers to present abortion as a choice to women with mental illness if federal funding is involved in supporting the agency that is dispensing care (see *Rust v. Sullivan* 1991). Also, women who are HIV positive as well as mentally ill may have limited choices. Private doctors and clinics may not perform abortions on women who disclose an HIV-positive serostatus. We must know what choices are really available to our patients before presenting them with options that cannot be implemented (Stotland et al. 1990).

Sterilization and genetic questions may be raised along with the discussion of abortion; although these are related topics, it is essential that any action about permanent sterilization be taken at another time. One major loss at a time is enough for any person to manage, especially a woman with long-term mental illness. The loss of a pregnancy needs to be separated in time from the loss of future reproductive capacity. Furthermore, prematurely concluding that a woman's mental illness (or her genetic makeup) demand permanent sterilization may preclude important discussion of fantasies and wishes that can take place when the possibility for the pregnancy continuing is taken seriously.

Abortion, if and when it does take place with the consent of the patient, does not end the necessity for therapeutic work. Following an abortion, the psychotic woman needs to mourn and needs help to do so. She also needs help in acknowledging her loss and in planning for her need to use birth control actively to prevent pregnancy. The relationship with a therapist who can help explore possibilities is also one that can see the woman through a pregnancy and delivery or through an abortion.

Case 16 : Postabortion Depression

A 31-year-old patient had been at the state hospital for the better part of 10 years. She became increasingly suicidal following an abortion to which she had readily agreed. She had thought she could never get pregnant because of her mental illness, the medication she took, and the street drugs she had used as a teenager. She had worked as a prostitute when she was out of the hospital and never used birth control. She was amazed and pleased to know she could be pregnant. She did not know who the father might be. She did know that she could not realistically have the baby, and maturely cooperated with the staff around arranging for a first trimester abortion. She was praised by the day staff for her decision; she told them they were her good mothers and had helped her make the right decision about not becoming a mother herself. However, at night, she cried herself to sleep, saved up her medications, and made suicide plans. She imagined her baby in Heaven, the perfect baby who never cried or dirtied his diapers, someone so easy that she would be capable of caring for him. She wanted to join this angel baby in Heaven and be a perfect mother. She began to imagine that her baby's real father was a deceased singer who had been popular, suave, and rich in his lifetime. She determined to kill herself to complete this ideal family.

When the nighttime suicide and reunion fantasies were openly discussed with the patient, she could begin to slowly confront her idealization and mourn the loss of this ideal family. When she saw that the staff could tolerate her grief and anger at them, at her real parents, and at her own inability to mother adequately, she slowly began to feel more self-accepting. She began to practice birth control. Over several years time, she began to give birth to her own best and most realistic self.

The father of the baby usually does not have a say in a decision to abort, especially if he is also a long-term psychiatric patient. Yet reactions of the men involved, as well as their yearnings, disappointments, and reactions, should not be underestimated.

It is important to keep open the possibility that any woman might be able to keep and care for her baby, at least as one of the options to consider. Once the diagnosis of pregnancy is made and the decision to keep the pregnancy has been determined, the work of managing the multiple high-risk pregnant woman begins in earnest.

Chapter 7

High-Risk Pregnancy: Management, Labor, and Delivery

*P*sychosis in pregnancy has been the subject of a great deal of wonder for centuries. Current acknowledgment of pregnancy in women with long-term mental illness creates a need to understand more about the management and treatment of these most difficult patients. Of all the psychoses associated with childbearing, schizophrenia is the most difficult and refractory to treat (Casiano and Hawkins 1987). In the past decade, there has been a special interest in the use of medications in pregnancy, an important subject about which there is continued discussion, research, and observation and an expanding literature. Some general principles of psychopharmacological treatment of pregnant patients have emerged, and some excellent reviews of the subject are now available and are summarized in Chapter 8.

Rare in the literature, however, are accounts of psychotherapy with the pregnant psychotic patient and honest descriptions of the anguish among caregivers working with her. Spielvogel and Wile (1986) have been unique in their presentation of practical clinical research that combines an examination of the complex clinical psychodynamic, medicolegal, and ethical issues with the pharmacological management. Only recently have Krener and her colleagues (1989a) and Miller (1989) described how women with multiple problems, including psychosis, actually deal with pregnancy and how daunting this population can be for even the most dedicated and competent caregivers.

Surprisingly, when anxiety of the pregnant psychotic mother about childbearing becomes available to consciousness, it is easier to develop an alliance that will help the patient to behave in ways that optimize the health of her unborn baby. It is important to recognize pregnancy as a normal crisis with changing physiology, body image, and social role, and to approach the woman with the assumption that she cares for her baby, and not to approach the patient with a punitive stance that might provoke guilt and anxiety (Rosett and Weiner 1984). The former approach may be helpful with many women who have long-term mental illness who also have the dual diagnosis of alcohol and drug abuse.

In this chapter, we will discuss 1) how the pregnancy affects emotional health and mental illness, 2) the prenatal care of pregnant psychiatric inpatients, 3) the prenatal care of pregnant psychiatric outpatients, and 4) the labor and delivery of women with severe mental illness.

Does Pregnancy Make Psychotic Illness Better or Worse?

There is a disagreement about the basic question of whether pregnancy worsens a psychosis or improves it. First psychotic episodes may occur in pregnancy and known psychosis can relapse in pregnancy, but sometimes ongoing psychosis may remit or be ameliorated by the pregnant state. There are many clinical manifestations of psychosis in pregnancy. As Chang and Renshaw (1986) concluded, there are no two cases alike and available findings are inconsistent. Pregnancy, with its hormonal and electrolyte changes, has been said to provide protection against schizophrenia (Preist 1978), but this finding is neither consistent nor causally understood (Seeman 1989a; Seeman and Lang 1990). Some schizophrenic patients who recall pregnancy as a time of remission of mental illness seek out the pregnant state and may have multiple pregnancies (Baker 1967).

While admission rates to mental hospitals rise to several times expected rates in the first 3 months postpartum, it is interesting to note that admission of women who are pregnant is less than expected for their age group (Pugh et al. 1963). The longitudinal investigations of McNeil and his colleagues (1983a, 1983b, 1984a, 1984b, 1984c) are outstanding in addressing the question of the relationship between pregnancy and psychosis. These investigators systematically followed 88 psychotic women and compared them with a demographically matched group of 104 control women during pregnancy. They chose the women during the years 1973 through 1977 from a comprehensive medical system in southern Sweden; the women had had a history of hospitalization for nonorganic psychosis. The authors collected the actual subjective concerns of the psychotic mothers-to-be and compared them to the observations of their (blind to diagnosis) interviewers and to the official psychiatric record. They hypothesized that the psychotic mothers would have increased mental disturbance during pregnancy compared with the control group. Indeed, the psychotic women had significantly more subjective problems with their mental condition than did control subjects. Significantly, only 35% of psychiatric records indicated any disturbance in mental condition during the pregnancy. To look at the records alone, fewer than a third of these quite troublesome and significant mental conditions would be identified (McNeil et al. 1983a, 1983b). There is some indication that comparisons of psychotic pregnancy with control subjects produce too large a disparity because of the socioeconomic variables and that psychotic women are more comparable to other poor women with few social supports and social skills.

When psychotic women are compared with themselves before and after pregnancy, they can show improvement largely because the services and attention to the pregnancy and baby provide relationships and organization for the mothers. When Krener et al. (1989a, 1989b) studied 27 pregnant women with psychosis, it was as part of an ongoing prospective study on the effects of social isolation of mother and infant. Methodological considerations are important in evaluating these studies, and results on the central questions of the effect of pregnancy on psychosis can vary depending on the variables and analysis chosen. The investigators asked whether pregnancy may constitute a separate or secondary affective syndrome beyond the primary diagnosis. They found that providing psychosocial support during pregnancy and the puerperium was necessary and did produce improved patient well-being.

Women with long-term mental illness, fearing advice or coercion for abortion, may drop out of view of the mental health profession during pregnancy. This protective disappearance gives a false impression to the psychiatrist, who may believe that the patient is in remission. Of course, the alert psychiatric program will follow up any person who has dropped out to discover such a pregnancy. When pregnant mentally ill women are followed assiduously, their need for enhanced mental and physical health services and the elaboration of their anxiety and depression regarding pregnancy become more apparent. In fact, some pregnant mental patients who are not hospitalized require so many support services that it is difficult even for the best motivated and endowed communities to keep up with these patients' needs (Krener et al. 1989a; Wrede et al. 1980).

Pregnancy is usually a time of emotional and physical turmoil. There is usually conflict about the pregnancy, about becoming a mother, and about one's own mother. All pregnant women must adapt to changing body shape and size, a varying hormonal environment, and a foreign creature living and moving within her. There is inevitably anxiety about life and death, labor and delivery, one's competence in mothering, and one's relationship with the father of the baby (Notman and Lester 1988). The side of pregnancy that is usually recognized is the opportunity to create new life, to "re-do" past losses, and this is very real. Less appreciated is the underside of pregnancy, invariably also a time of losses, imagined and actual—losses of the fantasies about being and having the idealized mother and baby. There is paradoxically the demand for enormous emotional and physical change along with an expectation of well-being and happiness (Cohen 1988). Women are willing to pay an enormous price for the fulfillment of the wish to be pregnant and to have the responsibility of motherhood (Kron 1989).

The stress of pregnancy taxes every woman to some extent. One large prospective study of an unselected sample in Sweden showed that almost 40% had a strikingly negative attitude toward the pregnancy for reasons related to the woman's own childhood or to the current emotional and social situation (Nilsson 1970). A vulnerable person who has a long-term mental illness would, of course, be at least as affected by the developmental crisis of pregnancy as would a healthy woman. Pregnant women with mental illness, and especially those women who have previously lost a child for reasons connected with psychiatric illness, show a great deal of anxiety and depression and concerns about the future (Krener 1989a, 1989b).

Pregnancy can also seem to be a time of great tranquillity, so much so that psychotherapy becomes impossible. However, this happiness may be illusory and transient. The pregnancy can be fulfilling a need for constant companionship, and the baby may be overidealized. An exclusive and excessive peacefulness can also represent a defense against mourning, often for the loss of a previous baby who was still-born, adopted away, or even aborted (Lewis 1979). Some patients may reduce their involvement with their therapists during pregnancy and put their full conscious attention on the medical aspects of prenatal care.

When queried about specific problem areas, surprisingly high numbers of even apparently normal prenatal patients report inadequacies, ambivalences, and anxieties that might be worrisome to the caregiver. Screening questions have been devised to help elicit some of these concerns (Cohen 1988):

1. Excessive concerns about adverse previous experience in childbearing or childrearing, e.g., "Has anything happened to you in the past or during this pregnancy that might affect the baby?"
2. Conflicts in the marriage, kinship, and support system, e.g., "Do you plan to raise your children any different from the way you were raised?"
3. Inadequate preparation for childbearing and childrearing, e.g., "How much experience have you had caring for children?"
4. Concerns about the mother's own health and how it can be adversely affected by the pregnancy, labor, delivery, or care of a baby, e.g., "Do you have any condition that you think could be made worse by the pregnancy?"

These questions are quite simple and open areas for more in-depth examination; they take into account that there are normal anxieties in pregnant women—anxieties about themselves and their babies.

The treatment of the pregnant woman with long-term mental illness is easiest when there is a previous relationship with the patient and knowledge of her capabilities; however, this is rarely so, and there are many surprises even to the experienced clinician. The treatment cannot be done alone and inevitably involves other medical specialties, particularly obstetrics, and legal counsel about the welfare of the fetus that may be at variance with the welfare of the mother (Muqtadir et al. 1986).

Prenatal Care of the Pregnant Psychotic Inpatient

The pregnant psychotic woman is best studied in the context of the normal pregnant woman. Burgess (1980) realistically summarized the tasks and emotions of each trimester. She noted, for instance, that ambivalence is always characteristic of the first trimester no matter how planned or wanted the conception. The second trimester is quiet and a good chance to rethink major relationships; the third trimester is for nesting. A psychotic pregnant woman requires more than traditional obstetrical service (Mirdal et al. 1977; Nurnberg 1980, 1984; Queenan 1980); she prefers a steady person at her prenatal visits, an understimulating environment, and frequent reality checks.

An inpatient psychiatric unit can be uneasy about hospitalizing a pregnant woman close to term, especially if she is psychotically denying her pregnancy or preventing examination. This presents mental health staff with an obstetrical problem and sometimes even the responsibility of determining when the patient is in labor—a determination that most psychiatric nurses are unaccustomed to making. A prior arrangement with a nearby obstetrical unit can ameliorate the anxiety of the psychiatric staff as well as provide optimal care for the patient. The physical proximity of the two places of care is quite important, because time may be of the essence once labor has started. At San Francisco General Hospital, for example, the psychiatric unit where pregnant patients are treated is adjacent to the high-risk maternity unit. The length of stay for pregnant psychotic patients must exceed that of nonpregnant patients. In one study, pregnant psychotic patients averaged 1 to 2 months instead of 1 to 2 weeks (Rudolph et al. 1990). The third trimester, nearing delivery, is the best time to hospitalize or rehospitalize when hospital length of stays may need to be limited. It is most important to provide adequate time to modify regimens and to help the patient prepare for labor, delivery, and mothering (Shapiro 1983).

Forcier (1990) and her psychiatric-mental health nursing staff at University of Illinois Hospital developed a treatment protocol for the inpatient prenatal care of psychotic women. In conjunction with the obstetric team, a plan was devised for each individual patient with the goal of the safe delivery of the mother and baby. In this model, the obstetric team made weekly visits to each patient to find potential obstetric complications, order diagnostic tests (nonstress, contraction stress, glucose tolerance, ultrasound), and order laboratory tests (for detection of sexually transmitted diseases, hepatitis). A primary nurse was assigned to the psychotic patient along with an obstetrics resident.

The psychiatric-mental health nursing team ensured completion of tests, prepared patients for weekly visits, did routine weight and blood pressure checks, requested urine tests, and listened to the fetal heart with the patient. The team notified labor and delivery of the onset of labor and transferred the patient when her contractions were 5 to 10 minutes apart and regular for an hour. A psychiatric nurse might stay with the patient throughout labor and delivery and later accompany the obstetric team on rounds to talk with psychotic patients. The focus is on reducing the anxiety for everyone. The nurse, acting as intermediary, can interpret the obstetrical experience for the patient and the patient's experience for the obstetric team.

The emphasis is on reality. Delusional beliefs about the fetus or the physical changes in pregnancy are the basis of much of the bizarre, difficult, and potentially dangerous behavior shown by pregnant women with mental illness (Miller 1990). When the underlying delusional beliefs are addressed, the need for other management techniques can be decreased.

Miller (1990) gives several striking examples of such delusions. One woman refused to shower or change her clothes for fear she would drown the baby or the baby would fall out when she pulled her pants down. Another patient thought the fetal parts were tumors on her body. One woman thought she should drink her urine to comfort the fetus with a familiar fluid that came from her body. A pregnant patient feared that the "people" living inside her were sucking out her nutrients and weakening her; this belief was transformed later in the pregnancy to be ghosts living inside who were poisoning her baby, then the devil who might be the father of the baby. In response to these delusions, the patient gorged and vomited her food. In the hospital setting, once the delusions were articulated, they did not have to be acted upon. It is always helpful for the staff to understand the behavior and be intellectually interested in it rather than to see the behavior as merely difficult to manage.

However, when a psychotic pregnant patient is treated as an inpatient, it is the responsibility of the mental health professional to see that prenatal care has been arranged and that there are adequate plans for the eventuality of the delivery. It is a type of coordinated planning that patients with long-term mental illness are rarely capable of themselves, but when it is done for and with them, a decrease in their psychotic symptoms is seen (Krener et al. 1989b).

Anxiety in the nursing staff increases as the patient's due date approaches, and with good reason. Despite all the careful preparation, 3 of 16 patients on Forcier's unit delivered precipitously. Because some of the patients do not feel their contractions, they do not call for assistance and instead attempt to self-deliver. These are emergency situations in which much of the stress falls on the nurses. Staff discussions and talks within the community of patients about the pregnancy and impending labor and delivery give all concerned a chance to express feelings, fears, and fantasies that are inevitable.

What of the patient who refuses to be examined? Everything possible should be done to encourage adequate prenatal care. However, fears and paranoia concerning the prenatal examination may prevent some psychotic women from consenting to an adequate examination. We concur with Spielvogel and Wile (1986), who strongly recommend the use of a court order, if necessary, to ensure proper medical care. It is important to be sensitive to what the examination represents for the woman and how particularly stressful it may be, especially in someone with a history of sexual abuse. However, the rule of thumb we recommend is to do what is medically right. Get the examination done to get the data that are needed. Do the minimal necessary examination to get the maximum data. Try to get as much data as possible. This is not always achievable. Some essential data may be historical (e.g., street drug intake) and difficult to ascertain by objective tests. Realize too that some of the objective tests (e.g., ultrasound) can be quite anxiety-provoking even to a nonpsychotic person; for the woman with mental illness, these tests can be profoundly disturbing and can reinforce and elicit delusional beliefs about the pregnancy or the caregivers. We feel that a useful principle is to treat the resistant psychotic pregnant woman as one might treat one's own recalcitrant teenage daughter. Be firm, gentle, understanding, persistent, and patient, and speak to the healthiest, most mature, most self-protective part of the patient.

Optimally, women who are pregnant and psychotic enough to require hospitalization will be cared for in a general hospital that has obstetrical and psychiatric services, or even better, at one of the few existent special units that welcome such patients. However, there will also be pregnant inpatients at state mental hospital facilities that are not medically equipped; in these cases, the staff will have to be creative in finding a solution that minimizes the difficulties for everyone concerned. So it was in the following case example:

Case 17: The Ward Milieu Prepares for a Delivery

A noncommunicative very psychotic patient on a women's ward was observed to be pregnant. She was a young unmarried woman, and there was no history of previous childbearing or of a relationship that led to the pregnancy, or of drug use in the first trimester. She was completely uncooperative with staff and would not permit physical examination of any kind. Her inability to take responsibility for the health of her baby and herself created a vacuum that was filled by other women patients and staff members. Other patients tried to care for and comfort her, and eagerly discussed the upcoming delivery with great interest. The staff psychiatrist tried to maintain the patient on medication that might diminish her psychotic thinking and increase her collaboration. The head nurse borrowed a fetoscope, recalled how to use it, and taught all shifts of nurses to be alert to signs of labor. The nearby general hospital obstetrical unit was warned to be ready for an emergency. The obstetrical unit personnel were fearful of managing an uncooperative probable primipara, but they were persuaded to do so when the patient went into labor. She appeared more agitated and reclusive but did not complain of pain, and she was rushed to the emergency room. Within the hour, she had delivered a healthy-appearing baby. The other patients waited anxiously for the news and greeted the arrival of a normal baby as a shared victory. The baby was immediately removed to foster care, and the patient returned to the unit. Although no one knew her, a circle of women—staff and patients—formed around this unfortunate patient to allow for the safe delivery of this baby.

When the pregnant psychotic patient is not approachable by a personal relationship or through teaching and talking with a supportive team in the hospital and is not held in chemical restraint by medication, the question arises about such practicalities as how to physically restrain the patient if necessary. Physical restraint may become necessary to prevent the patient from hurting other people, herself, and, in this case, her baby. Whenever possible, such contingency plans should be made before the need arises so that the staff and other patients can know what is happening and why. However, our mind-set is that a pregnant woman should not need such restraint, so we do not prepare for it in the usual manner. Old-fashioned techniques of sedation such as baths and quiet room are much preferred to physical restraining measures, which are required when the situation escalates or breaks too rapidly for gentler measures. Restraining should be done with one person in charge and four others firmly and gently holding the extremities of the woman. Care should be taken to subdue the patient without allowing trauma to the abdomen (i.e., to gently bring her onto her back or side rather than onto the abdomen). Talking to her during the restraining about how we will not permit her to hurt her baby or herself can be reassuring to even the most psychotic patient and to the other patients in the milieu. Talking with other patients and staff is essential because these events provoke everyone's deepest feelings about having basic security, being an infant, and having a mother. Short-acting medications, a chance for quiet, and the company of someone who can talk with and reassure the patient should follow.

Prenatal Care of Outpatients With Mental Illness

Women with mental illness who live in the community are more likely to come to prenatal or medical clinics when pregnant than to bring the pregnancy to the attention of the mental health clinic. They do what other women do in seeking the appropriate care when they are able to do so. They fear being judged or talked into an abortion because of the insensitivity of the mental health system to their wishes for parenthood. With some justification, they expect clinicians to be "policing their rights to parenthood" (Schwab et al. 1991).

The clinician who works with an outpatient in therapy should be in a unique position to advise the prenatal team. The therapist ideally has a good sense of a patient's reproductive history and the dynamics behind her yearning for a child, as well as the possible problems and pitfalls that may make full-time mothering an impossibility. However, the patient may not always allow the therapist's knowledge to be fully used, fearing, for example, invasion and control. The medical-obstetrical team may worry abstractly about the need for mental health services but will tend to move the patient through the normal obstetrical protocols. For the patient, this presents an opportunity to feel normal in a new normal role, and the patient may feel safer with the obstetrician than with the therapist. But, more commonly, the guidance the therapist can give the obstetrical team is useful and needed.

Case 18: Outpatient Pregnancy From Conception to Delivery

A long-term patient with schizophrenia had a range of services in place and lived in a halfway house. She had had one previous pregnancy in her teens that ended in a spontaneous miscarriage. Now, in her late 20s and in a stable 5-year relationship with a man who is not mentally ill, she wanted to have a baby. She was delighted to discover, with the aid of a drugstore pregnancy testing kit, that she was pregnant. She had already stopped taking all her lithium before conception. When she told her outpatient therapists her good news, they were clearly not as thrilled as she was. The psychiatrist asked her to discontinue carbamazepine and reduce her trifluoperazine, and to begin prenatal care.

The outpatient psychiatric staff, halfway house counselors, and case manager met to discuss the situation. They worried about the patient's ability to care for the child; her inability to consider abortion because of the psychological impact of the previous miscarriage; the problem of her residency, since she could not bring a baby to the halfway house; and their own sense of helplessness in the face of the patient's actions. The medical clinic staff consulted with the psychiatric staff and assigned a nurse clinician to coordinate and meet monthly with both groups. The psychiatrist discussed with the patient all the options and problems she could anticipate and offered the possibility of abortion, which the patient refused, as she was determined to go forward with the pregnancy.

In response, the team planned for the eventualities of the birth and the possible outcomes. They contacted social services to assess the mother at the time of delivery. They enrolled the patient in the high-risk infant-mother intervention program in a neighboring town, a program working with mothers and infants until the child is 1 year old. They arranged financing for the baby's prenatal and well-baby care. They met with the father and grandparents to involve them in planning. They started a search for housing for the couple and the baby. They sought supervision for themselves around their panic, their fear of having to care for the baby as well as the mother with mental illness, and the reactions of the staff people. For instance, the patient's therapist was not able to be sensitive to the patient's needs because of her own infertility and sense of loss. A senior staff member worried about a dynamic issue—the patient's withdrawal and secrecy whenever she became symptomatic—and how that would affect an infant.

While the staff was busy with all this, the patient, after 7 years of continuous treatment, stopped coming to the outpatient clinic. The clinicians worried about her judgment and about the need for more psychotropic medication. They were reassured to learn that she regularly attended the prenatal clinic and adhered to visits, diet, and exercise impeccably. At the time of the labor, her best friend and the father of the baby accompanied the patient, and she had an uneventful vaginal delivery. She selected epidural anesthesia so that she would feel minimal pain. The baby girl was born with an Apgar of 9. In the postpartum period, the patient chose not to breast-feed and asked for reinstatement of antipsychotic medications and for her long-time therapist and others from the psychiatric service to visit her.

This patient, and others like her, do not attend regular prenatal education programs because they are not encouraged to do so. Prenatal birth classes need to be encouraged to admit a psychotic pregnant participant who needs this type of childbirth education even more than most pregnant women do. If a class has a person with long-term mental illness in it, it is best for someone to accompany her who can interpret the realities. A patient with mental illness may not necessarily be as disruptive as is feared and, by asking innocent questions, may express what other pregnant women feel and fear but are too "sophisticated" to ask. Spielvogel and Wile (1988) have developed a teaching videotape to be used specifically by the pregnant psychotic patient and her family. The tape clearly orients patients about what will happen in terms of their prenatal care and introduces them to the multidisciplinary team.

Labor and Delivery

Most general hospital obstetrical units will be understandably reluctant to take on a patient with long-term mental illness, usually fearing that they will be overwhelmed by a patient who is out of control. They are more eager to do so if there is advance psychiatric input into the prenatal care and a promise that a mental health worker will accompany the patient through the labor and delivery. Psychotropic medications need to be readjusted after the delivery, depending on whether or not the mother is nursing her baby. Even when lactation is not present, it can take at least 1 to 6 weeks for full return of physiological homeostasis, during which time dosage needs are not stably predictable.

The topic of labor produces anxiety for all pregnant women, and even more so for the psychotic mother, and very much so for the nursing staff who will accompany and care for the psychotic patient during these laboring hours (Carmack and Corwin 1980). It is best to anticipate the labor problems, to the degree this is possible, and to have a psychiatric nurse or familiar mental health worker accompany the psychotic woman through the labor. It is well known that companionship in the labor situation reduces anxiety for the normal woman, and this is even more true for the psychotic patient. The nurses in the labor room need to understand about the psychosis and how it may manifest as delusions, hallucinations, paranoia, and violence during labor, and how to intervene in effective ways, both personally and pharmacologically (Fisher 1988).

When obstetrical care is preplanned and coordinated, women with long-term mental illness do not show more obstetrical complications than do other women (McNeil et al. 1974). About half of the women who are prepared for labor and delivery report a positive reaction to the birth process and a good rapport with the staff. Some are even able to adequately use relaxation techniques (Rudolph et al. 1990). However, even with the best possible program, precipitous deliveries do occur. Severely psychotic women may not experience labor pain and cannot report the contractions to the staff in the same way that most women do (Rosenthal 1990). As the expected date of confinement approaches, inpatient psychiatric nurses should institute 15-minute checks on the pregnant woman to reassure her and themselves that she is not yet in labor or to detect labor when it cannot be reported.

Every state hospital has had the traumatic and tragic experience of a patient who delivers in the toilet or the bed. The mother can be found inadvertently, bewildered about what happened. The baby may be dead or in critical condition. These events leave a scar on the entire unit.

Case 19: Precipitous Delivery in a State Hospital

A 40-year-old patient returned to the state hospital many times after she had precipitously delivered a baby in the toilet there when she was 18. The father of the baby was another patient. Their relationship had been recognized and responded to punitively by the staff, who proceeded to separate the couple by assigning them to different wards.

The patient's pregnancy was not recognized because she carried small, wore flowing dresses, never had regular periods, and had indignantly refused any pregnancy test or examination. She made a little scream in the toilet and dropped a full-term baby. A veteran mental health worker, who was also a Vietnam combat veteran, found the puzzled, bleeding mother and baby within an hour of the birth. Years later, still working on the same unit, he said it was worse than any of the many war tragedies he had experienced. The baby was resuscitated and transferred to a neonatal ICU where it survived and was adopted. The patient said nothing of the event and was able to leave the hospital only briefly to a halfway house where she was resistant to treatment. She was readmitted to the hospital many times until she came to stay on the chronic ward. At times when she was more in contact with her therapist, she talked and cried about her lost baby.

Even when the delivery is anticipated and accompanied by supportive staff, the stress of the actual childbirth can unleash further fear and aggression toward the baby. The psychotic woman may cross her legs in an attempt to keep the baby in, or try to strangle the head as it emerges. This is a time of increased disorganization when additional support and medication are necessary. Such traumatic delivery experiences confirm everyone's worst fears about psychosis and pregnancy, and can lead to a policy banning pregnant patients from the psychiatric unit, as if that could eliminate further trauma. These deliveries need to be discussed thoroughly as a critical incident in the life of the ward milieu. It is worthwhile going over what happened in great detail, hearing out everyone's feelings and fears, and thinking together about how to do better next time.

More reassurance can derive from some recent, practical, and thorough articles in nursing journals (Burgess 1980; Forcier 1990). Similarly useful is Oates' (1986) discussion of the use or suspension of medication in labor and delivery. In our experience, there is need for the most skilled obstetrical and anesthesiological care at the times of these deliveries. Major complications can arise from the interactions of psychotropic medications, current or residual, or from street drugs and alcohol used concurrently by the woman with major mental illness. Some women on tricyclic antidepressants have had dangerously precipitous labors. The tricyclics may inhibit not only the central nervous system uptake of dopamine but also the peripheral uptake that helps to initiate labor. A fetus can develop an extrapyramidal symptom—transient opisthotonos (i.e., head and neck muscles in spasm)—from transplacental phenothiazine, precluding vaginal delivery and requiring cesarean section. These are reasons to discontinue medication several weeks in advance of the due date, but even then complications may arise because of medications in the mother's (and baby's) system, or if the delivery occurs earlier than expected. A psychotic patient can be very uncooperative and may even require four-point restraints at the time of delivery.

We have described the prenatal care and labor and delivery issues for women with severe and long-term mental illness. We have seen that staff must prepare themselves to meet the special needs of this high-risk population both on the psychiatric service and in the liaison work that must be carried out with the obstetrical team. For this population the management of medications is especially important because psychiatrists must, in this high-risk situation, concern themselves with the welfare of two patients. In the next chapter we will discuss medication issues and their impact on both the pregnant patient and the unborn child.

Chapter 8

Pregnancy and Medications

*M*edication is crucial in the management of the pregnant psychotic patient. However, medication presents problems for therapists and patients alike. Many women with long-term mental illness who are actively psychotic and suicidal may refuse medications during a pregnancy because of their concern for their unborn babies. Clinicians, of course, worry about the teratogenic and behavioral effects of medication on the fetus while they try to keep the pregnant psychotic woman safe and minimize her damaging symptoms. In this chapter, we will provide a compendium of general principles to be followed for administration of psychotropics and other medications during pregnancy. These can serve as guidelines to clinicians who may want to consult with pharmacology experts about any individual case. Reassuring the patient and her family that care is being taken for both her and her unborn baby can help with compliance in any treatment regimen.

General Principles of Psychopharmacology in Pregnancy, Delivery, and Lactation

There are now some excellent and comprehensive guidelines available for the use of psychoactive drugs and ECT in pregnancy, but all of these articles will not be reviewed or repeated here (Ananth 1976; Boyd and Brown 1948; Burgess 1979; Clark 1977; Gelenberg 1986; Goldberg and DiMascio 1978; Hauser 1985; Kerns 1986; Lewis 1978; Slone et al. 1977; Onnis and Grella 1984). However, relying on Cohen et al. (1989a), on Oates (1986), on Miller (1991), and on the standardized classification of drugs in pregnancy by the United States Food and Drug Administration (FDA), we offer the following guidelines:

1. **All medications have a potential effect on the fetus, and the decision of whether to use a medication and which medication to use always requires that the clinician weigh risks and benefits in choosing what is clinically needed and useful for the**

pregnant psychotic patient while minimizing what can be dangerous for the developing fetus. The physical teratological risk, that of congenital malformations, is greatest in the first trimester; the behavioral teratological risk, that of brain maldevelopment, is greatest in the last trimester. The middle trimester is generally a time of low risk, during which most of the usual psychoactive medications used in a particular case can be reinstated. The first trimester problems usually are worst within the first few weeks prior to diagnosis of pregnancy, and those severe malformations generally are spontaneous miscarriages. Discontinuing medications or decreasing dose is important in the ninth month because it is a time of rapid brain development. Also, it is necessary to prepare the mother to be relatively drug-free as she enters labor and delivery. Drugs may need to be rapidly reinstituted at delivery to deal with the additional stress of the childbirth. Wait for symptoms and medicate accordingly. In a known patient, try to anticipate symptoms and prevent painful ones with medication. Guidebooks such as that of Briggs et al. (1990) are easier to follow and even more objective than the PDR as a source of data for the general clinician. It may be well worthwhile in complicated clinical situations to get a consultation from a clinical psychopharmacologist who is accustomed to prescribing for pregnant women and who can thereby share the responsibility of the case.

Risk factors (A, B, C, D, X) have been assigned to all drugs, based on the level of risk the drug poses to the fetus. Risk factors are designed to help a clinician quickly classify a drug for use during pregnancy. They do not, however, refer to breast-feeding risk, and they oversimplify a complex topic. Most drugs have not yet been given a letter rating by their manufacturers. These definitions used for the risk factors are the same as those put forth by the FDA:

> **Category A:** Controlled studies in women fail to demonstrate a risk to the fetus in the first trimester (and there is no evidence of a risk in later trimesters) and the possibility of fetal harm appears remote. [No psychotropic medication yet qualifies.]

> **Category B:** Either animal reproduction studies have not demonstrated a fetal risk, but there are no controlled

studies in pregnant women, or animal reproduction studies have shown an adverse effect other than a decrease in fertility that was not confirmed in controlled studies in women in the first trimester (and there is no evidence of a risk in later trimesters). [Includes fluoxetine.]

Category C: Either studies in animals have revealed adverse effects on the fetus (teratogenic or embryocidal or other) and there are no controlled studies in women, or studies in women and animals are not available. Drugs should be given only if the potential benefit justifies the potential risk to the fetus. [Includes haloperidol, chlorpromazine, and carbamazepine.]

Category D: There is positive evidence of human fetal risk, but the benefits from use in pregnant women may be acceptable despite the risk (e.g., if the drug is needed in a life-threatening situation or for a serious disease for which safer drugs cannot be used or are ineffective). [Includes lithium carbonate, middle trimester.]

Category X: Studies in animals or human beings have demonstrated fetal abnormalities or there is evidence of fetal risk based on human experience, or both, and the risk of the use of the drug in pregnant women clearly outweighs any possible benefit. The drug is contraindicated in women who are or may become pregnant. [Includes lithium carbonate, first trimester.]

2. **Medications are used in pregnancy, even when they are not prescribed.** The pregnant woman in different phases of pregnancy, the one in labor and delivery, and the lactating mother will all have varying medication needs that deserve changing consideration over time. The high mental health risk and the symptoms of pregnancy (e.g., nausea and insomnia, etc.) lead many women to seek medication. Some 80% of women take some medication (35% psychoactive) in pregnancy; many on their own initiative use over-the-counter medication (Apfel and Mazor 1989). The risk is not absolute, and to take a position of no drugs during pregnancy limits the armamentarium of the psychiatrist and the possibilities

for therapy of the pregnant patient. However, prudence is always in order, even erring on the side of caution; the total long-term effect of any drug passed transplacentally may not be known for many years to come (Apfel and Fisher 1984).

3. **Pregnancy changes the physiology of all women so that the pharmacokinetics are different.** A lower dose may be required than in the nonpregnant state because of slowed liver metabolism in pregnancy. A higher dose may be required if a pregnant woman is taking antacids that render a drug like chlorpromazine ineffective.

4. **Prescribing a weaker drug does not mean less danger.** It is an error to prescribe a minor tranquilizer when a major one is indicated. Small doses of a major tranquilizer can maintain the patient, offsetting the risk of relapse and the need for adjustments and higher doses. The minor tranquilizers (e.g., benzodiazepines) can have a worse effect in pregnancy (e.g., disinhibition and teratogenesis) than the major ones do. Reports of oral clefts following exposure to diazepam are alarming but not consistent. Panic disorders in pregnancy can be treated with tricyclic antidepressants or with alprazolam, which so far seem not to be harmful in pregnancy. Again, remember that for patients exhibiting anxiety symptoms, the use of psychotherapy and support, which can minimize the need for anxiolytic agents, is essential.

5. **Breast-feeding is relatively but not absolutely contraindicated for the psychotic new mother.** In fact, breast-feeding may be very important to continue for the preservation of the mother's self-esteem and to enhance the bonding relationship with the newborn. Lithium is the only absolutely contraindicated drug in this time period; tricyclic antidepressants seem to be the safest. Chlorpromazine, thioridazine, haloperidol, and even fluphenazine can be relatively safe (Nurnberg 1981). Use the lowest possible dose, and suspend if the baby gets drowsy, does not suck strongly, or is excessively wakeful and crying. Even when the dose is being adjusted, it is possible to pump the breast milk for a period of days or even weeks in an attempt to sustain the lactating function and spare the baby the drug side effects. Up-to-date registers of drugs in breast milk are available (see Briggs et al. 1990 and supplements).

6. **ECT is a well-tried and useful treatment in pregnancy and the puerperium.** It can be on occasion the treatment of choice (Varan et al. 1985; Wisner and Perel 1988). It is often delayed and used as a last resort even though it might be safer and more effective and work more rapidly than medications for relief of both florid psychosis and depression. The delay is caused in part by the countertransference reaction and the public view of ECT, a therapy that is stigmatized in all circumstances and seems especially anathema with a pregnant patient. Ideally, the ECT should be done in the presence of an obstetrician, with endotracheal intubation, low-voltage, nondominant ECT with electroencephalographic monitoring, electrocardiographic monitoring of the mother, evaluation of arterial blood gases during and immediately after ECT, Doppler ultrasonography of the fetal heart rate, tocodynamometer recording of uterine tone, administration of glycopyrrolate as an anticholinergic during anesthesia, and weekly nonstress tests—that is, all the currently available technology for monitoring the fetus, the mother, and the seizure. The literature contains several case reports that exemplify how ECT has been used to diminish violent psychosis in pregnant patients (Loke and Salleh 1983; Repke and Berger 1984; Wise et al. 1984). Even before these currently available safeguards, ECT was relatively safe for mother and baby. Presently, the use of ECT with pregnant women is becoming more refined and simplified. We can expect more acceptance and ease in its use as more clinical research and professional discussion among colleagues take place (Miller et al. 1991b).

7. **Smoking is a high-risk factor in pregnancy even though it is not generally considered a drug risk factor.**

8. **Plan pregnancy medications ahead whenever possible.** Ideally, in long-term work with long-term patients, plan a pregnancy with the patient and her husband/partner so that the medications can be diminished or discontinued in anticipation of getting pregnant. This prevents the rapid diminution of medication and a possible rebound effect. This requires a good deal of therapeutic alliance and trust. The psychiatrist or another member of the team must believe that pregnancy is a realistic alternative (though not perhaps ideal) and a desirable outcome for this patient. The patient must

have genuine conviction that the treating mental health professional can understand the yearning for pregnancy and the potential
meaning of a normal pregnancy for her. The discussions of the
wish to become pregnant, of the questions and longings for which
the pregnancy seems to be the answer, and of the mothering
received by the patient and its possible relation to her psychosis are
all important avenues for psychotherapy.

9. **Lithium is the most dangerous of the commonly used psychoactive drugs in pregnancy.** Women with affective disorders who
are taking lithium can collaborate on a drug-free time in order to
become pregnant (Cohen et al. 1988). Exposure in the first trimester has a clear teratogenic effect, especially an association with
cardiovascular malformations, and thus is contraindicated in the
first trimester of pregnancy for the sake of the baby. However,
mania and depression are injurious to the mother (and probably
indirectly to the baby) and must be treated with alternatives to
lithium (Van Gent and Nabarro 1987). It is now considered possible to reinstate lithium during the middle trimester but to taper,
then discontinue, prior to the estimated date of confinement. The
Lithium Information Center[1] maintains current information, and
the Massachusetts General Hospital's *Biological Therapies in Psychiatry*[2] has periodic reports on recommendations, the most recent
one in 1988 (Cohen 1988).

A register of lithium babies was started in 1970 by Morton R.
Weinstein, M.D., originally in collaboration with M. Schou in
Denmark, A. Villeneuve in Canada, and M. Goldfield in the United
States. The Register of Lithium Babies was to include all pregnancies exposed to lithium in the first trimester at least, and regardless
of outcome. The last published report from the Register appeared
in 1980 following the death of Dr. Weinstein.

At this writing there are 250 cases in the Register. Of these, 30
(12%) resulted in congenitally malformed infants, congenital malformations being defined as they were by Dr. Weinstein (1980), as

[1]Lithium Information Center, University of Wisconsin, Department of Psychiatry, Center for
Health Sciences, 600 Highland Street, Madison, Wisconsin 53792.
[2]Massachusetts General Hospital: *Biological Therapies in Psychiatry*. PSG Publishing Co.,
Inc., Littleton, MA 01460

macroscopic abnormalities of structure attributable to faulty development and present at birth. There is dramatic overrepresentation of severe cardiovascular anomalies, with 22 of the 30 of this type, and 10 of these are Ebstein's anomaly.

Reports to the Register have been retrospective, and such studies overrepresent pathology because cases in which there are problems are those that are reported. We have attempted to identify a population from which we could draw a statistically valid sample of incidence of malformations in exposures to lithium during the first trimester of pregnancy, but without success. We have thought that lithium was less teratogenic than Register results would indicate for these reasons (Jacobson et al. 1992). Recently published is a controlled study that points to an even lower risk of cardiac malformations, although one patient in the lithium group studied chose to terminate pregnancy after Ebstein's anomaly was detected by a prenatal echocardiogram. This study also noted an incidence of macrosomia, which was also found in work done by Yoder et al. (1984) using Register data.

Because the Register of Lithium Babies is not a source for statistically valid predictions, it was discontinued (R. A. Lannon, personal communication, April 1992).

10. **Depression in pregnancy (short of psychosis) should be treated actively with psychotherapy and antidepressant medication.** Cases with vegetative signs, not needing hospitalization or ECT, should preferably receive secondary amines, such as nortriptyline or desipramine, that can be easily monitored (Regan et al. 1981; Saks et al. 1985). Antidepressants should be discontinued late in pregnancy. They seem to interfere with the mechanism of labor and can also lead to urinary retention in the newborn.

11. **Antiparkinsonian agents can be used in pregnancy but, again, must be tapered prior to delivery, especially because of the atropine-like effect on the fetus.** A drug like diphenhydramine may be necessary to treat opisthotonos in the baby that can impede vaginal delivery.

12. **Propranolol seems to cause intrauterine growth retardation and as such is contraindicated in pregnancy.**

13. **Anticonvulsant medications, such as carbamazepine, that are used for schizophrenia and/or seizure control need to be evaluated for teratogenicity.** People with epilepsy, even without medication, produce babies with a higher-than-expected rate of congenital malformations.

14. **Street drugs of all types, including alcohol, can and do interact with medications that are prescribed.** The most complete history of the use of such substances should be obtained, and toxic screening tests should be done on admission and periodically throughout the pregnancy for anyone with a drug abuse history. People with major mental illness are often substance abusers as well. Street drugs may be used by a psychotic patient as self-medication, and they may even be misconstrued by the patient as being better for her fetus than prescription medications. Find out what the drugs are and what they mean to the patient, and work with her to stop the substance abuse.

15. **Pregnancy is a time when women can be better motivated to give up a drug habit** (Navarro 1991). Withdrawal under supervision is best done in the middle trimester slowly enough and early enough to spare the fetus withdrawal symptoms. The key is to provide prenatal care, including management of the pregnant woman's drug picture, without being punitive. In a climate in which some would prosecute pregnant addicted women for being drug pushers, it becomes even more difficult to maintain balanced medical attention to the patient's many needs. Prenatal care must include drug treatment, and drug treatment programs must make prenatal care available. Also, it is crucial that the clinician collaborate with obstetrics and medicine and with drug experts. Careful drug monitoring and minimization of drug effects are essential for the benefit of the optimal care of both mother and baby. Pediatric intensive care is usually required to detoxify the baby.

Opiate-addicted pregnant patients should be treated with methadone and only withdrawn from methadone in the most supportive milieu and before the third trimester; rapid and erratic withdrawal can cause uterine contractions and abortion (Lee 1983). Babies become passively addicted to the methadone in utero and undergo planned withdrawal at birth. They tend to be of low birth weight, have low Apgar scores, and show significant neonatal problems, including jaundice, infection, aspiration pneumonia, transient tachypnea, and hyaline membrane disease. Abstinence symptoms may last 3 months and include central nervous system irritability, gastrointestinal dysfunction, respiratory distress, tremors, fever, high-pitched cry, increased muscle tone, uncoordinated sucking and swallowing reflexes, dehydration, and electrolyte imbalances (Finnegan 1986, 1988). Infant morbidity is related to the maternal narcotic dependence and to the amount of prenatal care.

Finnegan (1979) has written an excellent and definitive guide on the clinical management of the drug-dependent mother and her child. Her guidelines still hold true today, although they might be updated to include crack and other more dangerous derivatives of the drugs that were originally described. The manual is based on her experience in a comprehensive program, the Jefferson Family Center, which she developed in Philadelphia in 1975. In summary, prenatal care was her key to reach women in time to adjust drugs and anticipate pediatric needs. Methadone maintenance in conjunction with intensive prenatal care reduced intrauterine death, neonatal death, prematurity, and the concomitants of low birth weight. When the babies were followed for 2 years, their function was well within the normal range of development, only slightly less than that of control infants born to nonaddicted mothers. This is an outstanding example of a nonjudgmental, compassionate program that takes the problem mother where she is, understands her plight, assumes part of her desires to do the best for her baby, and develops an alliance around that mothering instinct. Rosett and Weiner (1984) have demonstrated the same willingness of alcoholic mothers to care for their unborn babies in collaboration with nonjudgmental caregivers by decreasing alcohol consumption in pregnancy.

Crack cocaine addiction is quite different from opiate usage (Livesay et al. 1987). Cocaine addicts can also have sexually transmitted diseases and depression (Burns et al. 1985). They also have a short duration of labor and seem on the whole to be less inclined to care for their infants. Crack cocaine produces even higher levels of the drug than other forms of cocaine; it is cheaper, readily available, and more apt to be used by women with chronic mental illness. Crack, transferred to the fetus via maternal uterine blood flow, produces hypoxia and congenital malformations. Withdrawal is best done absolutely and totally. The earlier and more rapidly cocaine is withdrawn, the better for the baby (Chasnoff et al. 1987, 1990). Polydrug users usually do better than cocaine users because the dosage of cocaine is apt to be lower. Women on cocaine suffer more pregnancy loss, spontaneous abortion, stillbirths, prematurity, abruptio placentae, precipitous labors, and sudden infant deaths in the postnatal period.

16. **HIV-positive women may be taking medications relevant to AIDS or the AIDS-related complex, especially zidovudine (AZT).** This must be part of the record, and the interactions must be assessed. Also, HIV-infected women are more likely to be intravenous drug users or the partner of a person who is an intravenous drug user, and the assessments mentioned above are needed. Pregnant women who are HIV positive will deliver babies who have the maternal antibodies, but in approximately two-thirds of the cases the antibodies will not be present in 15 months. In a third of the babies with antibodies that do not disappear, some are born dying, some will die within the first year of life, and others may get sick any time during the first 5 years of life (Levine and Dubler 1990).

17. **Medication for any and all other medical conditions can and does interact with the psychoactive drugs and may require reassessment of type and dosage during pregnancy.**

As we have seen, managing the pregnancies of women with major mental illness is complicated by issues of psychology, psychiatry, psychopharmacology, law, and organization requiring the liaison of many specialties. These issues do not resolve, of course, once the delivery of the child occurs. The postpartum phase itself presents management issues, as addressed in the next chapter, for two distinct living patients, the mother and the baby.

Chapter 9

Postpartum Management of the Mother With Long-Term Mental Illness: Defining Postpartum Psychosis

> Childbirth is more than a biological event in women's lives. It is a vital component in the social definition of womanhood .... By understanding childbirth we can understand significant parts of the female experience.
>
> Judith Walzer Leavitt *Brought to Bed:*
> *Childbearing in America, 1750–1950* (1986)

> Pregnancy is a time of joy. For me it was full of sorrow. No one gave me presents for the baby and when I gave birth the baby was taken away.
>
> Woman with mental illness, 1989

*P*regnancy can be a greatly desired and gratifying state for the woman with mental illness. In proportion to how much she craves this emblem of normal womanhood, the postpartum period is a time of high risk for loss and for psychosis. Childbirth represents a loss of the pregnant symbiotic state for many women; but that loss is usually compensated by a baby. When there is a stillbirth or other tragic loss at the end of a pregnancy, the loss is devastating for all mothers. The woman with mental illness is statistically more vulnerable to every category of reproductive loss. In addition, she is less able to buffer the losses, and she may not be able to have another baby as compensation.

Stewart and Gangbar (1984) have written an excellent review of the general principles of evaluating the ability of a mother to care for her newborn at home. The authors showed that difficulty caring for the baby in the hospital is a serious danger signal; this difficulty only gets worse once a mother has left a protective environment. Very few new mothers for whom psychiatric consultation is requested (2 of 56 in

Stewart and Gangbar's series) actually have to relinquish their babies; most can do satisfactory mothering with supervision at home, psychiatric hospitalization, or both. Psychiatric assessment of competency to care for a newborn includes 1) collection of reports from nursery staff, obstetrical nurses, and attending/referring physician; 2) direct observation of the mother with her baby, both general responsiveness and specific tasks (e.g., feeding, bathing, diapering); 3) meeting with family; 4) checking on adequacy of housing; and 5) previous history of abuse and neglect. The report must be carefully written with clear documentation of the sources of information because some of these cases may proceed to court.

In this chapter, we will consider 1) management and care after childbirth on the obstetrical unit of the woman with long-term mental illness who is usually an outpatient and may keep her baby; 2) management of the patient who gives up the baby in the postpartum period on the obstetrical unit and on the psychiatric unit; 3) mother-baby units and other means of extended assessment postpartum; and 4) the question of how postpartum disorders overlap with long-term mental illness. The continuing assessment of the risk for infanticide will be the subject of the next chapter.

Postpartum Management of the Outpatient With Mental Illness on the Obstetrical Unit

The ability of a woman with long-term mental illness to take her baby home is based both on her own mental state and on the presence of at least one other adult in her environment who has competence and concern for the mother and baby. This can be the father, some other relative, a neighbor, or someone in daily life other than a member of the therapy team. Determining who that person is, as well as observing the mother and baby interacting, is best done on the maternity unit. These tasks require a longer time than the usual current 1-day maternity stay, as well as cooperation with the outpatient psychiatric and medical teams (Habgood 1985; Halonen and Passman 1985).

A woman who is not currently hospitalized but has a history of major mental illness might naturally fear this postpartum period as a time for relapse. Usually such a woman has a long-term therapist or treatment program, and the therapy can be used to anticipate and plan for the postpartum time (Hamilton and Sichel 1992; Petrick 1984; Seidenberg and Harris 1949). The therapist can work closely with the obstetrical team, arrange for a prolonged maternity hospitalization, and be available to work with the patient over the long haul of childrearing. Maternity unit staff are typically uncomfortable with the presence of new mothers who have a psychotic illness and often fear managing psychotic symptoms (Kumar 1984). The initial assessment of a woman's potential to care for her infant takes place during her pregnancy and optimally involves the patient, the father of the baby, the psychiatric team, a social services agency representative who will be the baby's advocate, the patient's family, and consultation from the hospital lawyer (Cox et al. 1987; Regan et al. 1987; Trad 1989). It is at this evaluation that all the possible plans should be considered: the patient can return home with the baby, the patient can go elsewhere with her baby, the patient can be hospitalized with the baby, or the patient can return to the psychiatric hospital while the baby goes to foster care or is cared for by another family member.

Whatever the ultimate decision about the baby, it is advisable for the mother to be able to see and hold her baby. She should not, however, be left totally alone with the baby. It is prudent to provide staff supervision to protect this vulnerable twosome. A staff member can also help the new mother with the care and handling of the baby and provide observations necessary to make a decision about her capacity to perform as a mother. It is important to observe the degree of bonding, eye contact, talking to the baby, and appropriate inspection and interest in the infant. Is the mother able to comfortably hold the baby? Does she seem distracted and far away from the infant? The maternity nurse, who is accustomed to seeing many new mothers, is the best person to make these observations. From experience and intuition, such nurses are able to quickly say, "This one is strange," and to ask for a fuller evaluation from a psychiatrist or psychologist trained in maternal-infant observation. Obstetricians in general are unaccustomed and less able to accurately assess this newly forming emotional bond between mother and baby. They should be encouraged, however, to become better observers. The observations should be made more than once and recorded in the patient's chart; they should be the responsibility of one member of the team but something to which all team members contribute. There will sometimes be different opinions about any given case. There is always need for staff coordination. Evaluation of the mother-child interaction should occur at several times of day and night over the first days postpartum.

Separation of the mother and child, on separate floors or in separate hospitals, should be avoided if possible so that bonding can occur. Interaction between the mother and the child (and the father if available) should be encouraged, and nursing staff can use these periods to educate and encourage behaviors that reinforce bonding. Finnegan (1979) suggests, even for drug-addicted mothers, that the woman should be treated as if she has the capability to learn proper mothering skills. We feel that the same benefit-of-the-doubt attitude should be applied to mentally ill mothers. Encouragement and support and patient teaching in an unhurried atmosphere can help to alleviate worries and doubts that every new mother experiences (Hartmann 1968).

Social service workers who evaluate the mother-child relationship should be in contact with the treatment team so that they are aware of the overall social supports that the patient has and the proposed treatment plan if the patient is able to return home with the child. In addition, the treatment team should be aware of the criteria utilized by social service workers to evaluate mother-child relationships, what the legal obligations are in the state regarding mandated reporting of child abuse and neglect, and what their role should be in that regard. Once it has been decided that the baby can go home with the mother, it is not clear that this will be a permanent arrangement. Social service and the treatment team will be obliged to continue to evaluate the mother-child relationship on an outpatient basis to make sure that the baby will not be rejected or harmed. However, the therapist of the new mother may need to be spared the reporting function in order to allow the mother to speak freely and fully. It is preferable that roles be separated and reporting be done by the social service clinicians assigned to the maternity unit and not by the patient's ongoing therapist. In any case, the patient must be fully informed about her obligations for the care of the baby and about the state laws on mandated reporting. Backup plans and alternative fantasies can be explored with the patient and may give her comfort, even if she cannot care for the baby.

It is essential that the woman with mental illness have her own advocate who can talk to her about her conflicts and can empathize with her whatever the outcome. When someone is psychotic or becomes more psychotic in the puerperium, it is crucial to assess why and to ask what is the meaning of the psychosis psychodynamically as well as biologically. It is important to minimize psychotic symptoms with chemical or other containment. The treatment in the postpartum period should optimally also include an appreciation and affirmation of the accomplishment of giving birth. There must then be enough time allowed and attention given for the woman to register this major milestone.

Psychotherapy helps to acknowledge the mother's feelings about her baby, including ambivalence, worries, and insecurities. The outpatient therapist must adjust to the patient's new maternal identity and to the realities of mothering. For instance, the patient can be encouraged to bring her new baby to sessions for continued observations. The therapist may want to be more available for phone calls and may be more likely to give concrete advice. Special outpatient clinics are being developed for those long-term mentally ill women who are now mothers. Miller and Raskin have begun such a clinic at the University of Illinois in Chicago as an aftercare service for the specialty inpatient unit.

Managing Loss in the Postpartum Period on the Maternity and Psychiatry Units

Some of the protocols that have been worked out for the treatment of loss in the case of a stillbirth might be applicable for dealing with loss of a live baby. These practices have been developed because they allow for appropriate attachment and then for grieving and working through the relationship (Herz 1984). These practices include 1) allowing the mother time alone with the baby (supervised if the mother's sanity is questioned), 2) urging the mother to keep a photograph of the baby and a lock of hair as concrete representations of the lost object, 3) encouraging the mother to name the baby, and 4) helping the mother to mourn (Bluglass 1988). The keystone of management of the psychotic patient in the puerperium is to minimize the losses for the woman and to maximize her sense of having experienced something that is human and normal.

In the past, especially when the mother was obviously psychotic, the baby was summarily removed. This left the mother with no one on whom to focus her mourning. Well-meaning people, determined to spare the mother the pain of separation after attachment, continued to argue that it was kinder and easier never to see the baby. This has not, however, been our experience with maternal loss. We believe that it is better to have actual memories, however painful, than any vague recollections and fantasies. If the mother is eager to breast-feed the baby, and if this is not medically contraindicated (Nurnberg 1981), she should also be given this opportunity. These early contacts are extremely important for bonding and are even more so in a woman with mental illness for whom the real baby can be easier to fathom if the baby is right there at her breast. The baby cannot be damaged by this contact if there is adequate supervision. Whether or not the baby stays with the natural mother, this interaction will probably serve both parties in good stead. Sometimes, however, the need for separating the mother from her baby can be underestimated, as in the following case:

Case 20: Assessment Hindered by Countertransference

A 40-year-old woman with a history of schizophrenia managed to live on her own in the community and work at a job in the hospital cafeteria. She was well known and liked by hospital personnel. When she became pregnant and came to the prenatal clinic at her hospital, she received enthusiastic support from the nurses who knew her. The social service department was notified to evaluate how the patient would manage the baby in the rooming house where she lived. The father of the baby and extended family were not available; the hospital person-nel had become her real family. House officers from psychiatry and obstetrics managed the pregnancy and labor and delivery, and took a personal interest in her case. Everyone was rather proud of this heroic single older woman, intrigued with her having gotten pregnant, and her determination to have the baby. The patient thrived with the attention. However, after her baby was born, the patient seemed more disorga-nized. She had trouble looking at her baby and difficulty holding and feeding him. She brightened and showed him off proudly when one of her hospital family came to visit. It was a new night nurse who pointed out how she and the baby were not doing well. A fresh look by the Department of Social Services' child protection worker revealed what most of her friends did not want to see: that she was not able to care for her baby, even in the hospital, and had not made any realistic plans for herself with a baby outside the hospital. When the baby was removed to a foster home, the cafeteria worker was very sad but relieved; many of her friends also experienced a loss.

More often babies of mothers with mental illness have been re-moved too quickly, without consideration for the long-term trauma experienced by the mother. The benefit of the early, albeit brief rela-tionship has been underestimated.

Case 21: Woman With Psychosis Separated From Her Baby Too Soon After Birth

The patient was psychotic when she gave birth at age 19 to her only baby. She held the baby briefly in the delivery room but then never saw him again. As her psychosis remitted, she was unsure whether she had actually had a baby or had imagined it. If she had given birth to the baby, it felt as if he had died, but there was no trace, no name. After many years, and 40 hospitalizations, a new therapist traced the medical records with the patient and was able to reconstruct what had happened. Now that she knows some of the facts of the childbirth and the age of her lost child, she is able to think and wonder about him in a more realistic way. The child's birthday season is recalled and the age of the child calculated yearly, so that the patient can, with support, mourn the real loss that she has endured. Even though the patient still becomes psychotic when confronted with a new baby in her environment, the opportunity to mourn her loss has helped her in many ways.

The patient with major mental illness requires at least 3 days on the maternity unit. This is difficult to arrange for any woman these days, and, especially for someone who may be a management problem for the staff, this is not an attractive recommendation. However, a 3-day stay works to everyone's advantage and is generally greeted with relief. This minimal time at a crucial crossroads is needed to give the mother-at-risk a protected setting to separate from the pregnancy or begin to integrate as a mother and, if she can, bond with her baby (Persson-Blennow et al. 1984). It also gives the staff an opportunity to assess more fully the strengths and wishes of the psychotic mother. Time will help with the bonding process for the mother who can keep her baby and with the separation process and mourning when the baby must be given up for adoption or foster care. When there is ambiguity, time will permit more supervision and intervention to be arranged.

Even women with long-term mental illness are aware of the importance of the early days of infancy and can feel remorse and guilt if they are unable to care for their babies. When the mothers can observe good baby care, even for a short time, they seem to feel less guilty later on. Postpartum women can be helped to feel good about what they have accomplished in the labor and delivery—for example, how they managed the pain, how they were able to cope in a normally stressful situation, and how it felt to identify with other women in this birth process. Developing a story of the birth with the patient close to the time of the facts can help to make a prideful story and to decrease the later development of delusions, shame, and confusion about this major life event. The reality can be more interesting and energizing than fantasies. Secondary depression caused by feeling badly about how one acted may thus be averted. Albretsen (1968) cited another advantage within the ward milieu: another patient who experienced postpartum psychosis in the past was able to effectively help with the baby and work through her own past trauma.

These situations can disrupt the smooth functioning of a maternity ward, which is set up to process "normal" mothers and babies. However, there are many high-risk categories that require special care in the maternity situation. In a general hospital, sometimes a functional compromise is to keep the baby-at-risk or the baby-in-question in the nursery while the mother is hospitalized on the psychiatric unit. The mother can be near her baby, and the maternity ward staff can feel less burdened by the presence of a mother with mental illness. The psychiatric staff can then get to know their patient and represent her viewpoint in the team discussions. Sometimes, even with all services cooperating and taking needed time, the need to separate mother and baby becomes evident, as in the following case:

Case 22: Time Reveals Need for Separation of Baby From Mother Postpartum

A new mother with schizophrenia was delighted with the plan that she be on the psychiatric unit that she knew from past hospitalizations while her baby stayed on another floor of the hospital. For her, it was having "the best of both worlds." After several days, she "forgot" to visit the baby, and the nursery staff could not rely on her to help with any care or feeding. After some discussion with the patient, it was decided by the staff that the baby should be placed for adoption. The patient agreed and signed the required papers. However, when the social worker came to take the baby from the nursery, the patient blocked the exit, then climbed to a window ledge, threatening to jump if anyone stole her baby. Her psychiatrist and the hospital security staff commiserated and talked with the patient and brought her to safety. The psychiatrist had forged a relationship with her around her wish for the idea of a baby, and her rage and loss could be genuinely appreciated. Meanwhile, the Social Services Department took the baby to court and placement.

When a mentally ill woman who has been hospitalized while pregnant delivers and returns to the unit without the baby, there is a postpartum reaction for all the patients and staff. The other patients will be curious to know about the baby and anxious about the baby's welfare. Patients will identify with the mother who lost her baby and with the baby who lost his or her mother, and staff will do the same. It is essential to discuss openly in the patient community what has actually taken place—the bare facts of the labor, delivery, and placement of the baby. Also, the baby should be described—its gender, name, size—and questions answered as much as possible. This can allow the mother-patient to have something, some accomplishment she can tell to other people. The loss of this baby is a loss for everyone. The gain of a healthy baby getting a new start in life is a gain and gift for everyone.

When it is clear that the mentally ill mother will not be able to keep and care for her baby, there are many considerations for the welfare of both the baby and the mother. Generally, schizophrenic mothers have been described as neglectful toward their babies immediately following delivery; they are not usually harmful or abusive and do not actively attack the baby or involve the baby in dangerous situations as a result of delusions. Furthermore, many are capable of giving quite adequate care to a newborn, holding and feeding with tenderness and warmth (Baker 1967). These capacities must be respected. On the other side, the actuality of caring for the baby—feeding, changing diapers, coping with the baby's crying—allows the woman more readily to acknowledge the difficulty she will have. She can then cooperate more with the separation, feeling she is being a good mother by doing what is in the best interests of the child. Having had the real baby to consider also lets her remember the sweetness of the baby.

When a psychotic woman must give up her baby, there has to be someone there for her to provide support. It is usually very wrenching and infuriating for the schizophrenic woman to lose her baby, just as it would be for any mother. Even if the patient has agreed about her inability to care for the baby, she will protest and be very pained, which is difficult for staff to experience. To anticipate the scene of separation, it is useful for the staff to assign jobs: one person in charge of the baby, removing the baby and protecting him or her; the other person an advocate for the mother, helping her to voice her pain and outrage at the separation. The parting scene is thus arranged to give the patient-mother the best chance to express herself at the time. Taking the baby when the mother is drugged or asleep, or before she has a chance to bond, has been done to spare the mother; these methods, however, actually prolong the agony for the mother. Not allowing her the chance to grieve at the time of the immediate loss only makes the grief more intense and last longer, even throughout the lifetime of the mother.

Mother-Baby Units and Other Extended Assessment Postpartum

The *mother-baby unit* is a hospital unit where women with psychosis can be hospitalized along with their babies. Most women, even those with severe postpartum psychosis, do not want to be separated from their newborns and may delay seeking treatment for fear of an enforced separation (Hurt and Ray 1985). Stewart (1989) reported that toleration of separation was a predictive factor in the women studied; those women who easily separated had not continued to care for the baby 2 years hence, whereas those who insisted on being with their infants were continuing to mother those babies. On a mother-baby unit, new mothers who are psychotic can come with their babies to receive 1) care for their own psychiatric illness, 2) care for their babies, 3) protected and professional nonjudgmental guidance, and 4) observation that can be used to maximally assess if and when the particular mother can assume care of the baby outside a hospital setting (Poole et al. 1980).

Nine of these units are now present throughout the United Kingdom, where this idea started in 1948, and operate together with substantial community nursing. In North America, the admission of mothers with their babies has been less consistent. Grunebaum and his colleagues admitted babies to the Massachusetts Mental Health Center in 1963 (Grunebaum et al. 1978, 1982). One admission was reported in New York City in 1966; London, Canada, admitted older children with mothers in 1967; and since 1969, Clarke Institute and St. Michael's in Toronto have had joint admissions of mother and baby (Stewart 1989). One group in Norway even hospitalizes the father and requires the new family to function under the protection of the hospital before leaving to pursue child care at home and participation in a postpartum couples group (Albretsen 1968). The University of Pittsburgh and Western Psychiatric Institute and Clinic have recently developed a hospital-based Pregnancy and Infant/Parent Center (K. Wisner, personal communication, 1991). The Newton-Wellesley Hospital is in the process of formalizing its capacity to serve this population better, and two other hospitals in Massachusetts have already opened several psychiatric beds for mother-baby admissions (D. A. Sichel, personal communication, 1991).

These mother-baby units tend to be very expensive and to require a high level of staff input. Even when a one-to-one nurse-to-patient ratio of staffing is available, it is difficult to find nursing staff who are able and willing to work on a psychiatric unit that requires newborn care. Jealousy and rage of the patient-mother are projected onto the nurses, making their role especially thankless. There is the fear of litigation because of the added liability in case of injury to the babies. The value of mother-baby units seems intuitively obvious, and they have their avid proponents. However, their effectiveness in regard to the health of mothers and babies has not yet been conclusively proven, which adds to the skepticism and resistance. Despite these factors, hospitals are responding to consumer demands for mother-baby psychiatric beds because the postpartum self-help advocacy organization Depression After Delivery (DAD) has helped women to validate the importance of professional recognition and treatment of this disorder.[1]

Sometimes, only an extended hospital observation can uncover the complexity of the situation, the ambivalence of the parents, and the lack of support on the outside, as illustrated by the following case:

**Case 23: Painful Separation of Baby From Mother
in Postpartum Period**

A young Asian woman of 16 left home to live with a non-Asian man with whom she became pregnant. By the time she delivered, she was hearing voices telling her the baby was an angel who would lead her back to her ancestors in China. She began to feel threatened by her boyfriend and took the opportunity of being in the hospital right after the delivery to break contact with the baby's father. While on antipsychotic medication, she expressed clear wishes to care for the baby herself in her family of origin. But later, when she refused medication

---

[1]See, for example, Heart Strings, The National Newsletter of Depression After Delivery, P.O. Box 1281, Morrisville, PA 19067.

because she wanted to nurse the baby, she sat and stared, seemingly not noticing the baby next to her.

She was transferred from the maternity unit to a general hospital psychiatry unit and placed in a room next to the nurses' station so that they could observe closely and help with baby care. Medication was suspended so that the patient could nurse her baby. The nurses felt burdened when most of the infant care fell to them, and they were angry at the psychiatrist for acquiescing to the cessation of medication. The patient's family came to visit once and, after much discussion through translators, indicated they would take her home alone, but could not accept her with this baby. She became even more unresponsive, almost catatonic. When medication was reinstated, the patient was furious with the psychiatrist and contacted her boyfriend to tell of the baby's birth and report that she was captive in the hospital and being forced to take drugs. These young, passionate parents tried to abduct the baby from the hospital but were intercepted. They had no plans, no possibility to care for the baby. After much discussion, it was decided that the baby would be sent to foster care and the teenage mother to her parents' home. The boyfriend appeared, threatening the staff, particularly voicing his intention to retaliate by kidnapping the doctor's children just as his son had, in his view, been kidnapped. His double loss was appreciated by a senior male psychiatrist who met with the young father through this crisis.

In most other cases where a psychosis is present in the postpartum period, a mother-baby unit geared toward the possibility of the mother eventually being able to go home with her baby may be able to provide interim support that helps achieve that goal. This is certainly true for many women whose psychotic illness only appears in the postpartum period, but it may also be true for a woman with long-term mental illness when an extended assessment of the dynamics of the family and patient is indicated. The following is an example of a contrasting case in which the hospitalization of mother and baby clarified strengths within a family that could then be mobilized:

Case 24: Mother-Baby Unit Reinforces Mother-Baby Relationship

A woman with mental illness had been discharged from the maternity unit to live with her mother and baby. When the baby started to have apneic episodes, the grandmother was not helpful, and the pediatrician noted that the new mother was frenzied, disorganized, and inadequate to the task. On the mother-baby unit, the mother had the assistance, competence, and commiseration of the nursing staff. They taught her to respond appropriately and how to evaluate her baby's needs. When the baby developed pneumonia and had to be hospitalized, the patient was able to visit him on the pediatric ward and to express to the other mothers on the unit, as well as to the staff, her fears of losing him. Family intervention and meetings with the patient's mother uncovered a heretofore unknown part of the history—that this grandmother had lost a child to crib death before the patient was born. Seeing her grandson apneic was more than she could bear, and she had withdrawn. When a treatment team and plan was set up, the grandmother could become available again to help care for her daughter and grandson. Steady extra pediatric support and community nursing were made available for a full year, until the baby was past the high risk of sudden infant death. A situation that might have compounded past losses with present ones thus was turned to a gain for everyone.

In most United States hospitals currently, joint hospitalization of mother and baby is not possible. The psychiatrist must do for the mother-patient what is best for her, but because of the timing of the illness, this will include careful consideration of what is best for the child as well. It is essential to talk with other family members and to realistically and individually assess the resources available. There is no one solution that is routine, easy, and clear for everyone involved.

Sichel and Driscoll (1992), who have developed an integrated approach for the general hospital setting, believe that hospitalization is only a small part of what is necessary for the adequate treatment of postpartum psychiatric disorders. Naming the problems as constituting an identifiable separate illness is important to patient and family. Ongoing education of families and work on the family dynamics, the couple relationship, and the mother-baby relationship can only *begin* in the hospital. These family interventions may need to continue for years after the delivery. Individual psychotherapy for the mother must address the loss of esteem that occurs whenever a psychiatric disease develops or is exacerbated.

Postpartum Disorders and Chronic Mental Illness

The risk of having a mental disease is 15 times greater in the immediate postpartum period than at other times for women who have never had a psychiatric history, and it is also a time of especially high risk for the woman with an established history of mental illness (Frank et al. 1987; Hays 1978; Hidas et al. 1989). The risk is greatest for the first 3 weeks but remains high for 1 year postpartum. All of the factors—psychological, dynamic-familial, social, and physiological—that go into this prevalence of postpartum disorders hold true for a woman who already has a long-term mental illness. However, this woman has fewer inner and outer resources to buffer her at all times, especially during times of stress. The medical staff must be alert to the possibility that psychological problems postpartum may occur more commonly than other postpartum problems such as infection and bleeding (Posner et al. 1985).

The parent with mental illness, even when in good remission and blessed with maximal support, can feel taxed by the normal demands of a healthy infant. The immediate postpartum period, the first 3 to 6 weeks, is a time during which the infant takes more than he or she returns. This is a trying time for every parent; a parent with low self-esteem, who cannot delay gratification, may easily feel rejected, depleted, and resentful. The biochemical factors that have been implicated in postpartum psychosis (e.g., precipitous drop in estrogen and progesterone) are further potentiated by psychotropic medications. For at least 2 years following the birth of a baby, women with mental illness who keep their babies will require additional interventions and support (Yarden 1988); for those who lose their babies early on, a lifetime of awareness of that loss may be required. Many women with long-term mental illness cannot easily be declared capable or incapable of taking care of the baby, and a continuing assessment of personal and social resources must be made for everybody's benefit.

There is a large and growing literature on the wide range of postpartum psychiatric disorders, from blues to depression to psychosis.[2] Postpartum psychiatric disorders are being considered for inclusion as a category in DSM-IV. There is not yet one accepted classification. There is much more interest and literature on these de

[2]See Braverman and Roux 1978; Brockington and Kumar 1982; Brockington et al. 1981; Cheetham et al. 1981; Cohn et al. 1977; Dalton 1980; Garvey et al. 1983; Gelder 1978; Halbreich and Endicott 1981; Inwood 1985; Kadrmas et al. 1979; Kendell et al. 1976, 1987; Kerfoot and Buckwalter 1981; Meltzer and Kumar 1985a, 1985b; O'Hara et al. 1983, 1984, 1990; Paffenbarger et al. 1961; Robinson and Stewart 1986; Schopf et al. 1984, 1985; Stern and Kruckman 1983; Zilboorg 1919, 1928; Ziporyn 1984).

novo postnatal psychiatric disorders than there is follow-up of women with mental illness who give birth to babies. Women with long-term mental illness can and do have a superimposed postpartum psychosis.

The days immediately following delivery of a baby have been known for some time to be a period of maximal risk for psychiatric disorder among the general obstetrical, nonpsychiatric patient population (Dunner et al. 1979; Marcé 1862; Sternbach 1982). As many as 50% of new mothers (higher among primiparas) experience some mild blues, 10% can have a major mood disorder, and 0.1%–0.2% develop a psychosis (Gotlib et al. 1989). Of those who develop a full psychotic disorder, 70% have never had any psychiatric disturbance, peurperal or nonpuerperal. Three-quarters of postpartum psychiatric disorders start within the first 2 weeks after childbirth, 80% of these acutely; the other quarter start either during the pregnancy or in the lactation time, up to a year following delivery.

Hamilton (1989) has made a more clinically descriptive classification. He reviewed postpartum syndromes and described five distinct pictures, all of which share common features of rapid onset-remission-recurrence and a high incidence of confusion, delirium, and sleep disturbances, with myriad physical complaints. Two of the five disorders are less severe: maternity blues and postnatal depression. Three are very severe: puerperal psychosis, major postpartum depression, and postpartum psychotic depression. These severe postpartum syndromes have an incidence of 1 in 1,000 births, a rate that has been constant in many places and times. After a woman has had such a psychosis, and for a woman with major mental illness, the incidence increases drastically to 1 in 3 or 4. These severe syndromes are all potentially life-threatening and require major intervention, hospitalization, medication, and even ECT. *Puerperal psychosis*, which can take the form of mania or depression, is marked especially by volatility and has its onset in the first 6 weeks postpartum. *Major postpartum depression* has its onset after the 20th day, a time well beyond the purview of the maternity hospitalization. *Postpartum psychotic depression* is differentiated by the persistence over time of recurring episodic delusions and hallucinations, which may be indistinguishable from the thought disorder of the ongoing mental illness.

Factors predisposing to severe postpartum psychoses have long been the subject of speculation. Recently, controlled studies have shown that there is a biological component to the most severe disorders.

The sharp drop in estrogen and progesterone at delivery and the rapid rise in prolactin seem to be the biological substratum, but there is not an exact correlation of hormone changes and behavior. There are also reports of other chemical markers (e.g., unusually severe depletion of endorphins after long labor, elevated serum calcium levels). These chemical changes are seen as causally related to the psychotic disorder in women who have no family or personal history of psychosis. The severe mood disorders seem to be correlated more with personality and with sociocultural variables.

It is important to note that most of the high-risk factors for severe postpartum illness are features of long-term mental illness. Significant risk factors include having seriously considered abortion in the current pregnancy; poor parenting; poor maternal care early in life; poor marriage or no partner; and chronic medical illness itself. There is a consistent correlation showing that women who have had severe menstrual disorders are somewhat more likely to develop postpartum disorders. Those with obsessive-compulsive characteristics and with a history of early parental loss are also more predisposed psychodynamically. In one study, although only 10% of the women who were hospitalized postpartum had schizophrenia, this was by far the most difficult and refractory group (Casiano and Hawkins 1987). Women with postpartum disorders can continue after the puerperium to be placed in diagnostic categories in which they were placed prior to the pregnancy. For our population, this means that a woman with a major psychotic illness may have an exacerbation of that illness postpartum. Her primary diagnosis will be schizophrenia or manic-depressive illness, and the pregnancy can be looked at as one more psychosocial-biological precipitant of the worsening of the ongoing condition.

Recent anecdotal clinical reports point to the possibility that some of these so-called "psychoses," or unusual experiences, are temporal lobe disorders that appear for the first time under the endocrinological and developmental stress of childbirth (Cohen et al. 1989b). Diagnosis is complicated and often delayed by the expectation of family and doctors that women will be "blue" and will even act strangely in the postpartum period. Panic disorders have also been described with onset in the puerperal period (Metz et al. 1988, 1989), and increasingly more postpartum disorders fit this description (Sichel and Cohen, in press). Most studies show a range of diagnoses among those women who are psychotic postpartum that is different from the range for all first-break psychotic patients and from the range of those patients with long-term mental illnesses. Fewer than 2% of the individuals in many series of postpartum psychotic women are called schizophrenic; most are placed in the schizoaffective, bipolar, or major depressive categories. We must wonder why—because they are women or new mothers, or because these psychoses are more affective than most? For instance, in a study of 100 patients with puerperal psychosis in the Soviet Union (Semenov and Pashutova 1976), the diagnosis of schizophrenia was used, but descriptively; these women were atypical for acute schizophrenia in that they had greater affect and repeatedly reenacted the childbirth and imagined scenes of child care such as singing lullabies and holding babies.

The risk of augmented psychosis following childbirth in women with schizophrenic illness has been carefully studied by Yarden et al. (1966). In this carefully matched study the authors followed 67 schizophrenic women for 5 years postdelivery and compared them with a control group. They showed that the immediate postpartum period was not significantly worse for the women with schizophrenia. However, it was the overall effect of childbirth and children over time that took a toll. Childbirth and children represented additional stresses for women with schizophrenia. These stresses were reflected in more hospital days and admissions compared with others having similar mental illnesses.

Genetic-familial studies suggest some important overlap between postpartum psychosis and major affective psychoses. The results are not all in, and those studies that have been done do not yield consistent findings. O'Hara and Zekoski, in their excellent review of all studies on the subject (1988), cite 10 studies that showed an increased risk for postpartum depression in patients with previous psychiatric history and 4 studies that showed no risk; a positive family history of psychiatric disorder was seen as a risk factor in 3 studies, but not so in Kumar and Robson's (1984) prospective study that showed no association between previous seeking of psychiatric therapy in the family and the occurrence of postpartum depression.

The overlap of major mental illness and postpartum psychosis appears to be especially present in manic-depressive illness. The postpartum period is known to be a time of especially high risk for women with manic-depressive illness. Reich and Winokur (1970) found that 50% of deliveries following a diagnosis of manic-depressive illness with evidence of mania had postpartum illness with depressive and/or manic components. There is some relationship between postpartum psychosis and manic-depressive illness, but postpartum psychosis is not simply a covariant of manic-depressive illness (Hays and Douglass 1984). It is not inevitable that all women with manic-depressive illness will have postpartum recurrences; most do not. Anticipatory guidance and timely medication (Stewart 1988) can be very helpful in preventing a major manic or depressive episode postpartum.

Case 25: Fear of Postpartum Psychotic Depression

A 35-year-old woman dreaded childbirth because her mother and two aunts had become psychotically depressed after the birth of their babies. She herself had already had a 2-year hospitalization at age 18 when she was psychotic, depressed, and suicidal. She had managed, with much help, to develop a career as a science editor and to marry. She very much wanted to have a baby but was afraid of a postpartum illness. Soon after she resumed psychotherapy she got pregnant. The pregnancy was uneventful, as were the labor and delivery. Her husband came to several therapy sessions to talk about his anxieties; he himself had no experience with babies and not too much understanding of his wife's anxieties or history. She spent much of the time remembering her mother's postpartum depression with a younger sibling. She was able to mourn the loss of her mother at that time, recalling her rage at the parents and new baby.

When her own baby boy was born, she became acutely anxious about how much she loved him, a totally unexpected reaction. She feared she would kiss him inappropriately on the mouth or the penis and would not be a good mother. With the baby, in front of the psychiatrist, the patient was stiff and nervous but obviously competent in her handling of the infant. She had used trifluoperazine in large doses as a teenager with some relief of psychotic anxiety and asked if she could try it again. With frequent phone contact, regular visits, and trifluoperazine, 2 mg prn, she coped very well with her baby. After the first 3 months she felt less anxious and very pleased with the beautiful baby she and her husband had produced. She was able to discontinue regular therapy with the understanding that she could call whenever she had further questions or discomfort for which she needed help. In addition, the therapist suggested a regular annual check-in time around the baby's birthday.

Although well-controlled treatment trials have not been done, treatment of puerperal psychosis seems to vary somewhat from that of other psychoses. Basically the treatment is symptomatic, with consideration of 1) alleviating psychotic symptoms and 2) allowing the mother maximal feasible contact with the baby, including breast-feeding. Brockington and colleagues (1981) recommend hospitalization with the baby and the use of lithium regardless of the symptomatic picture. If there is no improvement in a month or earlier and/or if there are significant depressive delusions, they use ECT. Perhaps because of the physicians' wish to preserve breast-feeding in mothers with postpartum psychosis or even to treat a pregnant woman with a safer option, ECT is likely to be tried in some centers before, or instead of, neuroleptic medications. Tricyclic antidepressants, fluoxetine, and antipsychotic medications are all useful and titrated according to symptom response (Brandon 1982).

Recovery from the acute phase of postpartum psychosis usually takes place within 3 months, but many women require continuing outpatient treatment and medication either because of continuing psychotic symptomatology while mourning the loss of the infancy of the baby or because of the frequent depression that follows a psychotic episode, especially at a time that was meant to be so joyous. There are residual tensions in the relationships with that baby and other family members. In patients who have had long-term mental illness, it may be difficult to distinguish the baseline from a continuing postpartum reaction. The following case illustrates how two severe mental illnesses can coexist and overlap:

Case 26: Repeated Postpartum Psychosis in a Woman With Long-Term Mental Illness

A 36-year-old woman was walking with her baby in a carriage on the grounds of a hospital where she was a patient at the mother-baby unit. She proudly introduced this baby as her fourth child and told the following story: She had had a first pregnancy during her freshman year in college; she arranged for an abortion, which seemed the only realistic option at the time, and even had the support of her boyfriend and parents. However, she became profoundly depressed following the abortion and had to drop out of school. Continuing suicidal thoughts and delusions about the baby she had killed required her to be hospitalized briefly. She never recovered fully, could not go back to college, and lived at home, working at menial jobs. She became pregnant again, out of wedlock, and she concealed the fact from her parents until late in the second trimester. After the baby was born, she had an exacerbation of her psychotic symptoms, became paranoid about the baby as the devil, and stayed away from him lest she be harmed by or harm him. Her parents took care of the baby and took custody legally when, during a prolonged hospitalization, the patient continued to seem unfit to mother. She became abusive and nasty with her parents, and they eventually told her that she could not return home. She lived in a halfway house and made a reasonable adjustment but required continuing neuroleptic medication. She was able to visit with her parents and baby for short periods of time, and, in therapy, she talked always about her lost children.

In a steady relationship with a man at the halfway house, she again became pregnant. She did well in the pregnancy and seemed less depressed. And even when her boyfriend required rehospitalization, she continued to be optimistic. She was able to take no medication first trimester and only small doses of thioridazine in the last two trimesters. Labor and delivery were uneventful, and she used the help of a maternity nurse to deliver a healthy daughter. In the hospital, she appeared to bond well with the infant, and they were discharged together to a subsidized apartment. However, by the third week, the visiting nurse saw the patient becoming slovenly and neglectful of herself and the baby, and called the Department of Social Services. The baby was removed, and the mother was hospitalized with a severe psychotic depression. Three years later, again pregnant, she presented asking for a mother-baby hospitalization after her delivery as part of the treatment. This was arranged prophylactically! She did become psychotically depressed but was in the hospital already, where she and the baby were protected. She was able eventually to keep her fourth baby.

This case illustrates how women with mental illness, given the chance to speak of their reproductive experiences, may organize their life histories around those major life events. For many women with postpartum illness, there are unhappy endings. In the next chapter, we will look at the tragedy of infanticide.

Chapter 10

Infanticide: A Fantasy More Than a Fact for Parents With Long-Term Mental Illness

*I*nfanticide is linked with psychosis in the popular imagination. One of the common fears about "mad" people is that they will do that which is unspeakable and which may not even be admitted into consciousness by many normal people. It is universal for parents to have angry impulses and not uncommon to even experience transient death wishes toward their children. Intense rage toward children is the underside of the intense love and attachment. Yet, the tragedy of acting on these fantasies is rare. The real question is not that anyone has such thoughts but why some people escalate angry thoughts and feelings into murderous impulses and finally into murderous deeds. Parents who have trouble bonding and attaching to their children, but are secretive about this problem, are at highest risk. Who are the people who do murder their babies? In what significant ways do they differ from ourselves? Do they have acute mental illness or chronic mental illness? Can these potential tragedies be averted? Parents with long-term mental illness may have the same ambivalence as normal parents do, ambivalence that does not lead to infanticide. Those parents who do murder their children need to be studied and understood as being at the extreme end of a spectrum of parents abusing children in our society. This problem overlaps with, but is not at all synonymous with, the problems of long-term mental illness.

In this chapter, we will discuss 1) the history and concept of infanticide, 2) its perpetrators, 3) the motives of its perpetrators, and 4) psychotherapeutic treatment after infanticide.

Infanticide: Its History and Concept

Infanticide is defined as killing an infant at or soon after its birth. Filicide refers to the killing at the hands of a parent of the child.

Neonaticide refers to killing of the newborn within the first 24 hours of life (Resnick 1969). The exact incidence and prevalence of these acts in our own society are difficult to ascertain because there is no federal or state statute dealing specifically with infanticide. Interpretation of figures from other cultures and times is even more difficult.

Actual documentation of infanticide has been best done in England, where there has been a long medicolegal debate on the subject. The British Infanticide Act in 1938 acknowledged a separate category for women who kill because of a disturbance in the balance of mind resulting from the effects of childbirth and lactation. The degree of abnormality in these cases is far less than necessary to prove psychiatric abnormality in most insanity defenses and provides for diminished responsibility of mothers during this vulnerable time. This act has been reevaluated and repeatedly discussed, but it is kept because other options appear to be too restrictive.

Some states in the United States have considered adopting such an act, but none has so far done so, and child murder is tried according to standards of insanity defense in each state. Bills are currently pending in several states to require that all women accused of infanticide be held in custody in a psychiatric hospital rather than be sent to prison (Toufexis 1988). These women are not considered a risk to society at large.

While there are special circumstances to explain infanticide, this behavior can also be considered as part of a continuum of child abuse and violence in our culture. As with other factors, such as the wish for babies, those persons who suffer with mental illness often reflect the views of the general culture in which they live. So it is with violence toward children. The United States is a violent culture; many children, and many persons with mental illness, go unprotected and are the victims in society. Federal Bureau of Investigation records for child homicide (Jason 1983) showed 6,301 reported homicides of children under age 18 between the years 1976 and 1979 out of a total of 73,931 homicides of all ages. Homicides reported to the FBI do not include those resulting from neglect, failure to thrive, malnutrition, exposure, and absence of care for medical problems.

The estimated risk of death at the hands of parents is five times greater in the first year of life than the risk of adult homicide (60 vs. 12 per million) (Kumar 1988). These killings appear to have more to do with the failure to bond than with maternal psychosis per se. Although psychosis can interfere with bonding, most mothers who fail to bond do not have diagnosed mental illness. Normal attachment may be disrupted under the following circumstances: when the child is unwanted, when there are major marital problems, when the mother's and baby's personalities are not a good match, when the infant has a physical defect, when the delivery is especially difficult, and when there is prolonged separation from the newborn.

Neonaticide has been known for centuries and has often been a social and cultural practice based on the needs of society (Tuteur and Glotzer 1959). In some societies this act was severely punished, despite its frequency. Midwives, themselves productive and normal members of society, were sometimes responsible for the disposal of infants who were defective, female (Jeffrey et al. 1984), or otherwise not desirable. In Japan, until 100 years ago, many healthy newborns and most defective ones were killed immediately after birth by masking their noses and mouths with wet paper, a practice called *mabiki* or "thinning out." This was the way for poor families to keep families small enough to feed and for all families to avoid the shame of a handicapped child (Kawashima 1988).

Over the years, motivations for infanticide have included illegitimacy, population control, inability to care for the newborn, greed for money and power, superstition, congenital defects, and ritual sacrifice (Myers 1967, 1979; Radbill 1968). Human beings who are vulnerable will seek out as targets those who are totally helpless and likely to be dependent for many years (Piers 1978). The dependency of infants has sometimes meant their "disposal" for family planning purposes. Proponents of euthanasia for babies in neonatal intensive care units claim that our present view of babies is deviant from that of most human societies over time, where infants have been killed for sex selection, population control, and removal of defective babies (Kuhse and Singer 1985). When we critically judge parents who are not fully committed to the rescue of a handicapped newborn, we forget that it is only recently in human history that we have expected to rescue all human offspring (Silverman 1981).

An opposing view is that history has been misjudged regarding infanticide and that it is a misuse and misreading of history to rationalize any taking of life such as killing of newborns (Post 1988). Euthanasia and active killing of extremely defective newborns can open the door to more genocidal acts, as has been shown in studies of medicalized killing in Nazi Germany (Lifton 1986; Proctor 1988).

In either view, few, if any, of the perpetrators of neonaticide—usually the mother, father, or birth attendant—were "mentally ill" or even culturally deviant at the time. We have no knowledge of what they felt at the moment or of what process of mourning or regret they might have experienced. These neonaticides were considered altruistic acts for their time and place; not to perform them would have been considered deviant.

Conflict within the person who kills a child has been poorly studied. Phenomenological accounts are given in literature, such as Euripides' *Medea* or Toni Morrison's *Beloved*. These great authors permit us to empathize with the inner turmoil of the heroines and to comprehend something more about their monstrous acts. Those clinicians working with people who perform infanticide would do well to read these works.

Who Are the Perpetrators of Infanticide?

The most extensive psychiatric study of infanticide came from Broadmoor State Criminal Lunatic Asylum in England, and the results of this study were instrumental in public recognition of postpartum vulnerability and the eventual passage of the 1938 Infanticide Act (Bender 1934; Hopwood 1927). The infant murders were impulsive and unplanned, and these women did not attempt to conceal the act. Preceding the killing of the baby, all of the mothers had been suicidal, and many tried suicide simultaneously with the homicide; the mothers who survived believed they would be punished for the baby's death.

Anthony (1959) has written about group psychotherapy at Maudsley Hospital in London with women who had compulsive murderous thoughts toward their children. There were 12 women treated by the group who represented four types: 1) severely obsessional women who appeared very nice by virtue of excessive reaction formation; 2) those women identified with an attacking parent and who tended to be more anxious and hysterical; 3) depressed, guilty, and suicidal women; 4) explosive psychopathic women who were aggressive and homicidal much of the time. The gap between thought and action was the major focus of the group. On the whole, the group process worked to allow the inhibited members to become more assertive and the aggressive ones to be more controlled. Eight of the women lost their symptoms and improved; for the most part, the group members helped each other. However, for three of the mothers, there was no improvement, and the psychological transmission of their wishes for their children's death became tragically enacted. The damage from such maternal hatred is reflected in the children's disorders and may be greatly underestimated; we later see it in our adult patients who felt the hatred and rejection. The most severe consequences for the children are in those whose mothers are depressed with unrecognized depression; studies of the mother-baby interaction demonstrate the subtle ways in which a baby, within the first year of life, will lose object constancy and appear distracted when the mother (or primary caregiver) has major depression (Lyons-Ruth et al. 1984; Murray 1988; Resnick 1970; Rosenbaum and Bimni 1986). A survey of the large and important literature on these high-risk infants, however, is beyond the scope of this book.

The mentally ill group who are at highest risk to commit homicide of all types are those with major depressive illnesses. Schizophrenia is less of a risk condition for filicide (Kaplan and Reich 1976). Brockington and colleagues (1981) noted that on the mother-baby unit at Manchester Hospital, only 3 of 93 women admitted with puerperal psychosis made any attack on the infant. When schizophrenic mothers do murder their children, it is generally in the context of feeling suicidal, and they become extremely depressed and at high risk for suicide after the filicide and again at the time of the anniversary of the child's death and the child's birthday. Some patients will admit themselves to the hospital prophylactically on these anniversaries.

Nine cases studied in Pennsylvania hospitals between 1965 and 1973 were cases in which there was a failure to bond from early pregnancy, attempts to abort, postpartum depression, revenge fantasies, and a belief that drowning (the modal method) was sparing the child unhappiness and pain (Browne and Palmer 1975). The murder may be done by a mentally ill person whose illness is unidentified and who, only following the tragedy, has a first contact with the psychiatric system.

Any murder of a child by a parent in our culture is a monumental event for the entire community; for the murdering parent, there is enormous pain and many complications and implications. Repeated filicide has been referred to as "a possible hereditary condition" (Bourget and Bradford 1987), but without postulating a murdering gene, we can understand the enormity of the event, the dynamic intrapsychic need to punish and repeat. Such major trauma cannot be underestimated. Let us turn to some actual cases to see the range of the problem and some examples of practical management and outcome.

Bender (1934), at Bellevue's Psychiatric Division, reviewed the cases of women with psychoses not associated with childbirth who murdered a child. She found that following the murder there was first a worsening of symptoms with greater depression and even stupor and catatonia. This first phase was characterized by amnesia, confusion, perseveration about punishment and death, and often denial of one's identity. The fact of the death was denied at the same time as the patient showed evidence of knowing that she had killed her baby. In a second phase, for some patients, there was recovery from the original and amplified symptoms. Bender concluded that the murdering mother saw her child as equivalent to herself and had severe delusional beliefs about the baby (e.g., the baby was getting smaller with age rather than larger). Child murder was then invariably a disguised suicide; psychodynamically, the mother projected her own self onto the baby, who became a "hypochondriacal organ," or representative of all that hurt within her.

These clinical observations hold true today. Psychodynamically, the meaning of the infanticide often seems to be an attempt to murder the unacceptable part of the self, a hated maternal (or other) introject. These acts usually occur during a symbiotic early infancy phase when many normal mothers experience a merger with their newborns. The intense dependency of the baby can realistically be quite depleting for a young parent, especially for someone with few inner resources. The large demands of a small baby can make the infant appear powerful and devilish. When (and perhaps only when) there are additionally the physiologic and chemical changes accompanying childbirth and lactation, these fantasies can escalate to delusions. The delusions, under the influence of sleep deprivation, few supports, and stress, can amplify into destructive acts. The murderous aggression unleashed can be expressed toward the baby and to older children as well as to the self (Pleshette et al. 1956).

In one study of 89 women who killed their children and were awaiting trial, it was concluded that the vast majority (over 80%) suffered from severe personality disorders and acute reactive depressions and suicidal feelings brought on by the loss of a love object (D'Orban 1979). Of the 14 psychotic women, 7 had postpartum psychosis with schizoaffective symptoms, 4 had schizophrenia, 2 had paranoid psychosis, and 1 had major depression. D'Orban cited a British research study showing that some 62% of mothers who kill their children commit suicide while awaiting trial; it is especially those women with depressive illnesses who are at risk of suicide. A series in the prison ward at Kings County Hospital in Brooklyn included 12 infanticides among 512 admissions of women and showed that only two of the women offenders suffered from long-term mental illness (McDermaid and Winkler 1955).

Reasons Underlying Infanticidal Acts

In a series of 131 cases of filicide, Resnick (1969) categorized five discernible explanations for the killing of the baby: 1) altruism, 2) acute psychosis, 3) unwanted baby, 4) accidental fatal battering, and 5) spouse revenge. The majority of murders were committed by women who had acute psychotic reactions, some epileptic, some organic. Altruistic filicides were described as usually being associated with a suicide attempt or as being a confused suicide attempt in which a psychotic mother identifies with the baby and does not know whom she is killing. These altruistic killings are, in the mother's mind, done to alleviate or spare the child suffering (Browne and Palmer 1975). The suffering may be imaginary and part of a psychotic delusion, but it may be quite real, as in infanticide committed in extreme situations (e.g., a concentration camp, slavery in the early 19th-century American South). Acute psychotic killings were done by parents, including those who did not have long-term mental illness.

However, several or even all of the above five categories may be present in any one given situation. The following is a case report in which all five contributing factors may have been present in a woman who killed her children but had not been known as a person with mental illness:

Case 27: Unreported, Repeated Filicide in a Woman With Undiagnosed Mental Illness

The newspaper reported the story of a 43-year-old pediatric nurse who was tried for murder after the death of her third child in 1988 and found not guilty by reason of insanity (Mansnerus 1988). She was described as "quiet and meticulous" as she detailed for the jury how she had seen hands she did not recognize as her own holding a pillow over the face of her infant in 1988, and before that, in 1980 and 1982. The first and second deaths went unnoticed as she seemed to be functioning well and managed to cover up signs of her illness and disastrous acts. This woman was working as a nurse and had never been diagnosed with mental illness. She did have a brother with schizophrenia. She was described by her examiners as childlike and having a transient and atypical psychosis at the time of the murders. She is someone who was unable to ask for help and whose desperate suffocated (and suffocating) screams for help went unheeded. Who along the way might have been able to perceive what was happening and gotten this woman some help before the repeated tragedies? Only after her trial was she able to receive psychiatric help.

Unwanted babies account for the vast majority of the neonaticides that take place within the first 24 hours of life, often as suffocation and stifling of the first breath (Resnick 1970). Now, in the United States, neonatal deaths are usually caused by nonpsychotic, very young and/or frightened mothers who want to conceal the birth and dispose of the evidence quickly. Incidents such as these are probably quite underreported and may be discovered only incidentally later on, perhaps in the course of a subsequent psychiatric examination. Only two newborns were killed by fathers according to Resnick's review of 168 cases reported in the literature between 1751 and 1968. One father was mentally retarded and jealous of the newborn; the other became overtly psychotic a year after the murder.

The nonpsychotic mother who realizes her difficulty with bonding and is not too paralyzed by her shame at this failure will get psychiatric help for herself and/or competently arrange for some other caregivers for the baby (e.g., father of the baby, relatives, friends, or hired helpers) so that the child can get loving, attentive care from other adults. The following case illustrates a failure of mother and infant to bond and a failure of family and caregivers to recognize a new mother's desperation. It also illustrates how the one factor of failure to bond is not a sufficient explanation; separation and bonding problems followed upon a depression that had started in pregnancy and continued postpartum.

Case 28: Unappreciated Depression and Failure to Bond After Separation as Background to Infanticide

A 32-year-old factory worker fatally shot her 6-week-old son (Elliott and Brookes 1989). She then shot herself, but just missed her heart, and she survived. She and her husband had planned and eagerly awaited this baby; neither had a history of mental illness. Her only prepregnancy disorder was a history of premenstrual tension. During the pregnancy she became especially physically uncomfortable in the eighth month; severe edema prevented her from going to work or even leaving her walk-up apartment. She felt housebound and depressed, and started to have strange ideas about the baby. The delivery followed a very difficult labor, and the baby was born with a medical problem that required him to be briefly hospitalized at an infant intensive care unit. The new mother became increasingly depressed and felt inadequate and helpless while separated from her baby.

Although she took the baby home after 4 weeks, she never felt able to bond with him. She began to think that the baby and her husband would be better off without her. Her mother took her to the family doctor because of her depression and fatigue; he underestimated her depression as the "blues" and advised the grandmother to help with the baby and provide relief care. While she visited her mother to get some sleep, the patient took an overdose of over-the-counter pills, wrote a suicide note, and went to sleep, hoping to die. Her long sleep was misinterpreted as "what she needs," and the note was ignored. The following day, feeling even more a failure, she attempted to kill herself with her husband's handgun, but first, in a fugue-like state, she shot her baby. Only then did she come to psychiatric attention. This couple still mourn for the baby they lost, with a grief that is even more intense because it is both for the loss of the baby and for the illness that was responsible for that loss.

Members of a self-help group for mothers with postpartum emotional illnesses answered an advertisement in their newsletter asking people to send in stories of their negative reactions to their babies. A questionnaire was sent to the 44 women with 87 children who responded to the ad. All the women thanked the investigator for the acknowledgment of their problem and for his interest, and expressed relief at being able to tell their stories—sometimes for the first time. Only 9 of the 87 childbirths had resulted in hospitalization; this was a largely ambulatory population, and 32 received no professional treatment at all. General practitioners had treated 43, and 3 of the women saw a psychiatrist for postnatal depression. There was only one factor (of many surveyed in a questionnaire) that retrospectively proved significant (though not necessarily causal) in disrupting affectionate bonding: severe pain at labor and delivery. Factors such as the baby's gender, previous consideration of abortion, history of infertility, cesarean section, delayed holding, and baby's health problem were insignificant. Most of the mothers now felt affection for the children, but one-third of the 87 children had mothers who had felt severe hatred and inability to take care of the child. One mother continued to have these feelings 11 years later. Twenty-eight mothers who had each had two children reported the same negative reaction to both. There was no individual study of the meaning of either of the children to them or the meaning of motherhood to that particular mother. These bonding disorders are not obvious because these mothers are usually emotionally and socially healthy enough to go through the motions of being "good-enough" mothers (Kumar 1988).

For the clinician working with mothers who are at high risk for infanticide, or even for those who are not known to be at high risk, there are a number of factors to keep in mind that will alert the clinician to the possibility of child abuse and worse:

1. Obsessional thoughts and complaints, especially concerning the baby. Be alert especially to somatic preoccupations.
2. Hostility toward the baby, husband, and those close to the patient.
3. Apathy to the baby and indifference to caregiving instruction.
4. Anxiety that produces excessive questioning about the same thing repeatedly.
5. Failure to bond in the first 3 days of life.
6. Difficulty responding appropriately to the baby's basic needs.
7. Projections of adult feelings onto the infant, e.g., "Look how angry he is at me!"
8. Neglect of basic baby care, such as feeding, diaper changing, and dressing of the baby.
9. Difficulty talking with the baby and/or maintaining eye contact and a conversation, even with a young baby.

Treatment

For the clinician, the most difficult part of the treatment of the woman who has killed her own child is the clinician's countertransference. The patient either experiences and conveys relentless sadness, or, even worse for patient and therapist, she exhibits defenses against that sadness (i.e., denial and projected rage). When sitting with a woman who has killed her baby, it is at first difficult to think of anything else. The magnitude of this event as an act of brutality and violence of the strong perpetrated on the weak can preclude all other impressions from the mind of the interviewer. This sense is further magnified when the patient is amnesic or unable to talk of the event, or is a person with whom it might have been difficult to empathize with before the event (e.g., a substance abuser). The following case vignette illustrates such a situation and the way in which hearing the story and hearing the continuing pain of the patient can help the clinician to feel empathy:

Case 29: Long-Term Treatment of a Woman Who Has Committed Infanticide

A 33-year-old woman had been at the state hospital for over a year before she was assigned to a clinician for long-term therapy. She had been transferred, everyone hoped temporarily, from a correctional institution where she was serving a term for murder of her 2-year-old child. In prison, she had been alternately abusive and suicidal, and the transfer had occurred after she tried to hang herself in her cell. In the hospital, she was belligerent and assaultive to staff and patients, and it was only after many months and treatment with carbamazepine, that she began to talk.

The therapist reconstructed the patient's history only slowly and incompletely; court records, prison records, and eventually the patient herself told of how she came to murder her child. The patient had been an abused child who had been abandoned by her own parents as a toddler and had spent much of her childhood in temporary foster homes. She had some learning disability and was not well liked, and only after puberty did she discover that she could trade sex for some attention and care. She married at an early age and was intent on having her own family, hoping she could rework and undo her traumatic childhood. She had three babies in 2 years, and her husband became increasingly abusive and alcoholic. One day, housebound and frustrated, after a beating from her husband, she picked up her 2-year-old child and threw him against the wall; he sustained multiple fractures and head injuries, and ultimately died. She was charged with manslaughter and sent to prison. Her husband divorced her, and the older children were removed permanently to protective custody. She lost her entire family at one time.

Over time, as she started to work with the therapist and staff, she had periods of overt psychotic thinking, especially on the child's birthday and death day. She hallucinated that the child was alive. She believed that he was the age he would have been at the present time and that he was living at home, taking care of the rest of the family while his mother was in the hospital. She also expected him to come to the hospital to visit her. She had total confusion at these times about who were her mother, her child, and her self. At other times, she appeared non-psychotic and was able to develop skills working on the hospital grounds in a clerical job. She repeatedly became involved in illicit sexual relationships with hospital patients and workmen; she was able to attract men to her but then felt inevitably disappointed, rageful, and vengeful when the relationships never provided everything she needed.

It was helpful to keep a focus on her sense of loss: not on the great sadness and tragedy that had occurred, but on the immediate disappointment when the child did not show up to visit or when the latest lover did not do what she wanted. This happened in the transference too, and the therapist could never do enough. It was a team effort, and many staff people were involved with very specific roles: monitoring medication, talking at particular set times, providing supervision on the job, etc. This type of approach permitted for the slow development of an alliance with this woman. She had a maternal figure in the therapist, but also many backup and foster parents available, who, unlike the first time around, were not abusive and communicated with each other. As she received firm and gentle treatment, she began to have fewer psychotic periods and to become more attentive and maternal herself to some of the neediest patients in the hospital. This provided her with a maternal role that was delimited and that could be appreciated genuinely by staff and patients. What started out to be a prolonged hospitalization (incarceration) by the authorities to protect society against this murderer became a safe, lifesaving setting for the patient where she could develop a sense of her capacity as a worker and caring person.

Such treatment must be ongoing over a lifetime and in a very structured setting. Despite all efforts, these women remain at high risk of suicide throughout their lives. Acknowledging the loss in whatever way the mother can acknowledge it allows for discussion and the gradual building of trust. At first, what is most on the clinician's mind about the murder and the attendant voyeurism can stifle the flow of conversation and impede developing a relationship. An alliance will develop only out of the willingness of the therapist to ask and listen and not to judge. It is easier not to judge when one hears about the pain, the anguish, the hallucinations that have preceded the murder, and those that continue. Over time, it can be useful to ask about the details of the death to start to fill out the story, even if there is some amnesia; the patient and therapist can satisfy their curiosity and then mourn for what actually did happen.

Not everyone can treat a child murderer or even speak to one. The intensity of the anger, the neediness, the patient's envy of the therapist, and the belief in the impossibility of empathy can be too much in the countertransference to bear. Team work and supervision are essential. Some therapists will be too voyeuristic and eager to hear the gory details and will not be attuned to the pain of the patient. A young therapist, especially one with a young baby of his or her own, may find the story too horrifying to fathom, the act too awful to permit the development of an alliance with the patient. It is wise to realize this and not force the issue but rather refer the patient to another therapist who is able to feel empathy for the patient. If one cannot feel the poignancy of the conflict and the pain of the loss, one cannot effectively treat and try to rehabilitate such a person. There is already such guilt and shame and self-loathing that the therapist must work at genuinely influencing the self-understanding and forgiveness in the patient and the family. The goal is to help everyone to see the infanticide as a side effect of a terrible illness that is treatable and is now under treatment.

Infanticide is a major concern with mentally ill parents even though it is an infrequent event. Until this point, we have discussed the female patient. Men with long-term mental illness also become parents and will be discussed in the next chapter.

Chapter 11

Fathers With Major Mental Illness: An Ignored Population

> I am a father, and I think of my boy every day of my life. The best thing I can do for my son is never to see him.
>
> A 35-year-old man with long-term mental illness whose biological son
> lives with the boy's mother and her new husband

*T*he importance of parenthood to men has been investigated in recent years as the role of fathers has begun to be highlighted in a new way by our society (Cath et al. 1982; Kutner 1990). The male role has expanded to include a greater participation in the pregnancy and childbirth experience and an increased nurturing of babies and young children. Male employees increasingly request paternity leave from employers in order to facilitate bonding with their new infants. Rights of birth fathers to custody of their children are now being acknowledged in the courts (Kolbert 1990), where fathers are openly advocating for their rights as parents.

We suggest that among men with long-term mental illness the issues of parenting and fatherhood are also extremely important. We have found, on an anecdotal and case-by-case basis, that men with long-term mental disabilities may have wishes for fatherhood and strong emotional responses to fatherhood, and may, in fact, play a role in parenting their children. In addition, for those men who have had children, even if they are now apart from them, fantasies about the children, wishes to be reunited with them, or thoughts regarding their health and happiness are important and valuable.

In recent studies of people with major mental illness who are living in the community, both men and women were asked about the importance of parenting and children in their lives. Godschalx (1987), in her Utah study, found that issues of parenting were emotionally central for the men who were fathers even though they had relinquished their children in divorce or separation. Test and her colleagues (1990) in Wisconsin indicated that there was a significant difference between the men and women in terms of the percentage of people having primary caregiving roles with their children; but in the sample of 82 men with long-term mental illness who were studied, four (4.9%) were acting as primary caregivers for their offspring. Schwab and colleagues (1991) in New Hampshire made participant observations of the lives of people with long-term mental illness and substance abuse and showed that for men as well as women issues concerning parenting and children were salient. By listening to conversations, seeing the time devoted to custody hearings, and observing visits to families and cemeteries, these authors saw the clear value of family and children to men with long-term mental illness.

From our own clinical observations, we have seen how reproductive issues can be intense and take on tremendous meaning and value in the lives of men. We expect that as data are gathered about the role of parenting for men with long-term mental illness, themes of longing, loss, and unfilled hopes and dreams will emerge. We encounter male patients whose ongoing connection with their children is of paramount importance in their daily lives. For other men, we see how reuniting with relinquished children even in fantasy can be an important therapeutic topic. Because of the psychological importance of the notion of parenting for men as well as women in this population as a sign of normalcy and as an identity that has respect and meaning, losses of parenting possibilities may well be devastating.

In this chapter we will 1) summarize the impact of parenting on men in the general population, 2) discuss male postpartum psychosis, and 3) describe the impact of various aspects of fatherhood on the course of illness in men with long-term and severe mental illness.

Impact of Parenting on Men in the General Population

Parenthood has been seen by psychoanalytic thinkers as a positive developmental stage in the maturation of both men and women (Ginath 1974; Jarvis 1962). Fatherhood, however, is also a time of stress, anxiety, and emotional difficulty (Kutner 1990; Raskin et al. 1990). Several studies have found that a partner's pregnancy and the birth of a child can create emotional and physical responses in men (Fawcett and York 1986; Shapiro and Nass 1986). For example, Lipkin and Lamb (1982) report that in a study of 267 men whose partners were pregnant, 60 (22.5%) had come to a general medical clinic with physical complaints that had no physiological basis. Fawcett and York (1986) note that some of the physical symptoms experienced by men during and after their partners' pregnancies included gastrointestinal disorders, abdominal bloating, increased or decreased appetite, and backache. Leg cramps, faintness, and lassitude were other complaints seen by these authors as a modern equivalent of couvade. Observations by Shapiro and Nass (1986) confirm that couvade is a spectrum disorder of pathological responses in males ranging from physical symptoms to psychosis as a reaction to pregnancy (Munroe et al. 1973).

Other authors studying patients without long-term mental illness have looked at the emotional responses of men to childbirth as being analogous to, and perhaps coincident with, emotional changes in the pregnant woman or in the couple dyad (Lomas 1959, 1960). Jarvis (1962) suggests that depressive postpartum reactions in the mother may be related to the emotional responses of her male partner to her pregnancy and to the birth of their child. Kaplan and Blackman (1969) carried out a study of 43 women with psychiatric illness in the postpartum period and found that 38 expressed problems in their relationship with their husbands. The difficulties stemmed from abusive, cruel, or neglectful behaviors on the part of the men. Upon examination of the male partners, the authors concluded that the men, in fact, were responding with negative emotions toward their wives because of the negative impact of the pregnancy and childbirth on their own emotional status. Harvey and McGrath (1988) also studied the male partners of women admitted to a psychiatric inpatient unit for postpartum illness and found that two-fifths of the husbands exhibited severe pathology. They postulated that the husbands' emotional response to the childbirth and new baby may have played a role in the etiology of the women's illnesses.

Raskin and her colleagues (1990) looked at depressive symptoms in both male and female partners during pregnancy and new parenthood. The authors studied 86 couples and found significant numbers of depressed men. Clearly an emotional response to pregnancy and childbirth exists for men, even those without major mental illness (Bieber and Bieber 1978). Other studies, as well as clinical observation, point to the positive and reparative role of childbirth for men and suggest how much the man's positive reactions may help buffer the woman's negative or depressive reaction (Cath et al. 1982).

Male Postpartum Psychosis

Psychotic responses to pregnancy and childbirth in fathers have often been reported (Benvenuti 1988; Cavenar and Weddington 1979; Davenport and Adland 1982; Ginath 1974; Retterstol 1968; Towne and Afterman 1955; Van Putten and LaWall 1981). Psychological disturbance in fathers with newborns was found by Wainwright (1966), who noted that in many of these cases, the underlying dynamics revealed that these new fathers were unable to take on the responsibilities and role of parent and became envious and rivalrous with the baby. In addition, these new fathers became rageful at the wife for being unable to fully care for them. Kaplan and Blackman (1969) contend that during the pregnancy a male partner may be more likely to equate his wife with his mother and that he may experience his wife's attention to her own pregnancy as a form of rejection and abandonment.

Wainwright (1966) reported on a series of 10 men whose psychological status after the birth of a child required hospitalization. At first, the patients did not associate their emotional difficulties with the new role of fatherhood, but, through psychotherapy, dynamic themes associated with fatherhood emerged. The themes centered around unresolved issues with their own parents, the added responsibility of the parenting role, and what Wainwright called the "disruption of dependency needs." We have found these themes in men with long-term mental illness who are faced with pregnancy or a new child either in their own family or elsewhere in their immediate environment (e.g., a pregnant staff member).

For men with emotional vulnerabilities, the pregnancy of their partner or the birth of their baby can precipitate an exacerbation of their psychiatric symptoms, as is seen in the following case:

Case 30: Male Postpartum Paranoid Psychosis

A couple had met on a psychiatric unit. The woman, a perky, energetic 22-year-old, had had one 2-week hospitalization for depression, recompensated well, and was able to continue in her career in the retail fashion industry. The man was 25 years old, attractive, and somewhat elegant in demeanor, and carried a diagnosis of atypical psychosis with paranoid features. He worked as an architectural draftsman and was talented at drawing and painting. He was also able to recompensate rapidly, but the course of his illness was rougher, and he did decompensate under stress.

The couple fell deeply in love and, with ongoing individual and couples therapy, were able to accommodate to each other and manage to stabilize their relationship. One year into their couples work, they married, and both seemed extremely happy. After another year, they decided to have a baby. Almost from the start, the husband began to have recurring symptoms. He became extremely paranoid and began to make accusations toward his wife. He was unable to continue his job and, in anger, stopped taking his antipsychotic medications. The wife became frightened of him and, during her second trimester, returned on some nights to her parents' house for safety.

Numerous attempts were made to try and reengage the husband in treatment. Finally, during the third trimester, his condition escalated, and he was committed to a psychiatric unit. The wife moved into her parents' home and began to plan for the birth of the baby and her subsequent return to work. She arranged for child care in her parents' neighborhood.

She was still in love with her husband and hoped that once the baby was born he would be able to acknowledge his child and they would be able to live together again. However, once he left the psychiatric hospital, the husband refused to see his wife and baby, did not even return his wife's calls, left the apartment they had lived in together, and moved out of state.

For this patient, fatherhood created an intolerable conflict. He needed his wife to be fully there to care for him and felt he could not survive with the addition of a child as well. The husband's illness was more severe than the wife's, and it was not possible for him to live with her and a baby. He was unable to see fatherhood as a role identity offering pride and self-confidence. Perhaps with additional support systems, he might one day be able to establish a connection with his child and with an experience of fathering. Psychotherapy, without the pressures of actual fathering, might help him to work on understanding the way in which fatherhood might be possible for him. The notion of fatherhood is premature when the person does not have enough sense of himself and feel adequately fathered.

Most often, the male postpartum psychotic episode is transient, a circumstantial reaction to the transition to fatherhood and the profound conflicts elicited. With treatment, short hospitalizations, neuroleptic medication, and clarifying psychotherapy, such reactive psychoses will resolve. Thus, pregnancy and childbirth create profound emotional responses in men, some of whom are at risk for serious psychiatric illness.

Impact of Parenting on Men With Long-Term Mental Illness

Apart from the specific male psychosis mentioned above, the many ways in which parenting makes an impact on men with mental illness will be illustrated in cases below. Fantasies that male patients have about parenting are important and must be explored by clinicians. Many male patients with long-term mental illness never actually father a child or have the real opportunity and challenge of parenthood, but nevertheless they have important fantasy connections to the notion of being fathers. The issues involve potency, generativity, and the concrete manifestations of male virility that a child may signify. For some men, there is rage at their own fathers for not protecting them from the ravages of mental illness. They may believe that they could be better fathers and could guarantee their offspring a healthy and productive life.

Procreation is also an act of creativity, and severe mental illness can massively diminish or even extinguish creative abilities; the birth of a child, then, might serve symbolically to replace that loss of creativity. The wish for health and vitality may be embodied in the idea of a child, as in the following case:

Case 31: The Importance of the Fantasy of a Child

A 30-year-old man with chronic schizophrenia had an early onset of his illness that cut short a promising career as a sculptor. Auditory hallucinations tormented him constantly so that concentration on both ordinary tasks and creative projects became almost impossible. Severe and long-standing mental illness had so handicapped him that he could no longer sculpt. The patient came from a large Chinese-American family in which sisters and brothers were married and there were many children. Although he lived in a halfway house, he was able to go home for family holidays and enjoy the many members of his family who were often assembled at his parents' home.

The patient was quite dysfunctional and was not able to maintain much of a day program or to participate in vocational rehabilitation. Yet, he was able to maintain a relationship with a woman who also suffered from a long-term mental illness. He talked openly of wanting to have a baby with her and became suicidal when she became pregnant with their child but decided to have an abortion. It was only when he was hospitalized on this occasion that his therapist realized how deeply this man wanted to actually have a child of his own and what this need represented.

Long discussions followed, in which the loss of the opportunity to father a child, the loss of his ability to follow a career, and the devastating toll that his illness had had upon his life were explored. He was able, at times, to admit to despair that made him wish to end his life. He joined a peer group and began to examine how one can be a man and have a long-term mental illness too. Others in the group had grappled with these issues and made strides in adapting to their losses and finding new avenues for personal growth and creativity.

Parenthood and pregnancies in the therapists and staff stimulate sexual and parenting fantasies for all patients. Male patients, however, may respond differently from female patients when faced with the knowledge that their therapist is about to have a baby and to take time off to begin the work of parenting. Sometimes these reactions are violent, especially for inpatients who are psychotic, and may occur when the inpatient unit has not been able to establish a sense of safety for staff involving the inevitable transitions associated with maternity leaves (Frank 1990). Barden (1985) wrote about her experience during her pregnancy of working with two men who were diagnosed with schizophrenia. She reported that both men responded in strong ways; neither tolerated the experience well. One patient dropped out of treatment dramatically by flying to another city, and the second became quite psychotic and bizarre as he struggled to overcome the issues of sexuality that emerged.

When a female therapist is pregnant, many feelings are stirred up for patients. For men with long-term mental illness, the pregnancy of a female therapist may be overwhelming. Not only may it stir up sexual feelings and fantasies that he has fathered the baby, but it may also elicit stirrings of identification with the baby, feelings of anger at the therapist for abandoning him for the baby, and identification with the pregnant woman. In this case, the yearning to be a parent or to have a child is not manifest. Instead, a more primitive merging with the therapist and mimicking of pregnancy symptoms are the ways in which the patient signals his fantasies about fatherhood. These powerful feelings, often terrifying for the male patient, must be addressed in the context of the therapy, as in the following case:

Case 32: Couvadelike Symptoms in Response to a Pregnant Therapist

The patient, at 45 years of age, had a diagnosis of chronic schizophrenia. He had never dated, but he lived independently, worked at a supermarket, and regularly attended outpatient vocational support groups and outings with the community social club. Weekends were usually spent at the nearby home of his parents, where he helped his father with household chores or watched television. He enjoyed the presence of his nieces and nephews when they came to visit their grandparents' home. However, at times, he resented the attention the children got from his parents and withdrew from the social activity.

When the leader of the vocational support group became pregnant, this patient became quite upset and began to skip some of his group sessions. When the group therapist was about 8 months pregnant, he requested an appointment with his psychiatrist to complain about a terrible bellyache. He asked to go into the hospital at the same time that his pregnant group leader delivered. The psychiatrist was able to make the connection between the patient's bellyache, his desire to be in the hospital, and the pregnant therapist's large belly and upcoming maternity leave. This man was so strongly identified with his pregnant therapist and so enraged at her leaving him that he left the group and was unable to return. He continued to discuss his loneliness and desire for a girlfriend with his psychiatrist. He was also able to start talking about his parents' relationship with their grandchildren, his jealousy of the children, and his realization that he would never have children himself. Airing these issues was frightening for the patient but became possible when the psychiatrist gently took the lead from the patient.

Just as pregnant female therapists bring issues of sexuality and reproduction into high relief, the paternity leave of male therapists also creates fantasies, envy, identification, and a sense of loss and depression for men with mental illness.

The current valuing of the parenting function of men in our society has created the possibility that male employees can take a paternity leave and begin to parent and bond with their child in the weeks following their partner's delivery (or the adoption of a child). Acknowledgment of the paternity leave is parallel to the female therapist's obvious pregnancy and will certainly stir up strong emotions in patients. Sometimes, the male therapist's paternity leave can stir up emotions of rage and jealousy against the patient's own father as well as toward the therapist. This can serve to reinforce the contrast between the health, virility, and positive future of the male therapist–father and the perceived dysfunction and hopeless and unproductive situation of the man with a long-term mental illness. The hopelessness fostered by this perception may be too much for the mentally ill man to bear. The approaching fatherhood of the therapist may provoke unbearable pain for the patient. Therapists must be sensitive to the power that the fantasy of fathering new life can have on men with major mental illness, as in the following case:

Case 33: Response to a Therapist's Paternity Leave

A 29-year-old man with a bipolar disorder had been married at age 19. He was quite handsome and courtly, and had been able to work and function when his illness was under control. His wife had adored him, but as his illness progressed and his depressive periods became more pronounced, she was unable to remain in the marriage and moved out of state. While this man was able to actively pursue his wife, she talked of reconciliation. But, eventually, his illness, his lack of ability to comply with taking medications, and his increasing street drug use put an end to her desire to recommit herself to the marriage.

As part of his repeated plans to win back the affection of his wife, he began supportive therapy and Narcotics Anonymous. His drug counselor was understanding and sensitive to him; the patient was able to comply with treatment and attend therapy meetings regularly, and to feel hopeful and pleased with his progress. But, when the male drug counselor announced his paternity leave, the patient felt shocked, betrayed, assaulted, abandoned, and angry. He stormed out of the group meeting room in a rage, began to take drugs, and drove out to see his wife, a day's drive away. When he arrived, he found her unavailable and socializing with a new boyfriend. Desolate and hopeless, he drove to a bridge not far from her house and jumped to his death. Although this impulsive act could not be attributed to any single cause, its juxtaposition with the announcement of the drug counselor's paternity leave underscored the vulnerability surrounding the issue of fatherhood in one man who was concurrently facing the loss of his wife.

Male patients can respond strongly to stories of pregnancy loss and relinquishment of children told by female patients. The idea of having a child or a family can feel especially good to those male patients who are now isolated and lonely but who originally came from warm, close families for whom children were a sign of family strength and vitality. The notion of relinquishment is usually associated with birth mothers who give up custody of their children to adoptive parents, but we believe it also applies to male patients who lose contact with children. When mental illness becomes severe and chronic, contacts with wife and children may cease. The break in contact may be the result of the action of the former wife and the children, or it may have been initiated by the father because of the severity of his illness and his shame due to his dysfunctional and dependent condition. Some men choose complete separation from their children because they believe (and/or are advised) that the children's best interests are furthered by ignorance of their fathers' condition, or they believe that they are unable to carry out any of the functions of the fatherhood role in a way that is satisfactory to them. In other cases, fathers with mental illness have reached out to children, only to be rebuffed repeatedly.

In the following situation, a man with mental illness in his mid-40s decided to try to reconnect with his two children whom he had not seen in a decade. He had voluntarily decided not to contact his children because of his fear that his condition would cause his children to reject him. However, once he had reached a stabilized condition and had a job, a cooperative apartment, and a certain pride in his accomplishments, he sought a reunion and desired a real and ongoing emotional connection to his children.

Case 34: Reunion After Relinquishment

A 42-year-old man had an affective disorder that had developed in his late 20s and was marked by mood swings and paranoia. Prior to his illness, he had married and had two children. However, once he became ill, his wife divorced him and remarried. Because the course of his illness was quite severe, he was hospitalized in a state hospital for 6 years and consequently lost touch with his children, whom he felt ashamed to contact. When the deinstitutionalization movement gave him the opportunity to live in the community, he was able to make the adjustment well and decided that the time had come to reconnect to his now-adult offspring.

The desire to know his children became the paramount motivating feature in his therapy. Over the years, working with his therapist, he was able to contact his children and successfully reunited with both of them. This achievement, which required him to overcome shame and stigma, was motivated by an overriding need to acknowledge his fatherhood and feeling of parental pride.

Family therapy provided a psychoeducational approach initially as family members were informed about the father's condition; both children and father needed a chance to talk about what it was like to lose touch with each other. Over many months, they got to know each other and talked about mutual feelings of anger, rejection, humiliation, and abandonment. Through the intervention of the family therapist, a growing trust developed, and a basis for ongoing relationships was established. Although this patient's daily life is marginal and lonely, reunification with his children and the ongoing sense of family helped to stabilize his condition and gave him pride and hope.

Clinicians must be especially alert to the role that the fantasy of parenting may play in the psychology of male patients because the feelings of men regarding parenthood are even more invisible and more difficult to acknowledge than those of women. Once looked at by the patient, this area is a painful one that may lead to a profound depression and sense of loss for the patient. These issues can be addressed in psychotherapy. Patients living in the community have an opportunity to actually connect with children by former marriages and to take on a father role in a concrete way. This may be an opportunity for a sense of pride and self-worth as patients see that their children are thriving, even if they themselves cannot. However, this opportunity has the risk of a major narcissistic trauma because of the shame and stigma associated with mental illness and the feelings of inadequacy and the possibilities of rejection that may accompany attempts at reunions. Such family therapy involves careful weighing of risks and benefits. Patients must be helped to realize how much of a role they are able to play and how much contact their children really do want. Inevitably, there are losses along with the gains of paternal involvement.

For some men with long-term mental illness whose lives are quite barren, a focus on their role as a father may serve as an organizing theme in their lives. By involving themselves with the raising of their child, they can nurture a healthy life force and at the same time achieve competency in their role as a father. So it was with the following case:

Case 35: The Passion to Be a Father

A 30-year-old man had a long-term atypical psychosis. Premorbidly, he was a hyperactive child, and, later, as a young adult, he enjoyed riding motorcycles and driving fast cars. He married at 18 and had a child. By age 20, he began to develop paranoid thoughts and was unable to maintain a job because of suspicions about his boss and co-workers. His marriage began to disintegrate and his wife left him. He became homeless and lived in a dumpster near his parents' home. Eventually, he was hospitalized after police discovered him trying to break into his parents' house.

Once recompensated, he continued to display some paranoid ideation, but he was able to work and live in a supportive community setting. Throughout his illness and recovery, he was obsessed with thoughts of his son and contacted a lawyer as soon as he was able to do so. He fought in the courts for the right to visit his son and was granted visitation rights every other week and was allowed to make one phone call to his son weekly.

During many hospitalizations and a difficult course of mental illness, he focused on his son in a steady way. He faithfully called his son weekly and kept up with his son's school and athletic accomplishments. He made sure that he was permitted to watch school athletic events in which his son participated. He always took the boy to his halfway house for major holidays. He negotiated sleepovers for his son at his parents' home, and he saved whatever money he could from his SSI check to pay a minimal amount in child support because he wanted to have the financial responsibility of parenthood.

This motivation to be a father to his son, in a very real way, has dominated this patient's life. When he got into another accident and the courts took away his license to drive a car, he was able to convince his parents to drive him to see his son so that his visits would not be interrupted. The severe course of his illness has made the challenge of connecting to his son an increasing burden. Yet, the value of the relationship and the normalcy of his son have given him pride and a sense of value in an otherwise quite empty world.

Supportive therapy helped him to acknowledge and validate his feelings of pride in fatherhood. Exploration of his fantasies and hopes about the relationship with his son was part of the work, and it helped him to plan for the realities in a systematic way. Therapy also became a place where small connections, such as appropriate presents purchased for birthdays and the son's achievements, could be shared and their meaning for the patient discussed. Ultimately, the patient was able to gain more emotional stability, to obtain work that was meaningful to him, and to attain a sense of self-worth in his vocational area as well as in parenting. However, throughout his darkest days, it was the notion that he could always, somehow, make some connection to his son that had instilled hope.

At the opposite end of the spectrum is the man who can never grow up, for whom a pregnancy is a reminder of an intense longing to return to the womb, the place of imagined perfect bliss. The following case illustrates this primitive yearning:

Case 36: The Wish to Be the Baby

A 50-year-old man with a diagnosis of hebephrenic schizophrenia was married for 1 year long ago and fathered a baby whom he had never seen. Each year, he reckoned the boy's age on the calendar. He was living in a rest home with a married couple who supervised eight patients. One day, when the patient came into the clinic for his regular depot medication appointment, he had completely shaven his head and was acting quite bizarre. In a long interview with the patient, the staff ascertained that the couple at his rest home just came home with a new baby. The patient wanted to identify with that baby and did so with his baldness. With this decompensation, he was returned to the state hospital, where he became completely regressed and had a long hospital stay.

For most male patients, the desire for parenthood may remain in the realm of fantasy; for others, connections with real biological children may be important to facilitate. Access to birth control and safe sex information, and access to medical clinics that can specifically address the special needs of the mentally ill male population, are essential resources for mental health clinicians.

Special care should be taken with male patients when staff maternity or paternity leaves are coming up. Staff must evaluate the impact of staff parenthood on the male patients with long-term mental illness and then help patients to grapple with the strong emotions that will be stirred up. The men's loss of the opportunity to parent can be a powerful reminder of the multiple losses in their lives and can lead to depression and/or an exacerbation of psychosis.

Parenthood for patients can be an enormous challenge for caregivers. We will next explore the range of choices available for patients who have had babies.

Chapter 12

Long-Term Treatments for Mothers With Long-Term Mental Illness

> HAVE YOU EVER . . . had your plans to marry interfered with by the mental health system? lost custody of your children or been labelled an "unfit parent" solely because of a psychiatric history? IF YOU HAVE EXPERIENCED ANY OF THESE SITUA-TIONS, OR OTHERS LIKE THEM, M-POWER IS FOR YOU!! M-POWER = Massachusetts People/Patients Organized for Wellness Empowerment and Rights.
>
> Brochure for M-POWER, 1990

*W*e have seen that men and women with long-term mental illness can and will have babies. Whatever involvement these parents with mental illness have with their children, the parents will always need special help from another adult who does not have a mental illness. There is a spectrum of parental involvement—from active daily parenting to a long-ago memory of a lost child. There is a spectrum of help—from daily supervision by a family member or mental health professional to a yearly check-in on an important anniversary. Situations in which people with mental illness parent long-term are difficult and can be painful, but may occasionally also be positive and joyful experiences for everyone. We have seen how complex the management of pregnancy in persons with long-term mental illness can be; all of those supports and more are necessary for continuous active parenting by this population.

Therapists may be caught off guard by the profound change in relationship that can occur when the patient's identity is expanded to include parenting and all that that role implies. The mental health professional can use help in adjusting to the new role identity of the patient and in working with the patient-parent in new, more collaborative ways. In this chapter we will discuss 1) principles of long-term treatment planning; 2) parenting options, including relinquishment (i.e., the adoption option), partial arrangements (i.e., open adoption and foster care), and family members as custodial parents (e.g., grandparents and fathers); and 3) the ideal components of a program for mothers with mental illness and an example of a model program.

Principles of Making Long-Term Treatment Plans: Weaving a System of Therapy and Support

The key to long-term treatment of the mother with chronic mental illness is the connection between the patient, her family, and all the professional groups and agencies that provide the full range of needed services (Schwab et al. 1988). To that end, communication and building of a team are essential. Long-term treatment has to be expert because of the high risk of these cases; it has to be consistent to ensure continuity of care (Bachrach 1988; Braham et al. 1975); and it has to be flexible enough to respond to changing needs of mother and/or child. Long-term treatment should be guided by the following principles:

1. Mothers who have major mental illness are a heterogeneous group, and treatment planning must reflect each individual situation. Despite the many emotional and social handicaps that these women endure, they usually respond best to an approach that appreciates the unique psychology of the person being treated.
2. The problems facing the mother with long-term mental illness are multifactorial and need thorough assessment. The psychological, fiscal, social, cultural, psychiatric, medical, and domestic situation must be included in any assessment.
3. The needed services are difficult to obtain. They may be offered by multiple resources, but they sometimes need to be created and creatively funded. Careful case management is essential and central to coordinating the many service providers.
4. Time is a key factor. Pregnancy is too brief and time-limited for the clinician to expect to mobilize a long-term support system, many caregivers, and a working treatment plan. Plans developed during pregnancy must be functional for that time. We can only anticipate some needs; most will await the coming of the baby. Then there is more time for the long view.

5. Ongoing attention must be paid to the legal status of the mother with long-term mental illness in relation to her baby, from before birth until the child has reached an independent age or been legally adopted by someone else. Birth mother rights, postadoption, require legal consultation and advocacy.
6. Ethical, moral, and emotional issues inevitably confront the staff caring for these patients. Openly addressing these issues is vital to patient care.
7. Liaison between psychiatry and other specialties, agencies, and professions is expedited by administrative support. Optimal treatment planning and delivery must depend on the local population, cultural values of the community, legal constraints in the state, and funding availability. Any or all of the following may be involved in treatment planning:

- Psychiatry, including both inpatient and outpatient services
- Obstetrics and gynecology
  — Birth control clinic
- Pediatrics and/or well-baby clinic
- Infection control
  — Assessment of HIV status and other sexually transmitted diseases
- Pharmacy
- Security
- Risk management
- Legal counsel
- Social service agencies—service and funding
- Department of Public Welfare (or other agencies involved in assessment for custody of children); entitlements and fiscal support for the new family
- Department of Public Health (or other agencies involved in treatment of alcoholism and drug abuse)
- Public housing office
- Self-help support groups (e.g., single mothers, grandparents raising grandchildren)
- Specialty programs for pregnancy loss
- Vocational specialists
- Child care and day care agencies
- Clergy

8. Documentation of the reproductive history for the psychiatric record gives continuity to the "mother" identity for a woman with long-term mental illness and alerts all clinicians to this part of her history. Standard psychiatric assessment is not sufficient; the present DSM-III-R (American Psychiatric Association 1987) can be used only if there is expansion of Axis III—for example, a face sheet that highlights reproductive experience for women and men, sexually transmitted diseases, drug and alcohol usage, and psychosocial supports.

Parenting Options

There are three overall options for the long-term plan for a mother with mental illness: 1) to relinquish her baby for permanent adoption at or close to birth; 2) to maintain some type of intermittent flexible arrangement of contact while someone else does the primary parenting; and 3) to be the primary parent with backup from other adults who recognize the mother's limitations. All of these options have long-term consequences for the mother with mental illness, and all require long-term attention in treatment.

Relinquishment (The Adoption Option)

We have argued in the discussion of pregnancy and postpartum assessment of mothering capacity that it is not possible to make a final choice of these options before the mother and baby have a chance to be together. In the past, and sometimes at present, permanent relinquishment of the infant seems the best, and maybe the only realistic, option. When the mother is clearly too psychotic to even consider alternative options, when she does not show interest in the newborn, when she is incapable of basic care for herself, when she is alone with no extended family or partner—these are all situations in which adoption will be the obvious choice. Such seemingly clear-cut cases give us the impression that the mother is relieved of an unwanted and impossible burden when the baby is safely placed with a competent adoptive family and the event ends. Today, we are realizing increasingly that there is a continuing cost to mothers who have relinquished their babies, especially to those mothers who were too psychotic at the time to fully participate in the decision. Birth mothers who give away their babies can hold onto lifelong grief. When their grief and loss are not acknowledged, these individuals are more likely to refuse contraception and to become pregnant repeatedly.

Adoption takes place in the context of the moral and cultural values of the society. In the past, prior to the major changes in cultural values of the last two decades, unmarried pregnancies were shrouded in secrecy. Women who were single and pregnant were many times sent away to homes for unwed mothers, and they signed affidavits during pregnancy agreeing to give up their babies for adoption. Women with mental illness who became pregnant and who were not married were stigmatized doubly.

Because of the secrecy of adoption and a method of childbirth using general anesthesia, many mothers never saw their newborns, who were taken away at birth. Birth mothers could be left with a profound loss that was fuzzy in memory and clouded in secrecy and shame. The birth mother then returned to her former life as a nonmother without the opportunity to mourn her profound loss. The shame and stigma surrounding the birth and delivery as well as the secrecy of the adoption prevented the birth mother from having sympathetic supporters who could help her to grieve and mourn her loss. Many of these birth mothers have been chronically depressed for years; until they are able to begin the grief process and come to terms with the very real loss they suffered, their symptoms of depression do not disappear (Pavao 1990).

Mentally ill women have been subject to the same sequence of events. Those who were institutionalized may have become pregnant by another patient or a hospital employee. In Massachusetts, they were transferred from their area hospital to a ward for pregnant women in another state hospital until the delivery of the baby (Apfel and Handel 1989). If no family member was available to take custody of the child, arrangements for adoption were made at the state hospital maternity unit, and the birth mother returned to her area hospital without her baby. She had no real opportunity to mourn her loss and was returned to the very situation in which she had gotten pregnant in the first place. These episodes were not well documented, and the patient was expected to carry on as usual. Enduring the double stigma of mental illness and out-of-wedlock status left these women quite outcast and isolated. Anniversary reactions and psychotic symptoms that reflected the profound sense of loss may have gone unnoticed by treaters who were unaware of the pregnancy and subsequent relinquishment of the child. Because all those involved in treating the women at the maternity unit as well as the birth mother herself believed that placement away was "best for the baby," little attention was paid to the mother's grieving process.

Rynearson (1982) interviewed 20 outpatient psychiatric patients who were not currently psychotic and had given up their babies. All those interviewed had anniversary symptoms of mourning and depression on the date that the relinquishment had taken place. These reactions subsided in intensity but never were extinguished. For a psychotic woman, as is seen in the following example, the effect of these losses can be even more profound and can lead to acute psychotic exacerbation or denial at anniversaries.

Case 37: A Birth Mother Mourns the Loss of Her Child Years After the Relinquishment

A patient with a diagnosis of paranoid schizophrenia had multiple admissions to a state hospital prior to a pregnancy at age 27. The stress of the pregnancy created an acute exacerbation. She was secretive about the father of the baby and refused to talk about him. The patient's parents were ashamed about her unmarried status and insisted that the baby be put up for adoption. When the patient went into labor, she was transferred from the psychiatric unit to a maternity unit, where she delivered a healthy baby boy. She named her baby and saw him and held him for just one day. A prearranged transfer to foster care followed, and the patient was returned to the state hospital.

In subsequent years, this woman had profound depressions on the anniversary of the relinquishment, several times necessitating rehospitalization. She could barely speak of her loss and had trouble trying to imagine her son. She has fantasized a reunion in which she and her son will be happy and he will come to love her and care for her in her old age. With long-term supportive psychotherapeutic work she can now use the anniversary of her son's birth to think about motherhood and her loss, and reflect on how her thoughts have changed over the years.

Psychotherapy with birth mothers who have long-term mental illness who were part of the era of secret adoptions and shame for unwed mothers should be carried out in much the same way as with less profoundly disturbed women. Just as with normal women, feelings of loss and mourning might be buried because they were not permitted prior acknowledgment (McCusker 1991). Relinquishment continues to be a necessary and viable option at times. Whenever this choice is made, the loss for the birth mother must be registered and discussed as a major part of her continuing treatment. The loss may also be experienced by the father of the baby and the grandparents, who may be included in the discussion over time. A short-term bereavement group geared to the general population may not be appropriate for the psychotic mother because of her illness and/or because the group cannot accept her presence. Further stigma and rejection could be devastating and should be avoided. Longer-term groups based in the psychiatric aftercare clinic that focus on common losses may be appropriate for the woman with mental illness who has lost a child.

Self-blame, shame, and guilt for not living up to an idealized notion of motherhood need to be explored. The patient's own sense of self-blame may be reinforced by staff and other patients who are unable to bear the realities of the mentally ill mother's limitations and the loss of her baby.

Open Adoptions and Foster Care

Cultural, moral, and legal changes in adoption have been brought about in large part by the actions of adoptees and birth parents who have searched for each other and often have had to fight agency regulations and closed adoption files (Caplan 1990a, 1990b). Protection of the identity of the birth mother was considered essential, especially in the case of birth mothers with long-term mental illness. Some state hospitals listed only a street address on the birth certificates of the babies born, to camouflage the status of the birth mother and her identity as a state hospital patient.

Recently, with the increased awareness of the profound consequences to the mother (and the adopted child) of secret adoptions, open adoptions have become more popular. Adoption by extended family, especially by grandparents, has been available for many years and has often been the adoption of choice. Now adoptions by nonfamily members are being opened so that the birth mother can know where her child is being raised and perhaps have some ongoing contact, the adopted child can have some knowledge of his or her birth mother, and the adoptive parents can know the origin of their child.

Open adoption: when birth parents can continue to see and know their children. A legacy of secrecy, shame, and anger on the part of all participants in the adoption triad (birth parents, adoptee, and adoptive parents) has led to this new approach to adoptions (Paveo 1989, 1990). The pain and loss for each of the parties are not eliminated by this openness, but, in many instances, it seems to be a better arrangement. This may also be true for the birth mother (and birth father) with mental illness. Such openness can also continue the yearnings and pain for the birth parent and can preclude grief and resolution (Watkins and Fisher 1992).

The advantage of open adoption for birth parents is the opportunity to watch their child grow and to gain pride and delight in parenthood. The birth mother has a more continuous experience with her pregnancy and birth process, allowing her a chance to integrate that part of life and to feel she has done something normal, rather than to have a disruption, loss, and more confusion around childbearing. She can feel herself to be part of an extended family with her baby; even if she is peripherally related, with visits only several times a year, she may think of the adoptive family as her own and vicariously experience growing up there as her child is doing. Parenting is a connection to the normal world, to a healthy and average family. Arrangements can potentially be made flexible and adjusted over time according to the needs and mental status of the birth mother as well as to the needs and developmental state of the adoptee and adoptive parents.

There are also considerable pitfalls and problems (Caplan 1990a, 1990b). Open adoption may be an improvement, but it is certainly not a panacea for the adoptive parents or for the child, and may not be helpful to the birth mother, especially the woman with long-term mental illness. Few adoptive families, other than the patient's own family, will want to continue contact with the birth mother over time. People who adopt a baby do not want to also adopt, for example, young adult schizophrenic birth parents and all the problems they may have. An initial contact may seem desirable, but adoptive parents want and need a chance to have the baby to themselves. The birth mother with mental illness may thus encounter further rejection, loss, and pain. The lack of clear structure in the arrangements can be anxiety-provoking and lead to uncertainty. There may be resentment, continuing dissatisfaction, sadness, and longing with each visit; ongoing and reenacted feelings of inadequacy about parenting; and grief—all of which need to be continuously worked on in psychotherapy. Women with serious mental illness who want to have babies are prey to agencies offering a loving home to a pregnant woman who will provide a baby for an ideal couple. These women can easily be exploited and need their own advocates—both mental health professionals and legal counsel. Adoption agencies may lure needy mentally ill women with offers of a family and a lifelong family approach to care of the birth parents. The agency may not be able to deliver what the birth mother needs and wants, opening her to profound disappointment and rage. Despite the problems that may be associated with an open adoption situation, sometimes a mother with a long-term mental illness finds that she must know her child in a very real way and is determined to establish a connection despite her inability to raise the child herself. The strong desire for this concrete maternal connection is illustrated by the following case:

Case 38: A Birth Mother Establishes an Open Adoption Arrangement So That She Can Continue to See Her Child

A 32-year-old woman with some material resources has had a persistent and severe mental illness for which she has been treated for many years in a state hospital setting. She became pregnant, deciding she wanted to try to keep the baby, but because of her severe disability, the baby was sent to a foster home at birth. The foster parents knew this would be a long-term placement leading to a legal adoption and that they might have ongoing contact with the birth mother. From the state hospital, the birth mother organized and mobilized her resources and hired a lawyer to petition for the right to see her baby regularly. She acknowledged that her severe mental illness and continuous hospitalization prevented her from receiving full custody from the courts, so she was given weekly visitation rights. At the same time, the foster parents were granted custody of the baby. This arrangement satisfied all parties.

The birth mother then enlisted her sister to help her get to the adoptive home every week; the sister picked her up at the hospital or halfway house, drove her to the adoptive home in a nearby town, and waited in a coffee shop while the patient visited her child for 1 hour. The adoptive parents supported her involvement with the child and monitored the visits. Although many staff members questioned the futility or the wisdom of these visits, they continued to give her passes because it was evident how the visits to the child motivated and organized the patient's mental and social life.

This case illustrates what one mother can do with both the emotional and the material ability to create a situation that would have seemed impossible. She mobilized her attorney, convinced the judges, and received the support of her family, the family who are parenting the child, and the hospital staff.

Foster care.   Foster care is often a good option for birth mothers who are mentally ill and their babies. If a clear assessment cannot be made during the hospital stay, and the birth mother needs time to stabilize her situation, foster care can provide both time and safety for all parties. In many cases, arrangements can be made for mother and baby to interact together in the structure and safety of special parenting programs so that every opportunity is made available to the mother who wants to try to parent her own child. Foster care ideally provides interim care for the child of a parent with mental illness when there is no available family alternative.

There are well-known problems for the foster child: lack of permanence, uncertainty, being subjected to sometimes abusive situations. There are also problems for foster parents: difficulty getting attached and involved with a child who is living with them on a transient basis, difficulty relinquishing a child to whom they have become attached. The foster care option for the mentally ill birth mother can present some of these same difficulties. Finding good foster care parents is an ongoing societal problem, and finding people willing and able to help out a mother with mental illness is even more problematic. Foster care may be used as a stopgap measure while a decision is being made about the mother's ability to raise her child and while other familial resources are researched. Foster care can provide respite for the mother who is hospitalized until she recompensates. Also, foster care can fill in skills in parenting when a birth mother is seen as contributing to her child's inadequate development.

Case 39: Foster Care as a Temporary Therapeutic Intervention

A 29-year-old woman with a diagnosis of chronic schizophrenia had a 22-month-old daughter, a second child who was not yet speaking. Her first child, a boy aged 9, was neglected as a baby and was given, by the courts, to his grandparents. This second child was also considered neglected and was removed by the Department of Social Services when the birth mother started a new relationship with a boyfriend who was a known drug abuser. The mother was very certain that she wanted to keep this daughter. The toddler was placed in foster care with a foster mother who was trained as a speech therapist; the foster mother and the birth mother met for instruction on talking to a young child, something the natural mother found interesting and novel in her experience. The mother and the toddler also attended weekly child care together. The mother was in therapy with and without the boyfriend. All these efforts were geared toward maximizing mothering skills to enable this patient to achieve what she felt was her most important goal: to resume full-time care of her daughter.

In the above case, the foster care was specific, time limited, goal focused, and clearly defined for all the players.

Open adoption by family members.   Grandparents who are parents of either the birth mother or the birth father may choose to keep and raise the baby and officially adopt the infant (Doten 1990). They may be granted temporary custody to give the birth mother time to learn to care for her baby or to see if she can or wants to gain custody herself. They also may serve as the supporting arm for a birth mother who chooses to care for her baby but needs supervision and additional help with parenting (Thurer 1983).

This arrangement has many advantages for families who choose it: The baby remains within the family of origin no matter what form of custody is finally decided upon, and the grandparents do not have to bear the loss of their grandchild. It is, of course, not optimal; grandparents will still grieve over the mental illness and the pain that everyone experiences because of it. If the infant remains with a family member, the birth mother will most likely have continued access to and knowledge of her child ("Relative's Home Sought" 1991). If the child is taken in by the parents of the birth mother, it is most likely that the upbringing of the child will be shared. If the baby is taken in by the parents of the birth father, the mother's access may not be guaranteed unless partial custody and visitation rights are built in.

Case 40: Grandparental Support Sees Parents and Baby Through Major Mental Illness of the Mother

The patient was a single woman living with her parents and sister in a middle-class suburb. She had had a bipolar disorder for 6 years, necessitating multiple hospitalizations both in private and in public hospitals. Her boyfriend was an alcoholic and often hospitalized in detoxification centers, and, unable to work, he moved in with the patient at her parents' home. The couple decided to have a baby, and the patient became pregnant before this decision could be discussed with anyone.

In the fifth month of her pregnancy, the patient became extremely depressed, overdosed on her antidepressant medication, and was hospitalized on the intensive care unit. After being medically cleared, she was transferred to the psychiatric unit, where she stated that she was still extraordinarily depressed and wanted to die. Simultaneously, she stated that she was concerned that she could not take care of her baby and was worried about the baby's welfare. Despite her depression, the patient continued to want to have a healthy baby and was cooperative with staff in that regard and was able to get prenatal care. Most importantly, her parents and boyfriend stood by her and her wish for the baby. Everyone wanted the baby; her parents and boyfriend promised to help her care for the child. Sonograms and other tests reassured them all that the fetus seemed to be in excellent health. The mother's continuing depression and suicidality necessitated ECT as a lifesaving measure for mother and baby.

After a prolonged psychiatric hospitalization, the patient gave birth to a healthy girl (Apgar 8–9) by a spontaneous vaginal delivery with local anesthesia. When the patient saw her daughter, she proclaimed, "She's beautiful." Nurses' notes observed her bonding with her baby and how she seemed to settle down as she learned to care for her newborn. Her parents assumed official custody of the baby while the patient and the baby's father continued to live with them and spend full time caring for the baby.

Not all grandparents can assume this responsibility. Some will be mentally or physically handicapped themselves and not in a position to consider raising a child. When parents of the birth mother are approached to take on the baby but feel unable to do so, there can be considerable long-term guilt and shame. Grandparents as Parents (GAP) is a self-help support group for those grandparents who take charge of grandchildren for many reasons. They have been officially recognized by the National Alliance for the Mentally Ill (NAMI), which is itself an organization composed of committed and concerned family members of those with major mental illness. These families have already endured enormous hardship with their mentally ill loved ones. It is difficult enough for healthy, prosperous people in their 50s to parent young children; those with mentally ill offspring may understandably decline to take on this role again. When they do, the grandparents may do so out of their affection and affiliation with the grandchild and antagonism with or alienation from their own child. The birth mother may be excluded from the grandparent-grandchild dyad and thus lose once again.

In many families, the grandparents begin the parenting process, and then it is assumed by one of the children, usually the oldest daughter, who becomes the parentified child (i.e., one who takes on parental responsibilities). She actually does much of the mothering for any subsequent children and may take daily care of the mother (and father) with mental illness. These children can do amazingly well, especially if there are siblings and some adults (grandparents, aunts or uncles, teachers, social workers) who validate the bizarreness of their parents, and when there is genuine love from the parents. The children can thus develop themselves and a compassion for their disabled parents.

The multiple losses that the patient with a long-term mental illness endures are shared by her family. The grandparents continue to mourn the loss of their healthy child throughout their lives. When they continue to support and care for a mentally ill daughter, they feel her pain and the profound effect of her reproductive losses. The additional loss of a grandchild affects the grandparents and siblings of the person with chronic mental illness. Acknowledging the families' losses and involving families is a central part of the long-term work with these patients.

Sometimes the father who is not mentally ill can be the key figure in managing the home environment, helping in child care, and, in some cases, when the couple is no longer a viable entity, raising the baby as a single parent. Coverdale and Aruffo (1989) interviewed 80 female outpatients and learned that 36 of the women had had a total of 75 children. Forty-five of these children (60%) were being raised by others, most commonly the child's own father. Chang and Renshaw (1986) recommend that staff on the inpatient unit attempt to engage the baby's father in treatment planning early on. The father can facilitate the patient's cooperation and recovery and help with decision making about infant care.

The following is a case of a healthy father who was able to take full care of his children and be generous to their mentally ill mother. As we have seen in the last chapter, even fathers who are themselves mentally ill can provide some adjunctive care.

Case 41: Primary Parenting by the Father

At age 30, a woman was diagnosed with a schizoaffective disorder and has been under continual psychiatric care since that time. She had previously been married and had two children. After years of severe bouts of illness, suicide attempts, and escapades in manic states, her husband divorced her and kept custody of their children. Yet, she has been able to see her children weekly. The daughters have visited her in every setting she has been in (hospitals, halfway houses, and vocational day programs) and have known and loved their mother over the many years of her illness and their growing up. Because she could not care for them herself, she was grateful that her husband and his new wife were able to do so.

In this case, the father of the children made it possible for this woman with chronic mental illness to be identified as a mother and have the joy of watching her children grow. The children are not strangers to her because both she and the children's father cooperated in allowing her to parent in whatever way seemed realistic and whenever she was able.

Supportive therapy allowed this patient to mourn the loss of her marriage as well as overcome the pain she experienced when her former husband remarried. Now, a mothers' group provides her with a forum to discuss with her peers the complexities of being a mother who is severely mentally ill.

Options for the Mother With Mental Illness Who Is the Primary Parent

There are now models that allow for women with mental illness to keep and mother their babies. Such programs are rare and still innovative. New models are being developed with current increasing attention to the reality that young adults with long-term mental illness are mothering and need continual support and surveillance to do so. The knowledge that her mothering skills will be observed with the possible consequence that the baby may be removed from her care adds an additional burden of anxiety to the new mother. However, it also provides her with the knowledge that if she is unable to care for her baby properly, she will be relieved of the obligation, at least temporarily, and she can have time to rethink her options. Furthermore, the desire to have her baby with her can be a positive motivating factor toward improvement of psychotic symptoms. All mothers with chronic mental illness need extra egos as well as hands to do the job of raising a child (Cohler and Musick 1984; Cohler et al. 1980).

Key Supports for Mothers With Mental Illness Who Are the Primary Caregiver

Certain factors enhance the ability of the mother with mental illness to raise children while continuing psychiatric care:

1. *Constant support person in the immediate social network to relieve the mother of 24-hour baby care and to monitor her well-being.* This is a parent, husband, friend, neighbor, or an organized respite service.
2. *Education about childrearing and child development* at home and in the community.
3. *Early intervention programs* to stimulate the children and provide group support for the mothers.
4. *Pediatric support,* with extra awareness to reinforce positive development, to guide mothers, and to be alert to early signs of neglect and/or abuse of baby and/or deterioration of mother's mental state.
5. *Primary care for the mother,* with special attention to her reproductive health and needs for contraception.
6. *Adequate housing arrangements* when the family does not and cannot provide housing. Halfway houses, board and care homes, nursing homes, and cooperative apartments usually have rules prohibiting intimacy between residents, and sexual partners are not permitted to stay overnight. Subsidized (Federal Section 8) housing is sparse and available only to the handicapped; fathers and babies are not welcome (Posey 1990). Many mothers with mental illness are homeless, making up some of the 20% to 47% of the homeless who are deemed to be mentally ill. Many live in welfare hotels and other temporary and inadequate housing that cities and towns provide for the homeless. There is now no known existing group home for mothers who are mentally ill and their babies. Homes for unwed mothers and their babies have been started by antiabortion supporters, but these are few and far between and are not set up for those mothers who are mentally ill (Hinds 1990).

7. *Adequate financial support.* Unemployed mothers with chronic mental illness will need all of the welfare services that are available for themselves and their children. Some combination of SSI disability, Medicaid, and Aid to Families With Dependent Children (AFDC) will have to be packaged to provide minimal livable income. Education about and assistance with money management are necessary parts of rehabilitation.

8. *Vocational training.* Mothers with mental illness can gain self-esteem and make better use of birth control services if they are trained to do something in addition to child care. State rehabilitation services and counseling are advisable.

9. *Legal counsel.* Mothers with mental illness will need legal advocacy from time to time to help protect their rights in custody disputes and during those periods when they are unable to care for their babies. These are delicate cases and the stakes are high. Competent and sensitive counsel can be therapeutic and is absolutely necessary for both the patient and the mental health professionals to feel secure.

10. *Psychotherapy and psychopharmacology.* These basic psychiatric services must continue, and even be increased, when a woman with mental illness becomes a mother and faces all the developmental demands of motherhood. Every new mother finds a new baby taxing of her physical and emotional well-being. The normal mature and healthy mother can experience infantile neediness, frustration, rage, panic, and anxiety; an older, experienced parental person is always important to help the mother keep things in perspective. These needs are all the more exaggerated for the mother with major mental illness. The psychotherapist has an auxiliary role as such an adult, someone who can help give a context to the patient's concerns (Fraiberg et al. 1975; Lieberman 1990). New psychiatric symptoms must be evaluated in light of the meaning for the woman patient in her new role as mother. It is especially valuable to have a therapist who knew the woman prior to her pregnancy continue to follow her long-term. Flexibility is necessary: there must be a willingness to talk in-depth at times, supportively at other times, and as a stern parent at still other times, and to include the father of the baby or the patient's parents or foster parents to her baby when that seems indicated. As always, the woman with long-term mental illness needs someone to listen

attentively to her, to value her perceptions (Strauss and Estroff 1989), and to help her make sense of her world, which has become far more complex with the arrival of a baby (Coursey 1989; Katz 1989).

Model Program

There are now a few centers in the United States that are models of programs that successfully combine all 10 of the supports described above. Project Child of the Providence Center for Counselling and Psychiatric Services in Providence, Rhode Island, is directed by Haven Miles, and the center is directed by Fredericka B. Bettinger. Another center, Loretta Finnegan's Jefferson Family Center in Philadelphia, provides comprehensive care for drug-addicted mothers, some of whom are also mentally ill. A third center, Alicia Lieberman's program at San Francisco General Hospital, is based on Selma Fraiberg's methods of working with high-risk mothers and children. In each case, one individual person has been the creator and continuing driving force of the program, but the system no longer hinges on only one person. One-stop care for women in these extremely complicated psychosocial/medical situations is ideal. All professionals giving services in these programs subscribe to the same orientation that advocates for the right of women with mental illness to be mothers and ensures the myriad supports needed to allow them to mother.

The best predictor of any woman's ability to mother is having been mothered well enough herself. This is also true for women who develop mental illness. Once other problems are present—for example, character problems, alcoholism, drug abuse, homelessness—the chances of being able to adequately be a mother diminish.

The basic philosophy of the model program is that the child's own mother is his or her best mother no matter how impaired the person is; therefore, bolstering the mother in every possible way is preferred to placing the child elsewhere. Project Child focuses on mothers with psychotic illnesses and their offspring from birth to age 5 years. For the child, the program addresses the high risk of cognitive and emotional developmental delay. For the mother, the program provides education about mothering, including nurturing and organizing. In the "moms-kids" group, mothers receive gentle example and a normal social context in which to learn. An individual treatment program is developed for each woman patient by the mental health counselors, child psychologist, and staff psychiatrist.

The following model program resources provide partial solutions for the long-term patient:

1. A teacher is identified as the constant support person within the program. The teacher and the other team members work in conjunction and do not compete with others in the mother's environment. Everything possible is done to encourage involvement of the father, the grandmother, or another person who shares the goal of caring for this mother and child. The program is part of an umbrella community mental health organization that has 24-hour emergency services available.

2. Education about childrearing is provided at the center, with a nursery program bringing mothers together with their children. Education is by example and by reinforcement of positive mother-child relations. There is direct instruction on interacting, for example, by playing a throw-and-catch beanbag game that increases the mother's interest, eye contact, and powers of observation. The program is highly structured, and the limits defined for activity and time give a sense of safety and predictability. Each mother keeps a journal at the center in which she writes about what she has observed that is new during that particular morning session; these are prized private documents, highly regarded by the mothers and respected by the staff. The mothers are actively invited to the program, even transported there, so that they and their children can regularly attend and can see the value of consistency and relationships. The mothers are not judged, punished, or excluded; their cooperation is genuinely sought out and desired.

3. Intervention starts at birth with mothers who have been identified in the maternity programs. The first meeting with a staff person takes place before the mother leaves the hospital. Staff visit in the home as needed, but, as soon as possible, mother and baby are expected to attend the center. This decreases the sense of isolation many new mothers experience. The transportation that the center provides is an essential service to permit full cooperation.

4. Pediatric care is arranged when needed to supplement well-child visits. There is continuous surveillance of the well-being of the child. Nutrition is taught through sharing meals and snacks to-

gether. Good child care can be reinforced and any suspicious lack of care can be explored. Although the program is only two mornings a week for less than 2 hours, when there is trouble in a family, home visits are arranged and contact can be daily. If and when a child needs to be removed from a dangerous family situation (e.g., when the mother decompensates or someone becomes abusive), the child can continue to come to the program from a temporary placement and meet the mother, under supervision, at the center.

5. Teachers inquire about the mother's well-being. When mothers need some medical help, they have each other and the staff to rely on for recommendations and for interested listeners afterward. Enhanced involvement with their young children increases mothers' motivation to use birth control in order to space children. Because the mothers derive so much from the program and see how fascinating and fulfilling a job mothering can be, they often elect to use birth control and even sometimes seek voluntary sterilization.

6. Psychotherapy and medication are available through the umbrella community mental health organization; the mother's psychiatric care is thus coordinated easily.

Housing, financial support, vocational training, and legal counsel, although important resources, are not directly available through Project Child. However, close connections to the relevant state agencies are maintained and utilization is encouraged.

Although this program is costly, in the long run it is cost-effective. Only one of 40 parents in 2 years required rehospitalization. Children who lagged behind peers in physical, social, and mental development (especially social and language skills) come to a par with their peers.

Even with sufficient supports, the combined stress of raising a child and having a mental illness is significant. Once the child is grown, and he or she leaves home, the mother with mental illness may be able to venture out into the world herself. She will continue to suffer from the mental illness and need to cope with life with her ongoing disease. One mother (E. Ohlrich, halfway house newsletter, 1990), now middle-aged, whose child is a young adult now out on his own, wrote about her own movement into the wider world outside of home:

> When I first realized that my mental illness might remain with me for many years, I wondered what to do. How could I get out into the world

when I had a disease that made me unable to be with others for long periods of time?

As I moved from a long period of isolation in my parents' home, during which I tried to be a parent, myself, to a son, into intensive group therapy, I found that my isolation distorted my perspective. I had developed a stigma.

Now, I have joined the Rehabilitation Program. It is communal, community oriented, and the talented staff are able to tap the talent which are resources within each one of its clients.

I still feel new here. I don't always show up. I am finally feeling like a human being, rather than feeling separate because of things in my mind.

The few existing programs that support and educate mothers with serious and long-term mental illness are still being developed. There is ample room for many more creative programs for this population that will not only support the parents with mental illness but also serve to buttress the work of the mental health clinicians. However, in order to know the directions that programming for this population of parents should take, we need to have greater understanding of the current psychological, medical, and genetic factors that are brought into play. If clinicians are to work most effectively, they need the support that research in the area of sex and reproductive issues for this population can provide. In the final chapter, we summarize those research areas that are key to providing more data for clinicians and for patients and their families.

Chapter 13

Conclusions and Recommendations

*W*e have shown how the treatment and care of pregnant women with long-term mental illness is challenging work for mental health clinicians. After surveying our own anecdotal experiences and that of others, we conclude that more systematic attention is needed and offer the following summary of further questions and recommendations.

Research Questions

Staff-Related Questions

1. What are the skills needed by psychiatric staff to better care for pregnant psychotic patients? What are the best ways of training both psychiatric staff and patients about human sexuality, sexually transmitted diseases, and contraception? How can this training be integrated as a basic service of all programs for the population with long-term mental illness?

2. How can we better work with families to address their concerns about their responsibilities for reproductive issues for their daughters with mental illness? How can we as professionals work more closely and constructively with families?

3. How can we keep abreast of the special treatment needs of women who abuse drugs and have mental illness? How can we program for women with dual diagnosis to address both concerns? How do we counsel about drugs and AIDS in a meaningful, nonpunitive way?

4. How can we face the realities of homeless mentally ill mothers and their sexual victimization and provide relevant interventions?

5. How can we identify women with mental illness during their first pregnancies and help to address their psychological needs with extra support and appropriate therapy to optimize care for mothers and children? How can we be present for our patients who make conscious reproductive choices?

6. How can we better motivate and train those women with mental illness who choose to mother to improve their parenting skills?
7. How can we provide anticipatory genetic counseling? How can mentally ill people, married or partnered and living in the community, receive appropriate and accurate information about genetic and other risks of having children? (Capron et al. 1979; Kessler 1979; Levine 1979)

Epidemiological-Demographic Questions

1. What is the incidence of pregnancies among patients with long-term mental illness in the hospital and in the community?
2. What is the prevalence of people with long-term mental illness providing primary and/or partial child care for their children?
3. What are the special needs of parents with mental illness who have infants? toddlers? school-age children? adolescent children?
4. How can data on pregnancy experiences of this population be routinely collected and collated?

Patient-Related Questions

1. What do female patients with long-term mental illness want in terms of the opportunity to have children? How can their needs be addressed both in psychological and in practical terms? Are there any forums that address these issues for patients? Can they be replicated?
2. Are pregnancies easy or difficult for these women? How do they respond to prepared childbirth? Are the labor and delivery easy, difficult, or remarkable in any way? For psychotic women, what percentage of deliveries are precipitous, and how can patients, working with professional staff, be taught to anticipate and feel labor more realistically?
3. What type of gynecological care do women with mental illness want? What is the optimal obstetrical-gynecological care for this population?
4. Who are the patients who most benefit from keeping their babies? What are the benefits and risks to the mental health of parents who have long-term mental illness?

5. What are the effects of psychotropic medications on the female reproductive cycle? (More and continued investigations are needed. Medications need to be routinely tested on women of different ages as well as on men.)

Recommendations

1. *Increase the visibility of patients with long-term mental illness and awareness of their concerns about sex, pregnancy, and parenting.* This needs to occur within national organizations and within local hospitals and training programs.
2. *Make updated information on psychotropic medications in pregnancy available to all psychiatrists.* In addition to the Lithium Registry, register all major pregnancy side effects of psychopharmacologic drugs.
3. *Develop resources that respect the rights of people with long-term mental illness to have normal sexual relationships.* These resources include private space in hospitals, permitting couples in halfway houses, and developing housing for one parent, or couples, with a child.
4. *Develop specialty inpatient programming and units to treat pregnant psychotic patients who may also have drug addictions.*
5. *Develop ongoing parenting support programs.*

This monograph has presented a compendium of the complex problems of sex and reproduction in patients with long-term mental illness that are currently facing clinicians today. Our hope is that increased awareness of the reproductive issues among persons with mental illness will lead to an atmosphere in which open discussion, clinical research, and mutual support will supplant long-standing denial of the existence of these issues. The natural reproductive life of women and men with long-term mental illness must be addressed by clinicians, patients, their families, and the public. It is a test of the maturity of our profession and of our society whether or not, and how, we face up to these deeply human challenges.

References

Abernethy V: Sexual knowledge, attitudes, and practices of young female psychiatric patients. Arch Gen Psychiatry 30:180–182, 1974

Abernethy VD, Grunebaum H: Toward a family planning program in psychiatric hospitals. Am J Public Health 62:1638–1646, 1972

Abernethy VD, Grunebaum H: Family planning in two psychiatric hospitals. Fam Plann Perspect 5:94–99, 1973

Akhtar S, Thomson JA Jr: Schizophrenia and sexuality: a review and a report of twelve unusual cases, Part I. J Clin Psychiatry 41:134–142, 1980a

Akhtar S, Thomson JA Jr: Schizophrenia and sexuality: a review and a report of twelve unusual cases, Part II. J Clin Psychiatry 41:166–174, 1980b

Akhtar S, Crocker E, Dickey N, et al: Overt sexual behavior among psychiatric inpatients. Diseases of the Nervous System 38:359–361, 1977

Albretsen CS: Hospitalization of post-partum psychotic patients, together with babies and husbands. Acta Psychiatr Scand Suppl 203:179–182, 1968

American Psychiatric Association: Diagnostic and Statistical Manual of Mental Disorders, 3rd Edition, Revised. Washington, DC, American Psychiatric Association, 1987

American Psychiatric Association, Task Force on DSM-IV: DSM-IV Options Book: Work in Progress. Washington, DC, American Psychiatric Association, 1991

Ananth J: Side effects on fetus and infant of psychotropic drugs used during pregnancy. Int J Pharmacopsychiatry 11:246–260, 1976

Anderson EW: A study of the sexual life in psychoses associated with childbirth. Journal of Mental Science 79:137–149, 1933

Anthony EJ: A group of murderous mothers. Acta Psychotherapeutica Psychosomatica 7(suppl):1–6, 1959

Apfel RJ, Fisher SM: To Do No Harm: DES and the Dilemmas of Modern Medicine. New Haven, CT, Yale University Press, 1984

Apfel R, Handel M: Madness and the loss of motherhood: the legacy of a double stigma. Paper presented at the 142nd annual meeting of the American Psychiatric Association, San Francisco, CA, May 1989

Apfel RJ, Mazor MD: Psychiatry and reproductive medicine, in Comprehensive Textbook of Psychiatry/V, Fifth Edition, Vol 2. Edited by Kaplan HI, Sadock BJ. Baltimore, MD, Williams & Wilkins, 1989, pp 1331–1339

Arras JD: HIV and childrearing. AIDS and reproductive decisions: having children in fear and trembling. Milbank Q 68:353–382, 1990

Aruffo JF, Coverdale JH, Chacko RC, et al: Knowledge about AIDS among women psychiatric outpatients. Hosp Community Psychiatry 41:326–328, 1990

Astrachan J: The psychological management of the family whose child is born dead (Chapter 81), in Gynecology and Obstetrics, Vol 6. Edited by Sciarra JJ. New York, Harper & Row, 1983, pp 1–9

Auchincloss E: Conflict among psychiatric residents in response to pregnancy. Am J Psychiatry 139:818–821, 1982

Bachrach LL: Deinstitutionalization and women: assessing the consequences of public policy. Am Psychol 39:1171–1177, 1984

Bachrach LL: Chronic mentally ill women: emergence and legitimation of program issues. Hosp Community Psychiatry 36:1063–1069, 1985

Bachrach LL: The context of care for the chronic mental patient with substance abuse problems. Psychiatr Q 58(1):3–14, 1986–1987

Bachrach LL: Defining chronic mental illness: a concept paper. Hosp Community Psychiatry 39:383–388, 1988

Bachrach LL, Nadelson CC (eds): Treating Chronically Mentally Ill Women. Washington, DC, American Psychiatric Press, 1988

Baer JW, Dwyer PC, Lewitter-Koehler S: Knowledge about AIDS among psychiatric inpatients. Hosp Community Psychiatry 39:986–988, 1988

Baker AA: Psychiatric Disorders in Obstetrics. Oxford, UK, Blackwell Scientific, 1967

Bancroft J: Sexual problems in psychiatric illness, in Human Sexuality and Its Problems. Edited by Bancroft J. Edinburgh, UK, Churchill, Livingstone, 1983, pp 360–362

Barden CA: The pregnant therapist. Journal of Psychosocial Mental Health Services 23(9):18–22, 1985

Bardenstein KK, McGlashan TH: Gender differences in schizophrenia. Poster presented at the 139th annual meeting of the American Psychiatric Association, Washington, DC, May 1986

Barton WE: Administration in Psychiatry. Springfield, IL, Charles C Thomas, 1962, pp 219–221 [on sexual misconduct]

Baum OE, Herring C: The pregnant psychotherapist in training: some preliminary findings and impressions. Am J Psychiatry 132:419–422, 1975

Beck JC, Van der Kolk B: Reports of childhood incest and current behavior of chronically hospitalized psychotic women. Am J Psychiatry 144:1474–1476, 1987

Bender L: Psychiatric mechanisms in child murderers. J Nerv Ment Dis 80:32–47, 1934

Benedek E: The fourth world of the pregnant therapist. J Am Med Wom Assoc 28:365–368, 1973

Bennett MB, Handel MH, Pearsall D: Behavioral differences between female and male hospitalized chronically mentally ill patients, in Treating Chronically Mentally Ill Women. Edited by Bachrach LL, Nadelson CC. Washington, DC, American Psychiatric Press, 1988, pp 29–43

Benvenuti P: Psychosis of fatherhood: a clinical study. Paper presented at the Marcé Society, Keele, UK, September 1988

Bieber I, Bieber TB: Post-partum reactions in men and women. J Am Acad Psychoanal 6:511–519, 1978

Bluglass K: Infant deaths, in Motherhood and Mental Illness: Causes and Consequences. Edited by Kumar R, Brockington IF. London, Wright, 1988, pp 212–246

Bourget D, Bradford JM: Affective disorder & homicide: a case of familial filicide: theoretical and clinical considerations. Can J Psychiatry 32:222–225, 1987

Boyd D, Brown DW: Electroconvulsive therapy in mental disorders associated with childbearing. Journal of the Missouri State Medical Association 45:573–579, 1948

Braham S, Houser HB, Cline A, et al: Evaluations of the social needs of nonhospitalized chronically ill persons. Journal of Chronic Diseases 28:401–419, 1975

Brandon S: Depression after childbirth. BMJ 284:613–614, 1982

Braverman A, Roux JD: Postpartum depression. Obstet Gynecol 52:730–736, 1978

Brewer C: Incidence of post-abortion psychosis: a prospective study. BMJ 1:476–477, 1977

Brewer C: Post abortion psychosis, in Mental Illness in Pregnancy and the Puerperium. Edited by Sandler M. New York, Oxford University Press, 1978, pp 52–58

Bridges NA, Smith JM: The pregnant therapist and the seriously disturbed patient: managing long-term psychotherapeutic treatment. Psychiatry 51:104–109, 1988

Briggs GC, Freeman RK, Yaffa SJ: Drugs in Pregnancy and Lactation, 3rd Edition. Baltimore, MD, Williams & Wilkins, 1990

Brockington IF, Kumar R (eds): Motherhood and Mental Illness. London, Academic Press; New York, Grune & Stratton, 1982

Brockington IF, Cernik KF, Schofield EM, et al: Puerperal psychosis: phenomena and diagnosis. Arch Gen Psychiatry 38:829–833, 1981

Brown K, Heidelberg S: For better or worse: intermarriage in the young adult chronic population. J Psychosoc Nurs Ment Health Serv 23(3):18–23, 1985

Browne WJ, Palmer AJ: A preliminary study of schizophrenic women who murdered their children. Hosp Community Psychiatry 26:71, 75, 1975

Browning DH: Patients' reactions to their therapists' pregnancies. Journal of the American Academy of Child Psychiatry 13:468–482, 1974

Burgess HA: When a patient on lithium is pregnant. Am J Nurs 79:1989–1990, 1979

Burgess HA: Schizophrenia in pregnancy. Issues in Health Care of Women 2:61–69, 1980

Burns K, Melamed J, Burns W, et al: Chemical dependence and clinical depression in pregnancy. J Clin Psychol 41:851–854, 1985

Burr WA, Falek A, Strauss LT, et al: Fertility in psychiatric outpatients. Hosp Community Psychiatry 30:527–531, 1979

Caplan L: A reporter at large—an open adoption, Part 1. New Yorker, May 21, 1990a, pp 40–68

Caplan L: A reporter at large—an open adoption, Part 2. New Yorker, May 28, 1990b, pp 73–75

Capron AM, Lapper M, Murray RF, et al: Genetic Counselling: Facts, Values, and Norms. New York, Alan R Liss, 1979

Carmack BJ, Corwin TA: Nursing care of the schizophrenic maternity patient during labor. Matern Child Nurs J 5:107–113, 1980

Carmen EH, Brady SM: AIDS risk and prevention for the chronic mentally ill. Hosp Community Psychiatry 41:652–657, 1990

Carmen EH, Rieker PP, Mills T: Victims of violence and psychiatric illness. Am J Psychiatry 141:378–383, 1984

Casiano ME, Hawkins DR: Major mental illness and childbearing: a role for the consultation-liaison psychiatrist in obstetrics. Psychiatr Clin North Am 10:35–51, 1987

Cath SH, Gurwitt AR, Ross JM (eds): Father and Child: Developmental and Clinical Perspectives. Boston, MA, Little, Brown, 1982

Cavenar JO, Weddington WW: Fatherhood and psychosis. Milit Med 144:490–491, 1979

Chamberlin J: On Our Own: Patient-Controlled Alternatives to the Mental Health System (1977). London, Mind Publications, 1988

Chang S, Renshaw D: Psychosis and pregnancy. Compr Ther 12(10):36–41, 1986

Chapman J, McGhie A: An approach to the psychotherapy of cognitive dysfunction in schizophrenia. Br J Med Psychol 36:253–260, 1963

Chasnoff IJ, Burns KA, Burne WJ: Cocaine use in pregnancy: perinatal morbidity and mortality. Neurotoxicol Teratol 9:291–293, 1987

Chasnoff IJ, Landress HJ, Barrett ME: The prevalence of illicit-drug or alcohol use during pregnancy and discrepancies in mandatory reporting in Pinellas County, Florida. N Engl J Med 322:1202–1206, 1990

Cheetham RWS, Rzadkowolski A, Rataemane S: Psychiatric disorders of the puerperium in South African women of Nguni origin: a pilot study. S Afr Med J 60:502–506, 1981

Chervenak FA, McCullough L: A practical method of analysis of the physician's ethical obligations to the fetus and pregnant woman in obstetrical care. Resident and Staff Physician 35:79–87, 1989

Chesler P: Mothers on Trial: The Battle for Children and Custody. Seattle, WA, Seal Press, 1987

Childers SE, Harding CM. Gender, premorbid social functioning, and long-term outcome in DSM-III schizophrenia. Schizophr Bull 16:309–318, 1990

Clare AW: Psychiatric and Social Aspects of Premenstrual Complaint (Psychological Medicine monograph supplement). Cambridge, UK, Cambridge University Press, 1983

Clark MR: Fluphenazine decanoate during pregnancy. Am J Psychiatry 134:815–816, 1977

Cohen DD, Tanenbaum RL: Sexuality education for staff in long-term psychiatric hospitals. Hosp Community Psychiatry 36:187–189, 1985

Cohen IM: Complication of chlorpromazine therapy. Am J Psychiatry 113:115–121, 1956

Cohen LM: A current perspective of pseudocyesis. Am J Psychiatry 139:1140–1144, 1982

Cohen LS, Rosenbaum JF, Heller VL: Prescribing lithium for pregnant women. Am J Psychiatry 145:772–773, 1988

Cohen LS, Heller VL, Rosenbaum JF: Treatment guidelines for psychotropic drug use in pregnancy. Psychosomatics 30:25–33, 1989a

Cohen LS, Rosenbaum JF, Heller VL: Panic attack–associated placental abruption: a case report. J Clin Psychiatry 50:266–267, 1989b

Cohen RL: Psychiatric Consultation in Childbirth Settings: Parent- and Child-Oriented Approaches. New York, Plenum, 1988

Cohen S, Taub N (eds): Reproductive Laws for the 1990s. Clifton, NJ, Humana Press, 1989a

Cohler BJ, Musick J (eds): Intervention Among Psychiatrically Impaired Parents and Their Young Children (New Directions for Mental Health Services, Vol 24). San Francisco, CA, Jossey-Bass, 1984

Cohler BJ, Gallant DH, Grunebaum H, et al: Child-care attitudes and development of young children of mentally ill and well mothers. Psychol Rep 46:31–46, 1980

Cohn CK, Rosenblatt S, Faillace LA: Capgras' syndrome presenting as postpartum psychosis. South Med J 70:942, 1977

Cook PE, Howe B: Unusual use of ultrasound in a paranoid patient (letter). Can Med Assoc J 131:539, 1984

Cournos F, Empfield M, Horwath E, et al: HIV infection in state hospitals: case reports and long-term management strategies. Hosp Community Psychiatry 41:163–166, 1990

Coursey RD: Psychotherapy with persons suffering from schizophrenia: the need for a new agenda. Schizophr Bull 15:349–353, 1989

Coverdale JH, Aruffo JA: Family planning needs of female chronic psychiatric outpatients. Am J Psychiatry 146:1489–1491, 1989

Cox JL, Holden JM, Sagovsky R: Detection of postnatal depression: development of the 10-item Edinburgh postnatal depression scale. Br J Psychiatry 150:782–786, 1987

Craine LS, Henson CE, Colliver JA, et al: Prevalence of a history of sexual abuse among female psychiatric patients in a state hospital system. Hosp Community Psychiatry 39:300–304, 1988

Cutting J: Physical illness and psychosis. Br J Psychiatry 136:109–119, 1980

DalPozzo EE, Marsh FH: Psychosis and pregnancy: some new ethical and legal dilemmas for the physician. Am J Obstet Gynecol 156:425–427, 1987

Dalton K: Depression After Childbirth. London, Oxford University Press, 1980

Davenport YB, Adland U: Postpartum psychoses in female and male bipolar manic-depressive patients. Am J Orthopsychiatry 52:288–297, 1982

David HP: Post abortion and post partum psychiatric hospitalizations. Ciba Found Symp 115:150–164, 1985

D'Ercole A, Skodol AE, Struening E, et al: Diagnosis of physical illness in psychiatric patients using Axis III and a standardized medical history. Hosp Community Psychiatry 42:395–400, 1991

DeLisi LE, Crow TJ: Evidence for a sex chromosome locus for schizophrenia. Schizophr Bull 15:431–440, 1989

Donlon PT: Sexual symptoms of incipient schizophrenic psychoses. Medical Aspects of Human Sexuality 10(11):69–70, 1976

D'Orban PT: Women who kill their children. Br J Psychiatry 134:560–571, 1979

Dorman BW, Schmidt JD: Association of priapism in phenothiazine therapy. J Urol 116:51–53, 1976

Doten P: When grandparents parent: a support group helps people who are raising their children's children. Boston Globe, July 3, 1990, pp 21, 27

Drew FL: The epidemiology of secondary amenorrhea. Journal of Chronic Diseases 14:396–407, 1961

Dunner DL, Vijayalakshmy P, Fieve R: Life events at the onset of bipolar affective illness. Am J Psychiatry 136:508–511, 1979

DuVal M: Giving Love . . . and Schizophrenia. The Experiences of Patients and Families: First Person Accounts. Arlington, VA, National Alliance for the Mentally Ill, Publ No 2 (Second Series), 1989

Dwyer E: Homes for the Mad: Life Inside Two Nineteenth-Century Asylums. New Brunswick, NJ, Rutgers University Press, 1987

Eastwood J, Spielvogel A, Wile J: Countertransference risks when women treat women. Paper presented at the 142nd annual meeting of the American Psychiatric Association, San Francisco, CA, May 1989

Eaton WW: Marital status and schizophrenia. Acta Psychiatr Scand 52:320–329, 1975

Eckerd M, Hurt S, Severino S: Late luteal phase dysphoric disorder: relationship to personality disorders. Journal of Personality Disorders 3:338–344, 1989

Elliott R, Brookes T: Beyond the blues. North by Northeast 4(4):6–12, 1989

Ely E: A special love. Boston Globe, December 26, 1990, p 13

Endicott J, Halbreich U, Schacht S, et al: Premenstrual changes and affective disorders. Psychosom Med 43:519–529, 1981

Endo M, Daiguji M, Asano Y, et al: Periodic psychosis recurring in association with menstrual cycle. J Clin Psychiatry 39:456–466, 1978

Erlenmeyer-Kimling L: Mortality rates in the offspring of schizophrenic parents and a physiological advantage hypothesis. Nature 220:798–800, 1968

Erlenmeyer-Kimling L, Nicol S, Rainer JD, et al: Changes in fertility rates of schizophrenic patients in New York State. Am J Psychiatry 125:916–927, 1968

Estroff SE: Making It Crazy: An Ethnology of Psychiatric Clients in an American Community. Berkeley, CA, University of California Press, 1981

Estroff SE: Self, identity and subjective experiences of schizophrenia: in search of the subject. Schizophr Bull 15:189–196, 1989

Fava M, Fava GA, Kellner R, et al: Depression and hostility in hyperprolactinemia. Progress in Neuro-Psychopharmacology and Biological Psychiatry 6:479–482, 1982

Fawcett J, York R: Spouses' physical and psychological symptoms during pregnancy and the postpartum. Nurs Res 35:144–148, 1986

Feinberg M: Being normal. The Boston Globe Magazine, November 20, 1988, p 24

Felthous AR, Robinson DB, Conroy RW: Prevention of recurrent menstrual psychosis by an oral contraceptive. Am J Psychiatry 137:245–246, 1980

Finnegan LP: Drug dependence in pregnancy: clinical management of mother and child. (Service Research Monograph Series; DHEW Publ No ADM-79-678). Washington, DC, Department of Health, Education and Welfare, 1979

Finnegan LP: Neonatal abstinence syndrome: assessment and pharmacotherapy, in Neonatal Therapy: An Update. Edited by Rubaltelli F, Granati B. New York, Elsevier (Biomedical Division), 1986, pp 122–146

Finnegan LP: Influence of maternal drug dependence on the newborn, in Toxicologic and Pharmacologic Principles in Pediatrics. Edited by Kacew S, Lock S. New York, Hemisphere Publishing, 1988, pp 184–198

Fisher LY: Nursing management of pregnant psychotic patients during labor and delivery. J Obstet Gynecol Neonatal Nurs 17:25–28, 1988

Flint N, Stewart RB: Amenorrhea in psychiatric patients. Arch Gen Psychiatry 40:589, 1983

Flynn L: The stigma of mental illness, in Families of the Mentally Ill: Coping and Adaptation (New Directions for Mental Health Services). Edited by Hatfield AB. San Francisco, CA, Jossey-Bass, 1987, pp 53–60

Food and Drug Administration: Risk factors of drugs. Federal Register 44:37434–37467, 1980

Forcier KI: Management and care of pregnant psychiatric patients. J Psychosoc Nurs Ment Health Serv 28(2):11–16, 1990

Fraiberg S, Adelson E, Shapiro V: Ghosts in the nursery: a psychoanalytic approach to the problems of impaired infant-mother relationships. Journal of the American Academy of Child Psychiatry 14:387–421, 1975

Frank E, Kupper DJ, Jacob M, et al: Pregnant-related affective episodes among women with recurrent depression. Am J Psychiatry 144:288–293, 1987

Frank JB: Pregnancy and leadership: case study from an inpatient unit. Psychiatry 53:77–84, 1990

Freud S: Psycho–analytic notes on an autobiographical account of a case of paranoia [The Schreber Case] (1911), in the Standard Edition of the Complete Psychological Works of Sigmund Freud, Vol 12. Translated and edited by Strachey J. London, Hogarth Press, 1958, pp 3–82

Friedman S, Harrison G: Sexual histories, attitudes, and behavior of schizophrenic and "normal" women. Arch Sex Behav 13:555–567, 1984

Frisch RE: Body fat, menarche, fitness, and fertility. Hum Reprod 2:521–533, 1987

Frisch RE: Fatness and fertility. Sci Am 3:88–95, 1988

Gallagher J: Fetus as patient, in Reproductive Laws for the 1990s. Edited by Cohen S, Taub N. Clifton, NJ, Humana Press, 1989, pp 185–235

Gartrell N: Increased libido in women receiving trazodone. Am J Psychiatry 143:781–782, 1986

Garvey MJ, Tuason VB, Lumry AE, et al: Occurrence of depression in the postpartum state. J Affective Disord 5:97–101, 1983

Gelder M: Hormones and post-partum depression, in Mental Illness in Pregnancy and the Puerperium. Edited by Sandler M. New York, Oxford University Press, 1978, pp 80–90

Gelenberg AJ: Pregnancy, psychotropic drugs, and psychiatric disorders. Psychosomatics 27:216–217, 1986

Geller JL: Women's accounts of psychiatric illness and institutionalization. Hosp Community Psychiatry 36:1056–1062, 1985

Ghadirian AM, Chouinard G, Annable L: Sexual dysfunction and plasma prolactin levels in neuroleptic-treated schizophrenic outpatients. J Nerv Ment Dis 170:463–467, 1982

Ginath Y: Psychoses in males in relation to their wives' pregnancy and childbirth. Israel Annals of Psychiatry 12:227–237, 1974

Gitlin MJ, Pasnau RO: Psychiatric syndromes linked to reproductive function in women: a review of current knowledge. Am J Psychiatry 146:1413–1422, 1989

Glick ID, Stewart D: A new drug treatment for premenstrual exacerbation of schizophrenia. Compr Psychiatry 21:281–287, 1980

Godschalx SM: Experiences and coping strategies of people with schizophrenia. Unpublished doctoral dissertation, University of Utah, College of Nursing, Salt Lake City, UT, 1987

Goffman E: Stigma: Notes on the Management of Spoiled Identity. Englewood Cliffs, NJ, Prentice-Hall, 1963

Gold JH (ed): The Psychiatric Implications of Menstruation. Washington, DC, American Psychiatric Press, 1985

Goldberg HL, DiMascio A: Psychotropic drugs in pregnancy, in Psychopharmacology: A Generation of Progress. Edited by Lipton MA, DiMascio A, Killam KF. New York, Raven, 1978, pp 1047–1055

Goldman N, Ravid R: Community surveys: sex differences in mental illness, in The Mental Health of Women. Edited by Guttentag M, Selasin S, Belle O. New York, Academic, 1980, pp 31–55

Goldstein JM: Gender differences in the course of schizophrenia. Am J Psychiatry 145:684–689, 1988

Goldstein JM, Kreisman D: Gender, family environment and schizophrenia. Psychol Med 18:861–872, 1988

Goldstein JM, Link B: Gender and the expression of schizophrenia. J Psychiatr Res 22:141–155, 1988

Goldstein JM, Tsuang MT: Gender and schizophrenia: an introduction and synthesis of findings. Schizophr Bull 16:179–183, 1990

Goldstein JM, Tsuang MT, Faraone S: Gender and schizophrenia: implications for understanding the heterogeneity of the illness. Psychiatry Res 28:243–253, 1989

Gotlib IH, Whiffen VE, Mount JH, et al: Prevalence rates and demographic characteristics associated with depression in pregnancy and the postpartum. J Consult Clin Psychol 57:269–274, 1989

Gottlieb JI, Lustberg T: Phenothiazine-induced priapism: a case report. Am J Psychiatry 134:1445–1446, 1977

Gregory BA: The menstrual cycle and its disorders in psychiatric patients, I. J Psychsom Res 2:61–79, 1957

Grob G: The Inner World of American Psychiatry, 1890–1940: Selected Correspondence. New Brunswick, NJ, Rutgers University Press, 1985

Grunebaum HU, Abernethy V: Ethical issues in family planning for hospitalized psychiatric patients. Am J Psychiatry 132:237–240, 1975

Grunebaum HU, Abernethy V, Rofman ES, et al: The family planning attitudes, practices, and motivations of mental patients. Am J Psychiatry 128:96, 1971

Grunebaum HU, Abernethy V, Clough L, et al: Staff attitudes toward a family planning service in the mental hospital. Community Ment Health J 11:280–285, 1975

Grunebaum HU, Cohler B, Kauffman C, et al: Children of depressed and schizophrenic mothers. Child Psychiatry Hum Dev 8:219–228, 1978

Grunebaum HU, Weiss JL, Cohler BJ, et al: Mentally Ill Mothers and Their Children. Chicago, IL, University of Chicago Press, 1982

Habgood J: Postnatal depression: exposing the blues . . . and treating them. Nursing Times, August 1985, pp 4–11

Halbreich U, Endicott J: Possible involvement of endorphin withdrawal or imbalance in specific premenstrual syndromes and postpartum depression. Med Hypotheses 7:1045–1058, 1981

Halbreich U, Endicott J, Nee J: Premenstrual depressive changes: value of differentiation. Arch Gen Psychiatry 40:535–542, 1983

Halbreich U, Rojansky N, Bakhai Y, et al: Menstrual irregularities associated with Bupropion treatment. J Clin Psychiatry 52:15–16, 1991

Halonen JS, Passman RH: Relaxation training and expectation in the treatment of postpartum distress. J Consult Clin Psychol 53:839–845, 1985

Hamilton JA: Postpartum psychiatric syndromes. Psychiatr Clin North Am 12:89–103, 1989

Hamilton JA, Parry BL: Sex-related differences in clinical drug response: implications for women's health. J Am Med Wom Assoc 38(5):126–132, 1983

Hamilton JA, Sichel DA: Prophylactic measures, in Postpartum Psychiatric Illness: A Picture Puzzle. Edited by Hamilton JA, Harberger PN. Baltimore, MD, University of Pennsylvania Press, 1992

Hamilton JA, Parry BL, Alagna S, et al: Premenstrual mood changes: a guide to evaluation and treatment. Psychiatric Annals 14:426–435, 1984

Handel MH: Deferred pelvic examinations: a purposeful omission in the care of mentally ill women. Hosp Community Psychiatry 36:1070–1074, 1985

Handel MH, Bennett MB: Development of a program to improve the care of chronically mentally ill women, in Treating Chronically Mentally Ill Women. Edited by Bachrach LL, Nadelson CC. Washington, DC, American Psychiatric Press, 1988, pp 111–123

Harrison M: Maternal-fetal conflict in proper perspective. Paper presented at the 143rd annual meeting of the American Psychiatric Association, New York, May 1990

Hartmann C: Psychotic mothers and their babies. Nurs Outlook 16:32–36, 1968

Hartocollis P: Hospital romances: some vicissitudes of transference. Bull Menninger Clin 28:62–71, 1964

Harvey I, McGrath G: Psychiatric morbidity in spouses of women admitted to a mother and baby unit. Br J Psychiatry 152:506–510, 1988

Hatfield AB: Patients' accounts of stress and coping in schizophrenia. Hosp Community Psychiatry 40:1141–1145, 1989

Hauser LA: Pregnancy and psychiatric drugs. Hosp Community Psychiatry 36:817–818, 1985

Haverkamp F, Propping P, Hilger T: Is there an increase of reproductive rates in schizophrenics? One critical review of the literature. Eur Arch Psychiatry Neurol Sci 232:439–450, 1982

Hays P: Taxonomic map of the schizophrenias, with special reference to puerperal psychosis. BMJ 2:755–757, 1978

Hays P, Douglass A: A comparison of puerperal psychosis and the schizophreniform variant of manic-depression. Acta Psychiatr Scand 69:177–181, 1984

Herz E: Psychological repercussions of pregnancy loss. Psychiatric Annals 14:454–457, 1984

Hidas G, Magal V, Epstein L: The risk of post-abortion psychosis and postpartum psychosis for the mental health of schizophrenic women. Unpublished manuscript, Department of Family & Community Health, Kupat Holim, Haifa, and Department of Psychiatry, Central Emek Hospital, Afula, 1989

Hilgard JR, Newman MF: Anniversaries in mental illness. Psychiatry 22:113–121, 1959

Hilger T, Propping P, Haverkamp F: Is there an increase of reproductive rates in schizophrenics? III: an investigation in Nordbaden (SW German): results and discussion. Archiv für Psychiatrie und Nervenkrankheiten 233:177–186, 1983

Hinds M: Abortion foes' centers guiding lives after births. New York Times (Sunday), May 13, 1990, Sect 1, pp 1, 22

Hodgson JE: Accurate pregnancy testing in tranquilized patients. JAMA 170:1890–1892, 1959

Hogarty GE, Goldberg SC, Schooler NR, et al: Drug and sociotherapy in the aftercare of schizophrenic patients, II: two–year relapse rates. Arch Gen Psychiatry 31:603–608, 1974a

Hogarty GE, Goldberg SC, Schooler NR, et al: Drug and sociotherapy in the aftercare of schizophrenic patients, III: adjustment of nonrelapsed patients. Arch Gen Psychiatry 31:609–618, 1974b

Holbrook T: Policing sexuality in a modern state hospital. Hosp Community Psychiatry 40:75–79, 1989

Hopwood JS: Child murder and insanity. Journal of Mental Science 73:95–108, 1927

Hubner MK: Cancer and infertility: longing for life. Journal of Psychosocial Oncology 7:1–19, 1989

Hurt LD, Ray CP: Postpartum disorders: mother-infant bonding on a psychiatric unit. J Psychosoc Nurs Ment Health Serv 23(2):15–20, 1985

Hurt SW, Schnurr PP, Severino SK, et al: Late luteal phase dysphoric disorder in 670 women evaluated for premenstrual complaints. Am J Psychiatry 149:525–530, 1992

Inwood DG (ed): Recent Advances in Postpartum Psychiatric Disorders. Washington, DC, American Psychiatric Association, 1985

Istvan J: Stress, anxiety, and birth outcomes: a critical review of the evidence. Psychol Bull 100:331–348, 1986

Jacobson SJ, Jones K, Johnson K, et al: Prospective multicentre study of pregnancy outcome after lithium exposure during first trimester. Lancet 339:530–533, 1992

Jarrahi-Zadeh AQ, Kane FJ Jr, Van de Castlf RL, et al: Emotional and cognitive changes in pregnancy and early puerperium. Br J Psychiatry 115:797–805, 1969

Jarvis W: Some effects of pregnancy and childbirth on men. J Am Psychoanal Assoc 10:689–701, 1962

Jason J: Child homicide spectrum. Am J Dis Child 137:579–581, 1983

Jeffrey R, Jeffrey P, Lyon A: Female infanticide and amniocentesis. Soc Sci Med 19:1207–1212, 1984

Jennings A, Jennings C, Sommer R, et al: A parents' survey of problems faced by mentally ill daughters. Hosp Community Psychiatry 38:668–670, 1987

Kadrmas A, Winokur G, Crowe R: Postpartum mania. Br J Psychiatry 135:551–554, 1979

Kallmann FJ: The Genetics of Schizophrenia: A Study of Heredity and Reproduction in the Families of 1,087 Schizophrenics. New York, JJ Augustin, 1938

Kane FJ, Treadway CR, Ewing JA: Emotional change associated with oral contraceptives in female psychiatric patients. Compr Psychiatry 10:16–30, 1969

Kaplan D: Disability rights perspectives on reproductive technologies and public policy, in Reproductive Laws for the 1990s. Edited by Cohen S, Taub N. Clifton, NJ, Humana Press, 1989, pp 241–247

Kaplan D, Reich R: The murdered child and his killers. Am J Psychiatry 133:809–813, 1976

Kaplan EH, Blackman LH: The husband's role in psychiatric illness associated with childrearing. Psychiatric Q 43:396–409, 1969

Kaplan HI, Sadock BJ (eds): Comprehensive Textbook of Psychiatry/V, 5th Edition. Baltimore, MD, Williams & Wilkins, 1989

Katz HM: A new agenda for psychotherapy of schizophrenia: response to Coursey. Schizophr Bull 15:355–359, 1989

Katz VL, Jenkins T, Haley L, et al: Catecholamine levels in pregnant physicians and nurses: a pilot study of stress and pregnancy. Obstet Gynecol 77:338–341, 1991

Kawashima H: Don't let my baby be like me (commentary). Hastings Cent Rep 18(4):27–28, 1988

Keitner G, Grof P: Sexual and emotional intimacy between psychiatric inpatients: formulating a policy. Hosp Community Psychiatry 32:188–193, 1981

Kendell RE, Wainwright S, Hailey A, et al: The influence of childbirth on psychiatric morbidity. Psychol Med 6:297–302, 1976

Kendell RE, Chalmers JC, Platz C: Epidemiology of puerperal psychoses. Br J Psychiatry 150:662–673, 1987

Kerfoot KM, Buckwalter KC: Postpartum affective disorders: the manias and depression of childbirth. Nurs Forum 20:296–317, 1981

Kerns LL: Treatment of mental disorders in pregnancy: a review of psychotropic drug risks and benefits. J Nerv Ment Dis 174:652–659, 1986

Kessler S: The genetic counselor as psychotherapist, in Genetic Counselling: Facts, Values, and Norms. Edited by Capron AM, Lapper M, Murray RF, et al. New York, Alan R Liss, 1979, pp 197–200

Klass P: Mothers with AIDS: a love story. New York Times Sunday Magazine, November 4, 1990, p 24

Kline CL: Emotional illness associated with childbirth: a study of 52 patients and the literature. Am J Obstet Gynecol 69(4):748–757, 1955

Kolbert E: Father's rights on adoption are expanded. New York Times, July 11, 1990, B1, 4

Kotkin J, Wilbert DE, Verburg D, et al: Thioridazine and sexual dysfunction. Am J Psychiatry 133:82–85, 1976

Kramer M: Menstrual epileptoid psychosis in an adolescent girl. Am J Dis Child 131:316–317, 1977

Krener P, Simmons MK, Hansen RL, et al: Effect of pregnancy on psychosis: life circumstances and psychiatric symptoms. Int J Psychiatry Med 19:65–84, 1989a

Krener P, Treat JN, Hansen RL, et al: Testing old wives' hypotheses: recent research advances in pregnancy and mental illness. Paper presented to the 4th International Congress on Pre- and Perinatal Psychology, Amherst, MA, August 1989b

Kron T: Pink Pajamas. Tel Aviv, Israel, Am Oved Publishers, 1989

Kuhse H, Singer P: Should the Baby Live? The Problem of Handicapped Infants. New York, Oxford University Press, 1985

Kumar R: Motherhood and mental illness: the role of the midwife in prevention and treatment. Midwives Chronicle and Nursing Notes, March 1984, pp 70–74

Kumar R: Report on questionnaire study at Marcé Society meeting, University of Keele, UK, September 1988

Kumar R, Brockington IF (eds): Motherhood and Mental Illness: Causes and Consequences. London, Wright, 1988

Kumar R, Robson KM: A prospective study of emotional disorders in childbearing women. Br J Psychiatry 144:35–47, 1984

Kutner L: Parent and child: when the father-to-be wakes up feeling sick. New York Times, February 8, 1990, C8

Landers S: Can jail protect a fetus of drug-addicted mom? APA Monitor, April
    1990, pp 26–27
Lazare A: Unresolved grief, in Outpatient Psychiatry Diagnosis and Treatment.
    Edited by Lazare A. Baltimore, MD, Williams & Wilkins, 1979, pp 498–512
Leavitt JW: Brought to Bed: Childbearing in America, 1750–1950. New York,
    Oxford University Press, 1986
Lee SR: Psychiatric disorders during pregnancy. American Family Physician
    128(3):187–194, 1983
Lefley HP: Aging parents as caregivers of mentally ill adult children: an emerg-
    ing social problem. Hosp Community Psychiatry 38:1063–1070, 1987
Leibenluft E: Staff responses to the pregnancy of a therapist on an inpatient unit.
    Hosp Community Psychiatry 35:1033–1036, 1984
Leridon H: Spontaneous fetal mortality: role of maternal age, parity and previous
    abortions. J Gynecol Obstet Biol Reprod (Paris) 16:425–431, 1987
Levine C: Genetic counseling: the client's viewpoint, in Genetic Counselling:
    Facts, Values, and Norms. Edited by Capron AM, Lapper M, Murray RF,
    et al. New York, Alan R Liss, 1979, pp 123–135
Levine C, Dubler NN: HIV and childbearing—uncertain risks and bitter realities:
    the reproductive choices of HIV-infected women. Milbank Q 68:321–351,
    1990
Lewine RJ: Sex differences in schizophrenia: a commentary. Schizophr Bull
    5:4–7, 1979
Lewine RJ: The group of schizophrenias, in Handbook of Behavioral Medicine
    for Women. Edited by Blechman EA, Brownell KD. New York, Pergamon,
    1988, pp 384–398
Lewine RJ, Gulley LR, Risch SC, et al: Sexual dimorphism, brain morphology
    and schizophrenia. Paper presented at the 142nd annual meeting of the
    American Psychiatric Association, San Francisco, CA, May 1989
Lewis A: Fertility and mental illness, in Inquiries in Psychiatry: Clinical and
    Social Investigations. New York, Service House, 1967, pp 295–305
Lewis E: Inhibition of mourning by pregnancy: psychopathology and manage-
    ment. BMJ 2:27–28, 1979
Lewis PJ: The effect of psychotropic drugs on the fetus, in Mental Illness in
    Pregnancy and the Puerperium. Edited by Sandler M. New York, Oxford
    University Press, 1978, pp 99–111
Lieberman A: Infant-parent treatment for women with psychiatric disorders.
    Workshop on Women's Treatment Issues, Hospital & Community Psychi-
    atry Symposium, Denver, October 1990
Lifton RJ: The Nazi Doctors: Medical Killing and the Psychology of Genocide.
    New York, Basic Books, 1986
Lipkin M, Lamb G: The couvade syndrome: an epidemiologic study. Ann Intern
    Med 96:509–511, 1982

Livesay S, Ehrlich S, Finnegan L: Cocaine and pregnancy: maternal and infant outcome. Pediatr Res 21:238A, 1987

Loeb FF Jr, Loeb LR: Psychoanalytic observations on the effect of lithium on manic attacks. J Am Psychoanal Assoc 35:877–902, 1987

Loeser AS: Effect of emotional shock on hormone release and endometrial development. Lancet 1:518, 1943

Loke KH, Salleh R: Electroconvulsive therapy for the acutely psychotic pregnant patient: a review of 3 cases. Med J Malaysia 38(2):131–133, 1983

Lomas P: The husband-wife relationship in cases of puerperal breakdown. Br J Med Psychol 32:117–123, 1959

Lomas P: Dread of envy as an aetiological factor in puerperal breakdown. Br J Med Psychol 33:105–112, 1960

Lukianowicz N: Sexual drive and its gratification in schizophrenia. Int J Social Psychiatry 9:250–258, 1963

Lukoff D, Gioia-Hasick D, Sullivan G, et al: Sex education and rehabilitation with schizophrenic male outpatients. Schizophr Bull 12:669–677, 1986

Lyketsos GC, Sakka P, Mailis A: Sexual adjustment of chronic schizophrenics: a preliminary study. Br J Psychiatry 143:376–382, 1983

Lyons-Ruth K, Botein S, Grunebaum HU: Reaching the hard-to-reach: serving isolated and depressed mothers with infants in the community, in Intervention Among Psychiatrically Impaired Parents and Their Young Children (New Directions for Mental Health Services, Vol 24). Edited by Cohler B, Musick J. San Francisco, CA, Jossey-Bass, 1984, pp 94–122

Mansnerus L: The darker side of the "baby blues." New York Times, October 12, 1988, C1, 8

Marcé LV: Traite Pratique des Maladies Mentales. Paris, Bailliere, 1862

Martin E: The Woman in the Body: A Cultural Analysis of Reproduction. Boston, MA, Beacon Press, 1987

McBurney R: Gynecologic care at a state hospital for the mentally ill. Am J Obstet Gynecol 95:345–349, 1966

McCarty T, Schneider-Braus K, Goodwin J: Use of alternative therapist during pregnancy leave. J Am Acad Psychoanal 14:377–383, 1986

McCusker EM: The bereavement experience among women who relinquish children for adoption: a qualitative study. Unpublished manuscript, 1991

McDermaid G, Winkler EG: Psychopathology of infanticide. Journal of Clinical and Experimental Psychopathology 16:22–41, 1955

McNeil TF: A prospective study of postpartum psychoses in a high risk group. Acta Psychiatr Scand 74:205–216, 1986

McNeil TF, Person-Blennow I, Kaij L: Reproduction in female psychiatric patients: severity of mental disturbance near reproduction and rates of obstetric complications. Acta Psychiatr Scand 50:23–32, 1974

McNeil TF, Kaij L, Malmquist-Larson A, et al: Offspring of women with nonorganic psychoses: development of a longitudinal study of children at high risk. Acta Psychiatr Scand 68:234–250, 1983a

McNeil TF, Kaij L, Malmquist-Larson A: Pregnant women with nonorganic psychosis: life situation and experience of pregnancy. Acta Psychiatr Scand 68:445–457, 1983b

McNeil TF, Kaij L, Malmquist-Larson A: Women with nonorganic psychosis: factors associated with pregnancy's effect on mental health. Acta Psychiatr Scand 70:209–219, 1984a

McNeil TF, Kaij L, Malmquist-Larson A: Women with nonorganic psychosis: mental disturbance during pregnancy. Acta Psychiatr Scand 70:127–139, 1984b

McNeil TF, Kaij L, Malmquist-Larson A: Women with nonorganic psychosis: pregnancy's effect on mental health during pregnancy. Acta Psychiatr Scand 70:140–148, 1984c

Meltzer D, Kumar R: Puerperal mental illness, clinical features and classification: a study of 142 mother-and-baby admissions. Br J Psychiatry 147:647–654, 1985

Meltzer ES, Kumar R: Puerperal mental illness, clinical features and classification: a study of 142 mother-and-baby admissions. Br J Psychiatry 147:647–654, 1985

Metz A, Sichel DA, Goff DC: Postpartum panic disorder. J Clin Psychiatry 49:278–279, 1988

Metz A, Goff DC, Sichel DA: Postpartum anxiety disorders—letters and response. J Clin Psychiatry 50:268–269, 1989

Miller LJ: Meeting the treatment needs of pregnant chronically mentally ill women. Paper presented at the annual meeting of the Illinois Psychiatric Society, October 1989

Miller LJ: Psychotic denial of pregnancy: phenomenology and clinical management. Hosp Community Psychiatry 41:1233–1237, 1990

Miller LJ: Clinical strategies for the use of psychotropic drugs during pregnancy. Psychiatr Med 9:275–298, 1991

Miller LJ, Spielvogel A, Raskin V, et al: Management of the high-risk pregnant patient. Hospital and Community Psychiatry Institute symposium, Los Angeles, CA, October 1991

Milstein KK, Milstein PS: Psychophysiologic aspects of denial in pregnancy: case report. J Clin Psychiatry 44:189–190, 1983

Minkoff HL, Holman S, Beller E, et al: Routinely offered prenatal HIV testing. N Engl J Med 319:1018, 1988

Minkoff K: Beyond deinstitutionalization: a new ideology for the postinstitutional era. Hosp Community Psychiatry 38:945–950, 1987

Mirdal MG, Rosenthal D, et al: Perinatal complications in psychotic patients. Br J Psychiatry 130:495–505, 1977

Mitchell JE, Pipkin MK: Antipsychotic drug therapy and sexual dysfunction in men. Am J Psychiatry 139:633–637, 1982

Modvig J, Schmidt L, Damsgaard MT: Measurement of total risk of spontaneous abortion: the virtue of conditional risk estimation. Am J Epidemiology 132:1021–1037, 1990

Mogul K: Psychological considerations in the use of psychotropic drugs with women patients. Hosp Community Psychiatry 36:1080–1085, 1985

Morgan R, Rogers J: Some results of the policy of integrating men and women patients in a mental hospital. Social Psychiatry 6(3):113–116, 1971

Morrison T: Beloved. New York, A Knopf, 1988

Mott FW: Normal and morbid conditions of the testes from birth to old age in one hundred asylum and hospital cases. BMJ 2:655, 698, 737, 1919

Mowbray CT, Chamberlain P: Sex differences among the long-term mentally disabled. Psychology of Women Quarterly 10:383–392, 1986

Munroe RL, Munroe RH, Whiting JWM: The couvade: a psychological analysis. Ethos 1(1):30–71, 1973

Muqtadir S, Hamann MW, Molnar G: Management of psychiatric pregnant patients in a medical-psychiatric unit. Psychosomatics 27:31–33, 1986

Murray L: Effects of postnatal depression on infant development, in Motherhood and Mental Illness: Causes and Consequences. Edited by Kumar R, Brockington IF. London, Wright, 1988, pp 159–190

Myers SA: The child slayer: a 25-year survey of homicide involving preadolescent victims. Arch Gen Psychiatry 17:211–213, 1967

Myers SA: Maternal filicide. Am J Dis Child 120:534–536, 1979

Nadelson C, Notman M, Arons E, et al: The pregnant therapist. Am J Psychiatry 131:1107–1111, 1974

Navarro M: Women with AIDS virus: hard choices on motherhood. New York Times, July 23, 1991, A1, 4

Nilsson A: Paranatal emotional adjustment: a prospective investigation of 165 women, I: a general account of background variables and attitudes towards childbirth and an appreciation of psychiatric morbidity. Acta Psychiatr Scand Suppl 220:9–61, 1970

Notman MT: Psychiatric disorders of menopause. Psychiatric Annals 14:448–453, 1984

Notman MT: The psychiatric implications of menopause, in The Psychiatric Implications of Menstruation. Edited by Gold JH. Washington, DC, American Psychiatric Press, 1985, pp 87–102

Notman MT, Lester E: Pregnancy: theoretical considerations. Psychoanalytic Inquiry 8:139–159, 1988

Notman MT, Nadelson CC (eds): The Woman Patient: Medical and Psychological Interfaces, Vol 1: Sexual and Reproductive Aspects of Women's Health Care. New York, Plenum, 1978

Notman MT, Nadelson CC (eds): Women and Men: New Perspectives on Gender Differences. Washington, DC, American Psychiatric Press, 1991

Nurnberg G: Treatment of mania in the last six months of pregnancy. Hosp Community Psychiatry 31:122–126, 1980

Nurnberg G: Breastfeeding and psychotropic agents (letter). Am J Psychiatry 138:120–121, 1981

Nurnberg G, Prudic J: Guidelines for treatment of psychosis during pregnancy. Hosp Community Psychiatry 35:67–71, 1984

Oates MR: Psychiatric disorders in pregnancy and the puerperium. Clinics in Obstetrics and Gynaecology 13:385–396, 1986

O'Boyle M, Severino S, Hurt S: Premenstrual syndromes and locus of control. Int J Psychiatry Med 18:67–74, 1988

Odegard O: Fertility of psychiatric first admissions in Norway, 1936–1975. Acta Psychiatr Scand 62:212–220, 1980

O'Hara MW: Postpartum "blues," depression and psychosis: a review. Journal of Psychosomatic Obstetrics and Gynaecology 7:205–227, 1987

O'Hara MW, Zekoski EM: Postpartum depression: a comprehensive review, in Motherhood and Mental Illness: Causes and Consequences. Edited by Kumar R, Brockington IF. London, Wright, 1988, pp 17–63

O'Hara MW, Rehm LP, Campbell SB: Postpartum depression: a role for social network and life stress variables. J Nerv Ment Dis 171:336–341, 1983

O'Hara MW, Neunaber DJ, Zekoski EM: Prospective study of postpartum depression: prevalence, course and predictive factors. J Abnorm Psychol 93:158–171, 1984

O'Hara MW, Zekoski EM, Phillips LH, et al: Controlled prospective study of postpartum mood disorders: comparison of childbearing and nonchildbearing women. J Abnorm Psychol 99:3–15, 1990

Ohlrich E: in Second Story Newsletter, Newton, MA, 1990

Onnis A, Grella P: The Biochemical Effects of Drugs in Pregnancy. New York, Wiley, 1984

Paffenbarger RS, Steinmetz CH, Pooler BG, et al: The picture puzzle of the postpartum psychoses. Journal of Chronic Diseases 13:161–173, 1961

Paltrow L: Maternal-fetal conflict and the law. Paper presented at the 143rd annual meeting of the American Psychiatric Association, New York, May 1990

Paltrow L, Goetz E, Shende S: Reproductive Freedom Project (memo). American Civil Liberties Union Foundation, New York, NY, October 3, 1990, pp 1–23

Paluszny M, Poznanski E: Reactions of patients during pregnancy of the psychotherapist. Child Psychiatry Hum Dev 1:266–274, 1971

Parnas J, Schulsinger F, Teasdale TW, et al: Perinatal complications and clinical outcome within the schizophrenic spectrum. Br J Psychiatry 140:416–420, 1982

Pavao J: Compact, The Family Center, Somerville, MA. Vol l, Fall 1989

Pavao J: Compact, The Family Center, Somerville, MA. Vol 2, Spring l990

Pepper B, Ryglewicz H: Schizophrenia: a constant brain disorder in a changing world. Paper presented at the 140th annual meeting of the American Psychiatric Association, Chicago, IL, May l987

Persson-Blennow I, Naslund B, McNeil TF, et al: Offspring of women with nonorganic psychosis: mother-infant interaction at three days of age. Acta Psychiatr Scand 70:149–159, 1984

Petrick JM: Postpartum depression: identification of high-risk mothers. ObGyn Nursing, January/February 1984, pp 37–40

Piers MW: Infanticide. New York, WW Norton, l978

Piker P: Psychoses complicating childbearing. Am J Obstet Gynecol 35:901–909, 1938

Pinderhughes CA, Grace EB, Reyna LJ: Psychiatric disorders and sexual functioning. Am J Psychiatry 125:1276–1283, 1972

Pivnick A, Jacobson A, Eric K, et al: Reproductive decisions among HIV-infected drug-using women: the importance of mother-child coresidence. Medical Anthropology Quarterly 5:153–169, 1991

Pleshette N, Asch SS, Chase J: A study of anxieties during pregnancy, labor and the early and late puerperium. Bull N Y Acad Med 32:436–455, 1956

Poole SR, Sharer, DR, Barbee MA, et al: Hospitalization of a psychotic mother and her breast-feeding infant. Hosp Community Psychiatry 31:412–414, 1980

Popovits RM: Criminalization of pregnant substance abusers: a health care perspective. Journal of Health and Hospital Law 24:169–181, 1991

Posey T: A home, not housing (guest editorial). Psychosocial Rehabilitation Journal 13:3–4, 1990

Posner NA, Unterman RR, Williams KN: Postpartum depression: the obstetricians' concerns, in Recent Advances in Postpartum Psychiatric Disorders. Edited by Inwood DG. Washington, DC, American Psychiatric Press, l985, pp 60–81

Post SG: History, infanticide and imperiled newborns. Hastings Cent Rep 18:14–17, 1988

Preist RG: Introduction, in Mental Illness in Pregnancy and the Puerperium. Edited by Sandler M. New York, Oxford University Press, l978, pp 7–8

Proctor RN: Racial Hygiene: Medicine Under the Nazis. Cambridge, MA, Harvard University Press, 1988

Propping P, Haverkamp F, Hilger T: Is there an increase of reproductive rates in schizophrenics? A critical review of the literature. Eur Arch Psychiatry Neurol Sci 232:439–450, 1982

Propping P, Hilger T, Haverkamp F: Is there an increase of reproductive rates in schizophrenics? Eur Arch Psychiatry Neurol Sci 233:167–175, 1983a

Propping P, Hilger T, Haverkamp E: Is there an increase of reproductive rates in schizophrenics? III, an investigation in Nordbaden (SW German): results and discussion. Eur Arch Psychiatry Neurol Sci 233:177–186, 1983b

Pugh TF, Jerath BK, Schmidt WM, et al: Rates of mental disease related to childbearing. N Engl J Med 268:1224–1228, 1963

Queenan JT (ed): Management of High-Risk Pregnancy. Oradell, NJ, Medical Economics Company, 1980

Raboch J: The sexual development and life of female schizophrenic patients. Arch Sex Behav 13:341–349, 1984

Radbill X: History of child abuse and infanticide, in The Battered Child. Edited by Helfer RE, Kempe CH. Chicago, IL, University of Chicago Press, 1968, pp 3–17

Raskin VD, Richman JA, Gaines C: Patterns of depressive symptoms in expectant and new patients. Am J Psychiatry 147:658–660, 1990

Recovering patient: "Can we talk?" The schizophrenic patient in psychotherapy. Am J Psychiatry 143:68–70, 1986

Reed SC, Hartley C, Anderson VE, et al: The Psychoses: Family Studies. Philadelphia, PA, WB Saunders, 1973

Regan DO, Rudrauff ME, Finnegan L: Parenting abilities in drug dependent women: the negative effect of depression. Pediatr Res 15:454, 1981

Regan DO, Ehrlich L, Finnegan L: Infants of drug addicts: at risk for child abuse, neglect, and placement in foster care. Neurotoxicol Teratol 9:315–319, 1987

Reich T, Winokur G: Postpartum psychoses in patients with manic depressive disease. J Nerv Ment Dis 157:60–68, 1970

Reider RO, Rosenthal D, Wender P, et al: The offspring of schizophrenics: fetal and neonatal deaths. Arch Gen Psychiatry 32:200–210, 1975

Relative's home sought for infant of mentally ill woman in Florida. Boston Globe, January 2, 1991, p 8

Repke JT, Berger NG: Electroconvulsive therapy in pregnancy. Obstet Gynecol 63:395–415, 1984

Resnick PJ: Child murder by parents: a psychiatric review of filicide. Am J Psychiatry 126:325–334, 1969

Resnick PJ: Murder of the newborn: a psychiatric review of neonaticide. Am J Psychiatry 126:1414–1420, 1970

Retterstol N: Paranoid psychoses associated with impending or newly established fatherhood. Acta Psychiatr Scand 44:57–61, 1968

Ripley HS, Papanicolaou GN: The menstrual cycle with vaginal smear studies in schizophrenia, depression, and elation. Am J Psychiatry 98:567–573, 1943

Roberts D: The bias in drug arrests of pregnant women. New York Times, August 11, 1990, 1

Robertson JA: Reconciling offspring and maternal interests during pregnancy, in Reproductive Laws for the 1990s. Edited by Cohen S, Taub N. Clifton, NJ, Humana Press, 1989, pp 259–274

Robinson AL: The effect of reproduction upon insanity. Journal of Obstetrics and Gynecology of the British Empire 40:39–66, 1933

Robinson GE, Stewart DE: Postpartum psychiatric disorders. J Can Med Assoc 134:31–37, 1986

Roca RP, Breakey WR, Fischer PJ: Medical care of chronic psychiatric outpatients. Hosp Community Psychiatry 38:741–749, 1987

Roe v Wade, 410 U.S. 113 (1973)

Rosenbaum M, Bimni B: Homicide and depression. Am J Psychiatry 143:367–370, 1986

Rosenthal M: Maternal-fetal conflicts: problems and perspectives. Paper presented at the 143th annual meeting of the American Psychiatric Association, New York, NY, May 1990

Rosenthal SH, Porter KA, Coffey B: Pain insensitivity in schizophrenia: case report and review of the literature. Gen Hosp Psychiatry 12:319–322, 1990

Rosett HL, Weiner L: Alcohol and the Fetus: A Clinical Perspective. New York, Oxford University Press, 1984

Royal College of General Practitioners: Oral Contraceptives and Health. New York, Pitman Corporation, 1974

Rozensky RH, Berman C: Sexual knowledge, attitudes, and experiences of chronic psychiatric patients. Psychosocial Rehabilitation Journal 8(2):21–27, 1984

Rubinow D, Roy-Byrne P, Hoban MC, et al: Prospective assessment of menstrually related mood disorders. Am J Psychiatry 141:684–686, 1984

Rudolph B, Larson GL, Sweeny S, et al: Hospitalized pregnant psychotic women: characteristics and treatment issues. Hosp Community Psychiatry 41:159–163, 1990

Ruocchio P: How psychotherapy can help the schizophrenic patient. Hosp Community Psychiatry 40:188–190, 1989

Rust v Sullivan, 111 S Ct 1759 (1991)

Rynearson EK: Relinquishment and its maternal complications: a preliminary study. Am J Psychiatry 139:338–340, 1982

Sacks MH, Perry S, Graver R, et al: Self-reported HIV-related risk behaviors in acute psychiatric inpatients: a pilot study. Hosp Community Psychiatry 41:1253–1255, 1990a

Sacks MH, Silberstein C, Weiler P, et al: HIV-related risk factors in acute psychiatric inpatients. Hosp Community Psychiatry 41:449–451, 1990b

Saks BR, Frank JB, Lowe TL, et al: Depressed mood during pregnancy and the puerperium: clinical recognition and implications for clinical practice. Am J Psychiatry 142:728–731, 1985

Sandison RA, Whitelaw E, Currie JD: Clinical trials with Mellaril (TP21) in the treatment of schizophrenia. Am J Psychiatry 106:732–741, 1960

Sandler M (ed): Mental Illness in Pregnancy and the Puerperium. New York, Oxford University Press, 1978

Saugstad LF: Social class, marriage, and fertility in schizophrenia. Schizophr Bull 15:9–43, 1989

Scheidt S, Thomas TJ, Thomas B: A survey of patient data on the women's issues Team B, Ward 7A, psychiatric inpatient unit, San Francisco General Hospital, July 1990

Schopf J, Bryois C, Le PK: On the nosology of severe psychiatric postpartum disorders: results of a catamnestic investigation. Eur Arch Psychiatry Neurol Sci 234:54–63, 1984

Schopf J, Bryois C, Jonquiere M, et al: A family hereditary study of postpartum "psychoses." Eur Arch Psychiatry Neurol Sci 235:164–170, 1985

Schwab B, Drake RE, Burghardt EM: Healthcare of the chronically mentally ill: the Broker model. Community Ment Health J 24:174–184, 1988

Schwab B, Clark RE, Drake RE: An ethnographic note on clients as parents. Psychosocial Rehabilitation Journal 15(2):95–99, 1991

Seeman MV: Gender differences in schizophrenia. Can J Psychiatry 27:107–112, 1982

Seeman MV: Interaction of sex, age and neuroleptic dose. Compr Psychiatry 24:125–128, 1983a

Seeman MV: Schizophrenic men and women require different treatment programs. Journal of Psychiatric Treatment and Evaluation 5:143–148, 1983b

Seeman MV: Neuroleptic drugs in men and women. Paper presented by Lang M at the 142nd annual meeting of the American Psychiatric Association, San Francisco, CA, May 1989a

Seeman MV: Neuroleptic prescription for men and women. Social Pharmacology 3:219–236, 1989b

Seeman MV, Lang M: The role of estrogens in schizophrenia gender differences. Schizophr Bull 16:185–194, 1990

Seeman MV, Littmann SK, Plummer E, et al: Living and Working With Schizophrenia. Toronto, University of Toronto Press, 1982

Segal SP, Everett-Dille L: Coping styles and factors in male/female social integration. Acta Psychiatr Scand 61:8–20, 1980

Segraves RT: Effects of psychotropic drugs on human erection and ejaculation. Arch Gen Psychiatry 46:275–284, 1989

Seidenberg R, Harris L: Prenatal symptoms in postpartum psychotic reaction. Psychiatric Q 23:715–719, 1949

Semenov SF, Pashutora EK: Clinical features and differential diagnosis of puerperal psychoses. Zh Nevropatol Psikhiatr 76:741–747, 1976

Severino SK, Moline M: Premenstrual Syndrome: A Clinician's Guide. New York, Guilford, 1989a

Severino S, Moline M: Temporary insanity and premenstrual syndrome (letter). N Y State J Med 89(2):94–95, 1989b

Severino SK, Moline M: Premenstrual syndrome. Obstet Gynecol Clin North Am 17:889–903, 1990

Severino S, Rado E: Legal implications of premenstrual syndrome. American Journal of Forensic Psychiatry 9:19–33, 1988

Severino S, Yonkers K: A review of psychotic symptoms associated with the premenstruum. Psychosomatics (in press)

Severino SK, Hurt S, Shindledecker R: Spectral analysis of cyclic symptoms in late luteal phase of dysphoric disorder. Am J Psychiatry 146:1155–1160, 1989

Shader RI: Sexual dysfunction associated with thioridazine hydrochloride. JAMA 88:1007–1008, 1964

Shapiro S: The pregnant patient on an inpatient psychiatric service. Journal of Psychiatric Treatment and Evaluation 5:363–370, 1983

Shapiro S, Nass J: Postpartum psychosis in the male. Psychopathology 19:138–142, 1986

Shearer ML, Davidson RT, Finch SM: Short communication: the sex ratio of offspring born to state hospitalized schizophrenic women. J Psychiatr Res 5:349–350, 1967

Shearer ML, Cain AC, Finch SM, et al: Unexpected effects of an "open door" policy on birth rates of women in state hospitals. Am J Orthopsychiatry 38:413–417, 1968

Shelter H: Gender sensitive CSP's needed. AMI of Wisconsin Newsletter, April 1991, p 5

Showalter E: The Female Malady: Women, Madness, and English Culture, 1930–1980. New York, Pantheon, 1985

Sichel DA, Cohen LS: Postpartum obsessive-compulsive disorder, a case report. Psychosomatics (in press)

Sichel DA, Driscoll JW: The integrated care of the hospitalized woman with a postpartum psychiatric illness, in Postpartum Psychiatric Illness: A Picture Puzzle. Edited by Hamilton JA, Harberger PN. Baltimore, MD, University of Pennsylvania Press, 1992, pp 115–125

Silverman WA: Medical "rescue" vs parental autonomy: mismatched attitudes about neonatal death. Hastings Cent Rep 11(6):12–16, 1981

Simon B: Mind and Madness in Ancient Greece: The Classical Roots of Modern Psychiatry. Ithaca, NY, Cornell University Press, 1978

Slayton RI, Soloff PH: Case reports: psychotic denial of third trimester pregnancy. J Clin Psychiatry 42:471–473, 1981

Slone D, Siskind Y, Heinonen OP: Phenothiazines in pregnancy. Am J Obstet Gynecol 128:486–488, 1977

Sobel DE: Infant mortality and malformations in children of schizophrenic women. Psychiatric Q 35:60–64, 1961

Soloff PH, Jewell S, Roth LH: Civil commitment and the rights of the newborn. Am J Psychiatry 136:114–115, 1979

Sontag S: Illness as Metaphor. New York, Farrar, Straus & Giroux, 1978

Sorel NC: Ever Since Eve: Personal Reflections on Childbirth. New York, Oxford University Press, 1984

Spaulding JG, Cavenar JO: Psychoses following therapeutic abortion. Am J Psychiatry 135:364–365, 1978

Spielvogel A, Wile J: Treatment of the psychotic pregnant patient. Psychosomatics 27:487–492, 1986

Spielvogel A, Wile J: Orientation to pregnancy and labor management for psychotic women. Women's Issues Consultation Team, San Francisco Hospital, San Francisco, CA, 1988

Starkman MN, Marshall JC, Ferla JL: Pseudocyesis: psychologic and neuroendocrine interrelationships. Psychosom Med 47:46–57, 1985

Statlender S: The impact of therapist pregnancy in a psychiatric aftercare service. Paper presented at the annual meeting of the American Psychological Association, Boston, MA, August 1990

Steadman H: Critically reassessing the accuracy of public perceptions of dangerousness of the mentally ill. J Health Soc Behav 22:310–316, 1981

Steiner M: Psychobiology of mental disorders associated with childbearing. Acta Psychiatr Scand 60:449–464, 1979

Stern G, Kruckman L: Multidisciplinary perspectives on postpartum depression: an anthropological critique. Soc Sci Med 17:1027–1041, 1983

Sternbach H: Puerperal psychosis in America—1847 (letter). Arch Gen Psychiatry 39:235–236, 1982

Stevens BC: Illegitimate fertility of psychotic women. J Biosoc Sci 2:17–30, 1970

Stevens BC: Psychosis associated with childbirth: a demographic survey since the development of community care. Social Services and Medicine 5:527–543, 1971

Stewart DE: Pregnancy and schizophrenia. Canadian Family Physician 30:1537–1542, 1984

Stewart DE: Prophylactic lithium in postpartum affective psychosis. J Nerv Ment Dis 176:485–489, 1988

Stewart DE: Psychiatric admission of mentally ill mothers with their infants. Can J Psychiatry 34:34–38, 1989

Stewart DE, Gangbar R: Psychiatric assessment of competency to care for a newborn. Can J Psychiatry 29:583–589, 1984

Stotland N: Contemporary issues in obstetrics and gynecology for the consultation-liaison psychiatrist. Hosp Community Psychiatry 36:1102–1108, 1985

Stotland N, Blumenthal SJ, Fullilove MJ, et al: Psychiatric impact of abortion law changes. Workshop presented at the 143rd annual meeting of the American Psychiatric Association, New York, May 1990

Strauss JS: Subjective experiences of schizophrenia: toward a new dynamic psychiatry—II. Schizophr Bull 15:179–187, 1989

Strauss JS, Estroff SE: Subjective experiences of schizophrenia and related disorders: implications for understanding and treatment. Schizophr Bull 2:177–178, 1989

Sullivan G, Lukoff D: Sexual side effects of antipsychotic medication: evaluation and interventions. Hosp Community Psychiatry 41:1238–1241, 1990

Talbott J: Reactions of schizophrenics to life-threatening disease. Psychiatric Q 50:218–227, 1978

Teja JS: Periodic psychosis of puberty. J Nerv Ment Dis 162:52–57, 1976

Test MA, Burke SS, Wallisch LS: Gender differences of young adults with schizophrenic disorders in community care. Schizophr Bull 16:331–344, 1990

Thurer S: Deinstitutionalization and women: where the buck stops. Hosp Community Psychiatry 34:1162–1163, 1983

Toufexis A: Why mothers kill their babies. Time, June 20, 1988, pp 81–83

Towne RD, Afterman J: Psychosis in males related to parenthood. Bull Menninger Clin 19:19–26, 1955

Trad PV: Self-mutilation in a new mother: a strategy for separating from her infant. Am J Psychother 43:414–426, 1989

Treethowan WH, Conlon MF: The couvade syndrome. Br J Psychiatry 111:57–66, 1965

Tuteur W, Glotzer J: Murdering mothers. Am J Psychiatry 116:447–452, 1959

Van Gent E, Nabarro G: Haloperidol as an alternative to lithium in pregnant women. Am J Psychiatry 144:1241, 1987

Van Putten R, LaWall J: Postpartum psychosis in an adoptive mother and in a father. Psychosomatics 22:1087–1089, 1981

Varan LR, Martin SG, Skenet DS, et al: ECT in an acutely psychotic pregnant woman with actively aggressive (homicidal) impulses. Can J Psychiatry 30:363–367, 1985

Verhulst J, Scheidman B: Schizophrenia and sexual functioning. Hosp Community Psychiatry 32:259–262, 1981

Wainwright WH: Fatherhood as a precipitant of mental illness. Am J Psychiatry 123:40–44, 1966

Watkins M, Fisher SM: "Mommy, Are You Really My Mommy?" Talking With Young Children About Adoption. New Haven, CT, Yale University Press, 1992

Weil C: The safety of bromocryptine in long-term use: a review of the literature. Curr Med Res Opin 10:25–51, 1986

Weinstein MR: Lithium treatment of women during pregnancy and in the post-delivery period, in Handbook of Lithium Therapy. Edited by Johnson FN. Baltimore, MD, University Park Press, 1980, pp 421–429

Welner A: Childbirth-related psychiatric illness. Compr Psychiatry 23:143–154, 1982

Wignall CM, Meredith CE: Illegitimate pregnancies in state institutions. Arch Gen Psychiatry 18:580–583, 1968

Wile J, Spielvogel A, Handel M: The impact of pregnancy on the care of the chronic patient. Paper presented at American Psychiatric Association 40th Institute on Hospital and Community Psychiatry, New Orleans, LA, October 1988

Williams EY, Weeks LR: Premenstrual tension associated with psychotic episodes. J Nerv Ment Dis 116:321–399, 1952

Willoughby A, Sutherland A, cited in Family Practice News 18(20):27, 1988

Wise MG, Ward SC, Townsend-Parchman W, et al: Case report of ECT during high risk pregnancy. Am J Psychiatry 141:99–101, 1984

Wisner KL, Perel JM: Psychopharmacologic agents and electroconvulsive therapy during pregnancy and the puerperium, in Psychiatric Consultation in Childbirth Settings: Parent- and Child-Oriented Approaches. Edited by Cohen RL. New York, Plenum, 1988, pp 165–206

Wrede G, Mednick SA, Huttunen MD, et al: Pregnancy and delivery complications in the births of an unselected series of Finnish children and schizophrenic mothers. Acta Psychiatr Scand 62:369–381, 1980

Wyatt RJ, Kirch DG, DeLisi LE: Schizophrenia: biochemical, endocrine and immunological studies: gender differences in schizophrenia, in Comprehensive Textbook of Psychiatry/V, 5th Edition. Edited by Kaplan HI, Sadock BJ. Baltimore, MD, Williams & Wilkins, 1989, pp 717–718

Yarden PE, Max DM, Eisenbach Z: The effect of childbirth on the prognosis of married schizophrenic women. Br J Psychiatry 112:491–499, 1966

Yoder MC, Belik J, Lannon RA, et al: Infants of mothers treated with lithium during pregnancy have an increased incidence of prematurity, macrosomia, and perinatal mortality. Pediatr Res 18:404A, 1984

Zambrana RE, Mogel W, Scrimshaw S: Gender and level of training differences in obstetricians' attitudes towards patients in childbirth. Women Health 12:5–24, 1987

Zilboorg G: The dynamics of schizophrenic reaction to pregnancy and childbirth. Am J Psychiatry 8:733–766, 1919

Zilboorg G: Malignant psychoses related to childbirth. Am J Obstet Gynecol 15:145, 1928

Ziporyn T: "Rip van Winkle period" ends for puerperal psychiatric problems. JAMA 16:2061–2067, 1984

Zola P, Meyerson AT, Reznikoff M, et al: Menstrual symptomatology and psychiatric admission. J Psychosom Res 23:241–245, 1979

Index of Case Examples

(by order of appearance)

Chapter 7

Chapter 9

Chapter 10

Chapter 11

Chapter 12

Index